ADVAN

"Compelling, entertaining, and inspiring! The personal and historical details the author shares about his father's unique relationship with Fidel Castro and their harrowing escape from Cuba are insightful and captivating. It is also an amazing story of how a kid from New York City develops an improbable relationship with the sport of golf, ultimately creating a successful corporate golfing career that is revealing, funny, and thought-provoking. *Out of the Rough* is a testament to the human journey, and an absolutely fascinating read for golfers and the historically curious."
—*Kent Smith, PGA Certified Professional*

"I wouldn't have thought that it was possible to weave together two totally different subjects, but somehow he manages to do it in an entertaining and educational way. His personal and familial anecdotes are hard to believe, even though we know they are true. As an avid golfer who has been to a few corporate outings over the years, I've now learned that I'm not a bad golfer, just an honest one. Keep hitting them straight and keep entertaining us."
—*Steve Fallack, Board Certified Plastic and Reconstructive Surgeon*

"*Out of the Rough* is a captivating and unique memoir that blends personal anecdotes with historical events. Author Eurice E. Rojas shares his family's experience during the Cuban Revolution and reveals the transformative power of golf within American corporate culture. This is a must-read book for anyone interested in history, sports, and personal journeys of triumph over adversity. Rojas' personal accounts close the loop for those readers who shared similar experiences and struggles associated with this dark chapter in Cuba's history. Additionally, the never-before-seen photos of Fidel Castro, add an extra layer of intrigue to an already compelling narrative, offering a unique personal and historical perspective."
—*Al Bernal, Strategic Sourcing Professional*

"Eurice Rojas explodes on the literary scene with his brilliantly written *Out of the Rough: The Cuban Revolution and its Effect on Golf*. He didn't escape from 111th Street in New York City, he evolved because of his experiences in that harsh environment. Rojas' description of growing up a Cuban refugee and his family's near-tragic escape adds to his remarkably captivating explanation of Fidel Castro's rise to power. His dissection of the amateur golf world takes the reader on a roller coaster ride which is both entertaining and unforgettable."
—*Louis Romano, Award-Winning Author*

LOU MENENDEZ
THANK you FOR your
SUPPORT! ALL the Best!
EURICE

OUT OF THE ROUGH

THE CUBAN REVOLUTION AND
ITS EFFECT ON GOLF

EURICE E. ROJAS

LIFE TO PAPER
PUBLISHING

First Edition 2023

Paperback ISBN: 978-1-990700-34-7
eBook ISBN: 978-1-990700-35-4

Library of Congress Control Number: 2023906142

Editing and Layout by Jennifer Goulden
Cover by Tabitha Rose

Printed in the USA.
1 2 3 4 5 6 7 8 9 10

Life to Paper Publishing Inc.
Toronto | Miami

www.lifetopaper.com

LIFE TO PAPER
PUBLISHING

This book is lovingly dedicated to my wife, Norma, along with our kids, Michael and Brian and my son Edward.
It is also in honor of my parents, Eurice and Onelia Rojas.

CONTENTS

OUT OF THE ROUGH

CHAPTER ONE

LIFE, LIBERTY, AND THE PURSUIT OF TRYING TO BE A FUCKUP

Without a doubt, America is the greatest country in the world. I am a Cuban American born in New York City in 1958. I lived on 111th Street between Broadway and Amsterdam Avenues until 1976—almost twenty years. New York City was going through another wonderfully dysfunctional grand renaissance, and as an impressionable young soul, I was fortuitously and gleefully absorbed in the city's never-ending attempts to craft its electric identity.

I was an only child, and as such, developed an autonomic, spoiled, and self-centered personality. Intrinsically, and by any technical definition, I would ultimately consider myself a classic underachiever who never truly capitalized on my intellectual capacity and natural talents. And why would I? As a spoiled brat, I just expected everything to be provided to me in order to continue my never-ending comfortable lifestyle, as if I were royalty. My mother would too often, in front of guests, refer to me as "El Rey," which meant "The King." Can you imagine living up to that royal decree? It was embarrassing, to say the least.

Nonetheless, I wasn't shy about yodeling my regal status and the ensuing complimentary egocentric, royal expectations and demands behind the scenes.

My parents were Cuban immigrants who worked their asses off to provide our family with a decent lifestyle and opportunities to better ourselves—through me, as a prominent example of generational progress in Cuba and then America. Even though my parents were immigrants and did not represent a privileged class in society, they sacrificed whatever they could to provide me with a privileged life.

Simply stated, I was a person who never had to work too hard for anything, and as a result, left a lot of what my potential could have garnered on the table—no doubt a self-inflicted mistake. In spite of my valiant efforts to the contrary, I may have been one of the luckier underachievers of my generation, in large part due to all the resources and opportunities that my parents invested toward me in their attempt to ensure that I would succeed in achieving the American dream. Their primary strategy was to construct and underwrite an educational path for me within prestigious schools where the environment filtered whatever attempts I would embrace to fuck things up. It was an intentionally fabricated habitat ensuring that many people would have their eyes on me, mentoring me through my immature sense of responsibility.

That being said, I was not a complete slug, and—not to pat myself on the back—I was innately astute enough to recognize otherwise glaring opportunities and accordingly applied the appropriate diligence on the rare occasions that I was inspired to achieve something. So, if you coupled my narcissistic and slacker tendencies along with my natural curiosities and consistent presentations of opportunistic good fortune, life for me seemed like a guaranteed yellow brick road paved with shit-eating smiles and winks. Frankly, because I felt that some kind of perverse, divine intervention was at play for me as no matter what kind of stupid shit I would try to pull off, be involved with, or engage in, I never got physically injured or got arrested, or came out on the wrong side of any situational equation. Rarely has someone with so much potential done so little yet so satisfyingly well with a career, education, relationships, and family—relatively speaking of course—compared to the effort put into it.

Additionally, as a recorded minority, I have also been fortunately and uniquely blessed with a mostly racism-free life experience. Is there some type of systemic racism embedded in our culture? Sure, but I ignored all those signs as if they weren't meant for me and kept setting my eyes on targets that would make me happy. A lot of my oblivious ignorance of racism had to do with the fact that my physical appearance reflected that of a classic

Anglo-European citizen rather than the stereotypical expectations of what a Hispanic—eh, "spic"—was expected to reflect. That does not mean that after gaining acceptance as a corporate citizen, I was not cognizant of the disparate balance minorities represented in senior leadership positions throughout Fortune 500 companies in America. There is no question that it is a tough grind for minorities to excel in the corporate world. These corporate cultural schisms have been embedded for decades and the only way to construct change is to be a productive team member that balances the existing cultural ecosystem with purposeful progressive contributions. Hammer-time tactics never yield long-lasting, meaningful outcomes. Yelling, screaming, and "canceling" only provide momentary muzzles and aimless distractions. You still have to prove your value amongst your peers.

Back to me.

Having things come as easily as they did for me in the corporate environment undoubtedly happened as a result of being sponsored and mentored by white senior executives with powerful businesses as well as philanthropic and political juice. And it was white guys who always helped me, not Hispanics who were in a position of influence. Surprising to me, unfortunately, was that most Hispanics who were able to intrude in powerful executive positions back then, as the corporate token, would not do much to support any other aspiring Hispanics on the desired road to success. They were simply looking over their shoulders twenty-four seven to ensure that they squirreled away their own path to success within a white man's world. Attaining mentoring and sponsorship by a white executive was absolutely the only way (given the lack of legal protection enforcement) any minority was able to survive and thrive with opportunities offered to them. I am one hundred percent convinced that my career opportunities came about as a result of the fact that I do not look Hispanic, and my mentors felt comfortable with me because I very much reflected the tapestry of the corporate population.

Unquestionably, the lack of Hispanic corporate connections and sponsors simply and understandably means that minorities go through a much more selective filtering process to attain corporate opportunities and career ascension than the general white prospects of the population. Think about it: generally speaking, minorities have significantly lower representations in the higher levels of elite educational institutions, where the socially and academically privileged conjoin to maintain the distinction of social classes. As a result of lower income levels amongst Hispanic households versus the general population, Hispanics have fewer options, fewer opportunities, and far less access to the selective or private educational institutions that are mostly designed for the exclusive segments of the population as glide paths for higher levels of elite training and education.

My parents recognized that aspect of society, and they worked like fanatics to integrate me within pedigreed academic circles. Of particular remembrance, after my parents and I participated in a series of professionally conducted but sterile interviews and interrogations, I was accepted into a newly distinguished but nonetheless prestigious private prep school on the Upper East Side of Manhattan that was managed by a fucking headmaster. I remember seeing my parents rejoice when they were informed of my acceptance to the school as if they had struck oil.

Neither I nor any of my friends in the neighborhood even knew what a headmaster was.

Despite being immigrants, my parents had amazing foresight into what would lead to a successful American assimilation. They felt that to effectively assimilate into American culture, they would continue to follow through on the ingrained values they had espoused during the pre-Castro revolution culture in Cuba—education and hard work. My parents intentionally and pragmatically constructed an academic launching pad for me that they hoped would ensure a successful future. They reasoned that if I were immersed in a social circle of rich friends, I would be exposed to the best New York had to offer. Now it was up to me. Jesus, I didn't want it to be up to me. I didn't want the responsibility of defining my future. I was a kid. I just wanted to keep fucking around.

My parents were correct in anticipating that most of my high school classmates would be the privileged offspring of rich families, children of corporate dynasties who were well taken care of in the comfort and security of generational wealth. What my parents did not realize was that these new friends would not provide me with the productive influence they were expecting. As a result of the all-consuming career and social demands of their parents, a lot of these "poor rich kids" also unfortunately experienced chronic parental disregard. The blithe attitude of irrelevancy exhibited by many of these parents toward their children resulted in them living an emotionally detached existence from their kids—one in which their kids were regarded as not much different than unremarkable furniture. These kids were left to themselves, almost abandoned, except for their caregivers (nannies), to haphazardly roam New York City in search of their identity.

They wandered in their loneliness in a world that was as perplexing as it was disconcerting as they were deprived of essential family values that would normally act as an emotional anchor for any young person pioneering the commonly anticipated juvenile crossroads of confusion. And these kids were very aware that they existed in a world that didn't altogether make sense to them. It was a seemingly beautiful, carefree, and secure lifestyle outwardly but a distressing echo chamber of fostered anxieties and insecurities inwardly. And since no parental guidance was evident in a meaningful way, they most often looked for answers through some form of popular rebellion—the most popular of which, during that era, was experimentation with drugs.

Understandably, drugs provided them with a convenient and numbing disguise, allowing them to be eccentric and irreverent with little compelling reason to thoughtfully reflect upon, or be accountable for, their actions and the resulting consequences. So, it was not unreasonable or unexpected behavior that when the lunch bell rang and friends gathered in front of our prestigious high school, they mostly remarked about where to go to smoke a joint instead of where to go to eat a sandwich. It also didn't help that our school didn't have a cafeteria. Ironically, although my parents' instinct to integrate me into the right social and academic circles was sound, it only served to reinforce my "only child," spoiled, nurturing halo of privileges via the inheritance of my eccentric—and very wealthy—group of high school cohorts.

By design, I simply surrendered to the environment and developed a characteristic of never establishing the drive or discipline necessary to develop the skills to be a good student. From a young age, I felt I did not have to work that hard to accomplish much or, as the popular phrase would have it, "work my way out of the ghetto," as I was already engulfed by rich kids from families representing the highest social and economic fabric of New York City. Shit, my adolescent academic environment was my "get out of the ghetto card." This characteristic misgiving was the devil on my shoulder, constantly whispering the assertion that my life was indeed nothing less than an idyllic journey. Fortunately, my maturing evolution, contemplation and inherent common sense eventually gained some traction and acknowledged my trait of ambivalent underachievement. This recognition helped me partially counter my disdain and self-proclaimed irrelevance for academics into a slightly more constructive focus.

I was lucky. Some of my friends were not.

The doubts and desperation that often accompany young people who do not have parental mentoring, guidance, wisdom, and, most importantly, love was evident with many of my gilded friends. Sadly, some of my closest high school friends befriended the shadows of despair and depression, ultimately succumbing to increasing levels of drug abuse and alcoholism in their search to find peace, compassion, and consideration.

These were young, smart kids whose age of innocence was blessed with meaningful potential and promise, but their drug abuse, which at first eased their subliminal parental psychological trauma, ultimately consumed them in a predictable mental and physical death spiral.

Once-promising athletes and students consequently transformed into users, dealers, pimps, and prostitutes. A talented basketball player who could have scored multiple college scholarships turned user, then dealer. A beautiful girl turned user, then prostitute, to support her habit. An intelligent student turned user, then dealer, and then started pimping. The next iteration of their collective evolution was intended or unintended death or jail. And some did die from situations that, directly or indirectly, were attributed to the use of drugs.

In high school, in those times, these kids escalated to abusing the hard drugs available—namely coke, PCP, heroin, and LSD (acid). Mind you, this was an elite high school that boasted parents of high society, corporate pedigrees living on the Park Avenues of the Upper East Side, West End Avenues of the Upper West Side, and Central Park West. These were heavily liberal-mindset parents who advocated for allowing their kids, during a significant transformative period in their lives, to initiate their own life-learning episodes and establish their personalities by carelessly being allowed to explore all the good and bad that the world has to offer without boundaries, without limits, and without worthy adult guidance. These parents were guilty of imposing their own lawless, ideological social experiment on their children under the misguided perception that their kids were better off left to find their identity guided by others who were also seeking meaningful guidance but were just as lost.

Unfortunately, this also made them easy marks for the unsavory predators in the neighborhood. Their collective confusion was a road map filled with forks in the road and dead ends. The saving grace, if any, may have been that they were all bewildered together. Not surprisingly, the affluent trappings of their environment did not immunize these parents from the catastrophic consequences of the callous disregard of loving and nurturing their children.

Some of these kids died at an early age without ever having realized most of what life had to offer them. However, not to worry, for the housekeepers, nannies, and valets looking after all their properties, including the children, allowed these parents to be unconscious of any emotional equity.

Other than smoking pot, I was never interested in venturing toward the serious drugs my friends in high school did. Weed was not a gateway drug for me. I did not feel the need to seek the fringes of experimentation because I very much enjoyed my home and very much embraced the love my parents shared with me. I wanted to be more like my parents instead of wanting to be like my private school friends. My very rich and privileged friends did not have anyone to emulate except their other lonely and isolated friends. Most maintained a fundamental dislike for their parents.

In contrast, I had not abandoned my friends and roots from my 111th Street community for the gold-paved streets of the New York City elite. Moreover, none of my less-entitled friends in my birth community were interested in harder drugs. Most of the 111th Street rabble were athletes whose parents were proud of their active participation in sports. And although most of the parents in my neighborhood were two-job, blue-collar people (which meant working a lot of hours keeping them away from home and their kids), they never neglected nor deprived their children of the emotional, spiritual, and loving investment of being their parent and friend. Most of my friends' parents devoted their precious spare time to participating in their children's athletic and academic activities. They were all dedicated athletic coaches and street counselors taking stock in and emotionally committed to providing well-rounded and heartfelt stages of education, wisdom, and life learning.

Another interesting component in my early development was how surprisingly progressive my parents were as I grew up with them—within parameters. My child-rearing exercise contrasted with most Cuban parents, who had proudly earned a reputation of being overbearing and controlling. More often than not, I would come home way after dinner, having eaten out at a friend's house because my mother didn't know how to cook. She didn't have the time due to owning her own business, and frankly, she had no interest in cooking.

She was not of a domestic nature and thought cooking was nothing more than broiling a steak. She would buy the best steak from the butcher and then do the unthinkable and simply throw the steak into the oven with a whole potato, turning the oven on to about 300 degrees, and when the potato was done, so was the steak. I never knew what it was like to eat a steak that was cooked "medium," much less "medium rare." They were more like burnt beef jerky.

My dad recognized this shortcoming and learned how to cook, not so much for his survival but for mine, and I subsequently learned how to cook from my dad.

So, I was always pretty much out on my own but always abided by a generous curfew. When I would return home for the evening, they never expressed any anxiety about my whereabouts. Both of my parents were always there when I came home. It seems kind of strange when compared to this day and age of technology, where we are in near-constant contact with our kids.

Without question, my blue-collar neighborhood is what ultimately provided me with a background in common sense and family values. These attributes helped me make some good decisions as I was growing up, and saved me from being absorbed in the whimsical, devoid-of-reality, and destructively-empty lifestyles of my poor rich friends. After figuring all of that out, I now just had to contemplate the most effective and results-oriented method to excel in academics while minimally applying myself to good old proven studying sweat equity.

CHAPTER TWO

THE 1970S SPORTS RENAISSANCE IN NEW YORK CITY: WHAT'S GOLF GOT TO DO WITH IT?

Understanding that there were significant cultural, social, economic, racial, and lifestyle revolutions occurring at the same time during the 1970s, those years represented a time capsule of dynamic, transformational experiences across the United States. Many of these social and cultural trends were pioneered, implemented, and magnified in New York City. It was a time when the combustible cocktail of sensory stimuli in the city took your breath away. It was a time when you didn't want to close your eyes because you were afraid a life-altering event would pass you by—or that someone was waiting to mug you at the same time. And as much as I can wax on about the colorfully different levels of cultural mosaics that city neighborhoods showcased, I was particularly enraptured by the magical era this city experienced with its many categories of professional sports.

I grew up watching, idolizing, and living through sports figures like Mohammed Ali, Joe Frazier, Hank Aaron, Kareem Abdul-Jabbar, Roberto Clemente, Tony Oliva, Tom Seaver, Thurman Munson, Joe Namath, Franco Harris, Mickey Mantle, Walt Frazier, Wilt Chamberlain, Oscar Robertson, Roger Staubach, Jerry West, Julius Erving, Willis Reed, Bruce Lee . . . you get the idea. Real men, real athletes, dripping with sweat and competing in real sports like basketball, baseball, boxing, martial arts, and football. Hockey is also a real man's sport, except it's not a sport played in the inner city, so who cared? Soccer? Is that played in New Zealand? Golf, swimming, or tennis? They were sports exclusively designed for rich white kids. Some of the notable athletes representing golf back then were Nicklaus, Palmer, Player, Trevino, Jacklin, Crenshaw, Floyd, Miller, Watson, Irwin—athletes? Seriously, to an inner-city kid? Trust me, not one kid within the proximity of my urban neighborhood was emulating any golf "athletes." Golfers, at that time, were analogous to the old repairman in the Maytag appliances commercial. It was an individual, lonely, old-man sport that was pretty much isolated from the mainstream, urban American sports ideology. And at that time, it was acutely true for minority kids existing on 111th Street in Manhattan.

One could argue that almost any individual sport had greater appeal than golf in our small world. For example, a relatable individual city sport was track, as it was a sport in motion and mainly free to practice for inner-city kids. I mean, we all ran at various speeds and distances at various times depending on who was chasing us. Running represented nonstop action, with our arms pumping or trying to catch air, springboarding or vaulting over fences, fire hydrants, or metal garbage cans while running swiftly through back alleys. Track and field excitement prevailed when an athlete broke the four-minute mile, ran a hundred-yard dash in less than 9.5 seconds, or set records in the 220 or 440 hurdles, or long jump, or by chucking a javelin, and on and on.

Golf, on the other hand, was quite the contrast to action and motion. In golf, you walked. And you smoked cigarettes. You got to see someone putt, politely clap, whisper, wave, and then, of course, walk some more. Occasionally, someone would hit the ball waywardly into the water, and you would see the splash. Now that was exciting. The wardrobe was also potentially very exciting. Especially to firemen. Golfers would walk the course wearing polyester ensembles consisting of wide-collar shirts and pants accompanied by snazzy white, brown, or black wingtip shoes. And since the polyester outfits weren't fireproof, I would always imagine them spontaneously combusting on very hot days or flaming up from a carelessly flicked cigarette. Was this intended to be exciting, inspiring, and motivational stuff for inner-city kids? I don't think so.

At that moment in time, the PGA of America and the United States Golf Association (USGA) could not have been more exclusively dismissive of kids in the inner city. Also, consider that with respect to the other professional sports, kids in urban areas had practical access to venues that supported baseball, football, basketball, and track-and-field sporting activities. There were recreational resources provided by municipalities for those particular sports. In distinct contrast, golf was pretty much removed and isolated from the general masses. Almost everyone could get on a track, a basketball court, or a field somewhere, while the sport of golf—well, it was a secret society. Golf, with its overbearing social class distinction, was very much like what was showcased in one of the best golf movies made: *The Greatest Game Ever Played.*

Remember when you were a kid, and you would see an old man in an expensive and cool car and wonder why every time you saw these particular autos, you only saw older people driving them? Did you have to be an old white man to drive an expensive car? Golf was akin to that. We were not aware of any "real" athletes that played golf as a pastime or indulgence. Older, rich, fat white men played golf. Back in my time, golfers may as well have been sumo wrestlers representing attractive athletes for us to emulate. In our sports universe, golf was not considered a "real man's sport."

And unlike today, golf back then was not a young man's sport either. No kid on our block was running out in their Converse to buy polyester plaid pants or golf shirts with big collars like they do today with Nike, Puma, TaylorMade, or Under Armour wardrobes. Over time, the sport of golf has thankfully evolved to mostly remedy that perspective. The majority of professional golfers now train with proven coaches as dedicated athletes in their pursuit to gain physical and mental advantages over their competitors. In addition, many professional athletes from other commercialized sports are now familiar with golf and golfers, and even actively play golf themselves. This has increased awareness amongst sports fans and contributed to legitimizing golf as a "real man's sport."

Back then, if we were to buy, or steal, a golf club, it was as a stick to be used as a weapon, not as sports equipment. Moreover, our socioeconomic blue-collar, urban reality imposed financial and other restrictions on any thoughts of playing golf—especially given the consideration that our parents usually held two jobs and didn't have time for anything other than working and taking care of chores alongside managing our recreational and academic activities. If they were going to pay for anything extravagant, it would be an investment in education and not green fees. Lastly, golf was an individual sport presiding in mostly affluent, suburban communities that was not accessible to any type of urban setting, especially for minorities surviving in a slum. Face it, there was almost no access to be able to play, much less practice for minorities when it came to golf. You would be more likely to find a five-legged unicorn around our area than a golf course or practice range.

In any case, bicycles were our main form of transportation throughout the city. So, it would have been difficult, even if we owned a set of clubs, to strap a golf bag, which at that time was not constructed of the lightweight materials you find today, to the banana seat of a Sting-Ray bike. If we took trains or buses, it was either to go to school or to go to one of the city beaches. Beaches and manhole covers in the city streets were the closest we came to sand bunkers or actual "golf holes." Golf never ever entered the equation for us when we considered any type of social, athletic, or recreational activity—although I am sure they could have carved out a nice nine-hole golf course in Central Park and still left plenty of room for its zoo, bike trails, fountains, and kite flying.

Golf is not a team sport and our neighborhood embraced team-related sports. Team sports were the athletic and social connection for the kids throughout our communities and schools because everybody could play. So, if someone was going to swing a stick, it would be at a hardball, a Spalding rubber ball, or someone's head. Not a chance it would be at a golf ball. Moreover, adding to the sport's unappealing lack of action and movement, there was no place in the sport of golf where you got to throw a ball, catch a ball, or run with a ball. We were into sports where you had to hit or catch a ball in motion. The ball is not in motion in golf. It is sitting still. It is like playing T-ball with a field hockey stick.

Golf was not the default sport for urban kids who were not picked to participate in a team-related sports activity. One-on-one street handball was the default sport, and it was the lowest you could go while still maintaining any sense of street rep (forget about rope skipping—uh-uh). And at least with handball, you were playing with a Spalding ball that you hopefully owned and which other kids would have to borrow to play stickball, allowing you to squirm into a stickball game here and there. Being the owner of a Spalding ball was the essential element needed to ensure your playing time. People might also play with you if they had nothing to do or as a sympathy play because you were not talented enough to do anything else.

But golf?!

Golf, back then, was not the sports commodity—if you can refer to it as such—that it is now. When I was young, the sports that were both accessible to me and accepted by my pediatric ensemble were basketball, baseball, stickball, stoop-ball, handball, ringolevio, and tackle football—on the streets or in a field. That's right. We often played tackle football on the streets of Manhattan. Not the sidewalk—we were smarter than that. The sidewalks were narrow and constructed of cement, which would result in deeper scrapes when tackled as the uneven and rough surface contributed to digging deeper into flesh. Whereas streets were wider and the asphalt was smooth, which would result, more often than not, in raspberries and bruising rather than indiscriminately tearing into our skin. We quickly learned how to roll and fall as gently as possible when being tackled. Parked automobiles would help cushion the blow before you hit the street, or if you were lucky (not lucky for the owner of a car), you'd get tackled on a car. The play would be called dead, and you would never hit the street. It really was amazing that there were never any serious injuries resulting from what we were doing—which was downright stupid. It's also amazing that cops weren't called to arrest us for, in some cases, damaging or destroying private property.

So, given the juvenile mentality and accessible resources dictating the sports activities that we would participate in, how could golf—the equivalent of shuffleboard matches at a retirement home in our eyes—ever fit into this formula? I eventually gained a level of deep respect for professional golfers because as they say, they have "skin in the game." Their own dollars. I know, I know. The top tier professional golfers have some stately, and well-deserved, sponsorship support, but a majority do not have that type of guaranteed income. Unlike team sport athletes in football, basketball, baseball, and so on, professional golfers do not have the luxury of having guaranteed professional performance contracts, with all expenses paid including meal allowances irrespective of lackluster performances. If contracted professional sports team athletes have a bad year, so what? If they get hurt, "we'll get 'em next year!" These guys get paid pretty much no matter what happens to them.

In contrast, golfers pay all their own expenses, and if they don't show up and perform, they are simply not cashing out—unless you become a professionally contracted employee that has signed on to play exhibition matches with the LIV golf series, which is bankrolled by questionable money, and whose front man is a disgruntled individual who is still bitter over choking away almost every major championship he was in a position to win. The rationale used by golfers who have resigned from the PGA Tour and signed up to be employed by an illegitimate golfing enterprise that pays for all player expenses and rewards mediocrity is nothing short of hypocritical, demeaning, and insulting to true golf competition. Not to be deterred, most professional golfers religiously clock in every day in their loyal pilgrimage to win tournaments, in particular major championships, to earn respect and honor within the legitimate annals of golf.

But what did the sport of golf have to do with the professional, amateur, and aspiring junior sports lore of inner-city kids in the Big Apple? Nada.

CHAPTER THREE

TURF WARS AND THE CUBAN EMBARGO OF 109TH STREET

I grew up on 111th Street between Broadway and Amsterdam in Manhattan in New York City. I was befriended, and literally protected, by a colorfully diverse ethnic mix of teenagers who were self-deputized, unofficial vigilantes sworn to uphold the sanctity and integrity of their version of the neighborhood. (There existed a predominant culture of "turf" sections in New York City at the time I grew up.) These self-appointed guardians maintained the safety and harmony of "their" village by thwarting any attempts of trespassing and incursions from unwanted and unwelcome guests traversing from other "turfs."

We looked up to these deputies as they enforced a brand of street law designed to protect us. They were an inspiration to all the younger kids and were considered local superheroes while also performing as our senior mentors. There was even one guy who resembled Fonzie from the 1970s sitcom *Happy Days*. Our neighborhood vigilante deputies were an immigrant enclave composed of Germans, Italians, Irish, and some Puerto Ricans protecting a younger crew (me and my friends) consisting of Puerto Ricans, Cubans, Dominicans, South Americans, and a few African Americans. Oh, yeah, there was also a Jamaican kid who ran with us. This was the new generation of immigrants that the teenage immigrants from another generation were protecting. Our racial or cultural makeup didn't matter and didn't clash. Turf did not represent a color or religion—we were family.

Golf?! We had gangs.

Make no mistake, in circa 1970 in New York City, anyone who did not live in the neighborhood was not allowed to venture into our hallowed, coveted 'hood. Allow me to share a harrowing childhood experience that occurred because of me, so that you have a sense of the type of neighborhood lifestyle we experienced when I was growing up. Some friends and I were playing basketball on a court located at St. John the Divine Cathedral on 111th Street, right off Amsterdam Avenue. The cathedral is situated right next to Morningside Heights which served as a boundary line of demarcation between our neighborhood and Black Harlem. The priests at St. John the Divine were always very gracious and welcoming to the kids in our neighborhood and often gave us access to their athletic resources, which included indoor and outdoor basketball courts and a baseball/football field. No other kids really knew about or used these facilities because the basketball courts were pretty much removed from view of the outside world, and the baseball/football field was fenced in and therefore didn't offer the easiest access from the street. To a great extent, it was almost like they were our own proprietary fields as there was never anyone that we didn't know using them.

One day, six of us were playing on the outside court on the cathedral grounds (there was only one outdoor basketball court), and seemingly from nowhere, a group of about eleven or twelve black guys, ranging in ages from teenagers to adults, strolled up to the court. We had never seen these guys in all our years hanging around there. And even though the court was just two blocks away from our apartments, our neighborhood deputies did not have jurisdiction over this area because they were technically out of their neighborhood boundaries. They performed more as a defensive force field for our block and not as an offensive armada outside of their claimed jurisdiction. They were not there to gain new ground, just to protect two narrow blocks of real estate—111th and 112th Streets between Broadway and Amsterdam avenues.

All of my friends were between twelve and thirteen years old and younger than the youngest member of the group that had landed on the basketball court, so we were at a severe developmental disadvantage. They basically walked unto our court, deliberately moved us aside—"get the fuck outta here!"—and took over the whole court, including our basketball. They started playing a full-court game while we watched from the sidelines. We were pissed. We had been thrown aside like rodents. Who the fuck were these guys, and how dare they throw us off "our" court?

I wasn't going to stand for any of this. "I'll be right back," I said, and got on my Sting-Ray and rode over to 109th street to reach out to some of the more recklessly hostile guys to explain what had happened and request some assistance. I spoke to a "captain"—a Dominican guy I had come to know from friends that lived on 109th street—and explained that these guys had come into our neighborhood and kicked us young kids off the court.

What do I mean by "captain?" This guy was in his late twenties, had a family, and all he did was hang out and give orders to other people of varying ages who would hang out with him throughout the day, every day. I had no idea what he did for a living, how he fed his family, or how he paid his rent. And I certainly did not want to know. I only knew that he commanded a lot of people on that block and that things would or would not happen based on his approval.

Most noteworthy is that no one would ever fuck with this guy. He was respected and feared for reasons I wasn't privy to at my age and he did not take kindly to outsiders coming into this Spanish neighborhood—especially from Harlem. And even though most of the Dominicans in our neighborhood had dark skin color, they did not consider themselves to be black. They considered themselves Hispanic. In my time, referring to Dominicans as "black" was insulting to them. I would imagine referring to an African American as being Dominican would have been equally insulting to them as well. After I made my case, the Dominican guy said, "Don't worry. Ride back. Keep an eye on them, and we'll be up there soon." Feeling relieved and somewhat vindicated, I rode my bike back to the courts confidently and on the winds of impending vengeance and victory. I didn't realize at the time the implications of my actions and what activities I had actually set in motion.

"This'll show these guys who the neighborhood belongs to," I said to myself.

I got back to the court, and the guys were still playing, and my friends were still there staring helplessly at the court action. My friends asked me what happened, and I gleefully whispered that the Dominican guy was coming with a bunch of his boys, and I wouldn't want to be these guys. After five or ten minutes of being there and whispering back-and-forth with my friends about the forthcoming hostilities these guys were about to experience, they dropped the basketball, stopped playing, and started to slowly walk away.

They leisurely wandered back toward Morningside Heights and their territory. It was like they had never been there. They had stayed for less than an hour. Who would have figured that?! I almost felt compelled to stop them—and mind you, for an instant, I was trying to figure out a way for them to stay there while calculating their walk-away pace compared to the pace of the mass of hurt that was coming our way.

I then realized my greatest fear. *Holy shit! I've set an army in motion, and they'll get here and there won't be anyone to inflict pain on—EXCEPT ME!* I hadn't even given a thought to how the priests would comprehend the consequences of this activity. I decided to wheel my ass back to 109th Street as fast as possible to call off the attack. As I rounded the corner just south of 111th Street, I witnessed a wave of bobbing heads along with shiny reflections off the sun from what I thought were thick metal chains. I saw bats being held up at arm's length, some resting on shoulders, others pointing toward the sky. There was a pilgrimage of about twenty people marching in a rowdy and confrontational manner toward St. John the Divine Cathedral. I immediately braked and side skidded to a stop because I also saw my ass getting the shit beat out of me and dragged in the street. This was now evolving into the closest near-death event I would experience in my young life. I panicked and pedaled home as fast as I could, lowered the shades in my bedroom, closed the door, and hid under my bed. So much for the young, savvy, badass, orchestrator-of-revenge, know-it-all turk.

About twenty minutes passed, and I was thinking I was in the clear, when I heard all kinds of commotion going on outside my parents' second-story window. The commotion included yelling out my name. My father came into my room to see what the hell was going on, and I fearfully explained the circumstances to him. He just said "OK" and left my room. My dad had a great reputation in our neighborhood because of all the things he did with the kids, like volunteering his time to coach baseball. He was a respected person who had earned that respect through his genuine interaction and presence within our community.

But that wasn't all; he also made it a point to get to know and befriend, in a wise and fatherly sort of way, all of the influencers in and around our community, good and bad. I learned a lot from him, and this was one day where his noble and astute efforts in the community paid off.

I peeked out my window, barely opening the slits of my shades to witness my father talking to the captain of the pack—the Dominican guy I had originally communicated with—who was yelling, "I don't give a fuck! I'm kicking somebody's ass today!"

I scurried back down under my bed when I heard that. You might have thought I would have been concerned about my father's safety and well-being, but I wasn't that mature yet. And yes, by the way, his mob was still with him. My friends who had been with me at the basketball court were also with this mob to see what would happen to me. Fucking assholes led these guys to where I lived.

I don't know what my father said or did, but in the subsequent minutes after that outburst, everyone left, and nothing had happened to my father. Afterward, my father bestowed on me the realities of the consequences that arise when requesting help from such individuals and contributing to the coordination of what could have been an unnecessarily tragic outcome to a situation. "Think about what you want to do. But don't do it right away. Sit back, take a breath for a good while before you respond hastily to something. And don't ever approach this guy again for anything. Ever." He was a wise man, this man. And this boy was a very lucky boy. As the sun set, I looked forward to staying away from 109th Street for a prolonged period. It would be a self-imposed exile and 109th Street was my version of a Cuban embargo.

CHAPTER FOUR

SCRATCH HANDICAP BULLSHITTER

Growing up in the city taught me a lot about survival of the fittest. If you paid attention, the different cultures, lifestyles, neighborhoods, ethnicities, and perspectives that intricately composed an urban existence provided one with a dynamic and stimulating landscape. And throughout the streets of New York City, informally appointed and self-proclaimed community gang leaders seemed to have the freedom, within somewhat lawless community autonomous zones, to shape themselves and their respective "turfs" into their own sovereign domains. These were tough neighborhoods where individuals also had an unwritten obligation to robustly defend themselves from any hostile threats to their physical well-being and street reputation.

After the St. John the Divine basketball court debacle, I instinctively resolved never to run away from challenges and adversity again because I theorized that the related anxieties attributed to always running away would continue to haunt you in some real or imagined capacity. If you were confronted with a fight, then you were literally required to fight for your respect—even if you lost. Otherwise, you could bank on surrendering your freedom and dignity because the same cowardly retreats running away from different sets of assholes would assuredly persist. And running away and hiding repeatedly was not a plausible life pathway. Most importantly, you could depend on no one but yourself. You had to stand up for yourself because you had to begin with the basic assumption that no one else was going to get your back. And that was especially true if you didn't have anyone's respect.

As a consequence, I enthusiastically decided to commit myself to developing the skill of *personable* communication—frankly, *bullshit*—as my path to enlightenment and, hopefully, success. I began to foster this skill in grade school and, as time passed, deliberately increased my energies toward attempting to influence and manipulate people, young and old, in one way or another. High school would ultimately prove to be the environment where my real developmental experience occurred and where I really sharpened my skills in social choreography. Good looking, athletic, and charismatic to boot, I forged friends and relationships with people from every walk of life: rich and poor, young and old, black, white, Hispanic, Jewish, Catholic, Protestant, feminist, gay, et cetera.

It was a wonderfully stimulating embrace of diversity at a time in life when the expression or lifestyle of the "politically correct" and "cancel culture" did not exist.

Everyone was a minority in NYC in one form or another. We were all ingredients in a large, experimental stew of racial, sexual orientation, and religious expression, where potentially insulting cultural comments were the expected part of the colorful commentary and largely ignored as meaningless banter. No one gave a shit if they were called names.

Of course, that perspective is strictly related to the relationships you had with your friends. One could not blindly approach strangers and bestow indignities upon them. It was very much like family: family has guidelines in which they can insult each other, but no one outside of family can insult your family. We were all close friends who shared our vulnerabilities and innermost thoughts with each other more than anyone else involved in our world.

And our closeness was reflected by our ability to denigrate, ridicule, and accept each other—no matter what—for what we each stood for and represented. No one cared if anyone of us referred to themselves, or each other, in what others would consider to be racially insensitive and derogatory terms—as long as it was within our circle of friends.

For us, these seemingly offensive references were evidence of our brotherhood, respect, and affection for each other. Nothing was out of line or out of bounds. We were all proud to be united under a common flag, and we laughed about the racial and cultural indignities directed at each other because we facetiously embraced the comedy of stereotypes and the shortcomings of ignorance.

We knew who we were, we were confident in ourselves, and we trusted each other, and that was enough for us. We had bigger issues to deal with. We were trying to fucking survive in, and ultimately get out of, these streets. Our crew today would probably be banished from school and would have made media headlines due to the crassness and insensitivity of our ethnic, religious, and cultural lifestyle perspectives and commentaries.

In addition to a once-in-a-lifetime crew of friends, my educational and social evolution would not have been complete without my parents. I was blessed to have had parents who spared no expense in providing me with access to the most prestigious educational forums available.

Almost every weekday, I would transform from a "spic" living on 111th Street in Manhattan to an upper-crust prep student in a school located in the mid-eighties between Lexington and Park Avenues. I wasn't born with "white privilege." I possessed hardworking "spic" privilege! Most impressive was that the school was managed by a headmaster. I mean, this was like Hogwarts before *Harry Potter*.

Prep schools in Manhattan exist in rarified air. The financial and social elites and their familial misanthropes attended, and continue to attend, these schools. Children of presidents of multinational corporations, Wall Street barons, and lineages of aristocracy filled the pipeline of students attending these prep schools, and although many were socially fit and stable, too many were social misfits because of the separation of a traditional family atmosphere and the presence of nannies rather than parents steering their childhood development.

However, that prep school was a significant contributor to my communications development because the curriculum leaned heavily on literature. Learning about the evolution of literature and the power of prose was an inspiring and meaningful experience that, in combination with my urban ethnic diversity experience, substantially expanded my exposure to include a three-hundred-and-sixty-degree view of society.

This factual and fictional literary enlightenment facilitated my ability to comprehend the characteristics that comprised a wide range of characters present in real life, as they were also portrayed in novels, short stories, and other forms of literature. In effect, it was life reflecting art and vice versa. The curriculum and the interaction with professors who, for a large part, were young and relatable (not far from having gotten their graduate degrees from

Ivy League academia) accelerated my ability to become articulate, insightful, inquisitive, and engaging. It was like performing in lifestyle theater—my '70s version of reality TV. Our professors even smoked pot with us on occasion.

CHAPTER FIVE

PERFECTING SCRAMBLING TECHNIQUES AT A YOUNG AGE

My best friend in my junior and senior years in high school, a Jewish kid—let's call him Alan—and I were on our way to a party somewhere in Long Island City. Like most city kids that traveled throughout the city, we had taken the subway there. After departing from the train station on our way to the party, I had noticed that we were passing through a seemingly nasty neighborhood with abandoned buildings and storefronts that transformed to pool rooms and bars at night. I was convinced this would be a different neighborhood at night when we came back this way to go home—versus what we were experiencing as we jaunted through it during the afternoon. Alan, on the other hand, didn't notice much as he wouldn't shut up about who was going to the party and which girl he was going to try to woo in his attempt to get laid that night.

Alan was sporting his finest nicely pressed jeans, a shirt unbuttoned three buttons down to show he had no hair on his chest, a corduroy jacket (the coolest kind of corduroy jacket, with suede elbow pads), and the signature footwear that was the fashion statement of our time, other than Converse—Frye boots. Any guy in our age group had to have Frye boots because they were established footwear for "studs." Earth shoes ran a distant second. And let me not forget one other jewelry accessory that he was sporting: he had a huge Star of David marqueed on his hairless chest like a walking, shouting-from-the-mountaintops, Jewish billboard parading around in a less-than-impoverished neighborhood. A neighborhood where trash cans were set ablaze at night to provide for intermittent heat and ground-level street lights. But for now, we were on our way to the party during daytime, and not too much could go wrong. I suspected that the walk back home at night would paint a different proposition as the streetlights were probably not going to be working.

We had a great time at the party, and as expected, Alan didn't pick up any girls or get laid. He would return, as he often did, disillusioned, empty-handed, and somewhat bitterly reflective. It was 10 p.m., and although streetlights were buzzing on and off (as I expected), our walk back through the suspect area was proceeding in an uneventful manner. It was kind of chilly out and the streets seemed deserted. But that in itself made my neck hairs stand on end because it wasn't cold enough outside to force people to stay indoors. I surmised that concerns about criminal activity were keeping everyone off the streets. This then led to my consideration that if there weren't many people on these streets, then how fucking stupid was it for two dumb-ass white—well one that was pretending to be white—guys to be strolling these streets at night? This situation presented Alan and I with a disturbing opportunity to get ambushed.

Three blocks away from the train station, closely approaching our safe zone, we passed a down-and-dirty hamburger restaurant that was about one hundred and fifty feet away from us. Outside of the strongly illuminated hamburger joint, was a skinny Black kid, standing in a spotlight by himself, hanging around dribbling a basketball.

It was innocuous enough for Alan and me to ignore, and I didn't get a sense of any perceived threats until the kid yelled, "Hey, ya fucking honkies. What the fuck are ya fucking crackers doing here? Get the fuck outta here before you get your asses kicked!"

I coyly and intelligently chose to ignore the remarks and continued our stroll. Alan indignantly turned to me indicating he wanted to confront the kid, and I told him without turning my head, maintaining my focus, and looking straight ahead, "Don't say a goddamn word and keep going." Alan, having grown up in a nice bubble of a neighborhood on the Lower East Side of Manhattan, wasn't particularly astute or cognizant of the consequences that could unfurl when you challenge people in a neighborhood that you are unfamiliar with—and a neighborhood that is completely composed of skin color that does not even closely resemble the color of your skin. He was acutely unaware of the fact that he was out of his comfort zone.

I quickly unraveled what was going on in his mind without him having said a word, and repeated, "Don't say a fucking word and keep walking."

The skinny Black kid who was all of five foot, three inches, proceeded to yell again, "That's right. Keep walking you white faggots!" And then again, "You White boys are all faggots!"

The kid obviously did not know that I was only impersonating a white boy and that Alan and I were not dating.

Unfortunately, or fortunately, I don't look like a stereotypical "spic." I have a lot of "White" features that kind of distinguish me from other Hispanics, to the point that when I am with white people, they don't feel I'm Hispanic. They think I am more like them. In a way, it makes them feel more comfortable associating with someone homogenous. It's just the way it is. My thinking was that Alan had built up too much testosterone because he hadn't gotten laid at the party, or that he actually thought he was tough, or he had no clue that what he was about to do would result in a high probability of an unfavorable outcome—or all the above. It was too late. The genie was about to be let out of the bottle.

Alan had surrendered any common sense to sophomoric emotion. He suddenly jerked around, took a couple of steps toward the kid, and loudly blurted back, "You little Black shit! Get the fuck over here and these White boys will kick your fucking ass!"

"*Ummm . . . We'll what?!*"

It was now too late to manage what Alan had put in motion by employing rudimentary escape tactics. My next thought was that I was now stuck with Alan no matter what. *Or was I?* I quickly flipped through my options. I could just turn and run to the train and abandon him here to meet his fate, like throwing chum in the water. I mean, I ran much faster than he did, and I wasn't wearing Frye boots. My other thought was to start yelling in Spanish and just kick Alan's ass for the Black kid and drag his torso with me to the train. But I chose my third option and turned back to Alan, grabbed his arm, and swung him ninety degrees to face me.

"What the fuck do you think you are doing, you stupid fuck?!" I demanded.

Astoundingly, Alan's response to me was, "He's a skinny fucking kid. We can kick his ass."

"We're not going anywhere or kicking anyone's ass, you fucking shithead. We're going home." I forcefully pointed Alan toward the train station and kept moving at a prescribed, for the situation, pace. It was a ballroom dancing move. My mind was now racing, waiting for the proverbial other shoe to drop as it painfully occurred to me that, first, we were in the Black kid's neighborhood, and second, I knew how it worked in any inner-city neighborhood: you did not instigate confrontations like this without the appropriate backup. Yet we—fucking Alan—let ourselves get baited into a potential confrontation. Not exactly what you would describe as a favorable, inspiring position. Not one I would bet on.

As I finished our choreographed turn, my hopes and prayers to our heavenly father, mother, aunts, uncles, cousins, stepbrothers, and any future children, were that the current situation would be benign and that the potential for disaster would subside if we just ignored the circumstances. At that moment in time, I resorted to playing make-believe and kept walking. Five or six steps into our retreat, I heard a glass shattering whistle. And no, it was not a train whistle, or the grinding of metal wheels screeching from the train station, or a male bird romantically chirping for the chance to attract a female bird. No. The whistle was emanating from the little Black kid replicating his very own bird call. As I turned to observe the unfolding musical event, I made note that the whistle was being directed toward the hamburger joint. I stopped us in our tracks and slowly turned completely around so that we could both anxiously observe six other Black guys in varying types of body masses, heights, and ages pour out of the restaurant. Four out of the six were *big* dudes. Like, all pro, defensive-line dudes. The other two were of medium height and girth. I looked at Alan, who noticed this and was now paralytically speechless—the badass that he was—and watched the blood drain from his face, transforming his skin into a blob of pizza dough. Obviously, whatever testosterone-powered confidence he mistakenly thought he possessed had understandably evaporated along with the unrecoverable deep body retraction of his testicles. Because of the unfolding circumstance and having created this uncalled-for dilemma, Alan was now idiotically scared shitless. I could see by his flaccid expression that he thought his final resting spot would occur in a slum next to this restaurant. In his naïveté, he was unable to comprehend the consequences of a momentary lapse of judgment. Remember that Alan was not raised in a slum. He was simply a clumsy white boy trying to fit in with guys from the street.

"Ohhhhh shit," he proclaimed out loud in an involuntary, autonomic reaction.

"Oh shit? No shit, you fucking idiot!"

At this point, Alan appeared to be in a self-induced coma complemented by glassy eyes that did not respond to any external stimulus. He had morphed into a useless lava lamp. A barnacle on a pier.

He used both his hands to harshly grab my arm and managed to exhale a terrified, zombies-are-attacking-us, gut-wrenching, whisper-shriek of "Let's run for it!!"

My experience from growing up and traversing these neighborhoods pointed to a psychological strategy of never running away from a fight unless you had a clear and unmistakable exit strategy that successfully ensured your safe harbor. Otherwise, you were no different from wounded prey trying to evade the hunter while leaving a trail of blood, which meant that the wounded prey attempting to escape had little time left in this world. In our case, we weren't familiar with the territory and consequently our physical surroundings. There was no apparent or designated "safe house" in the foreseeable distance, and no one we could rely on for backup. Not to mention the fact that no one in this 'hood was going to open their doors to provide sanctuary for two "White guys" in favor of their noteworthy, upstanding community brethren.

Nowhere to run. Nowhere to hide. No one to ask for help. And remember, this was also before cell phones.

"Listen to me asshole! We're not running anywhere," I declared.

Man, you should have seen Alan's eyes light up at that moment. If there was ever a face that would collectively illustrate fear, panic, nausea, diarrhea, confusion, and the effects of a stroke, it was Alan's face.

"We're going straight to them and dealing with this face to face!"

Our only choices were stark, and I felt our odds were vastly better played out by going on offense. Also, I had noticed something unusual that was now quickly factoring into my calculations. Even though they had assembled into a pack, they were not moving toward us. We had started moving toward them but they weren't moving at all.

This was a very important sign. In my opinion, it was a reflection that *they* were waiting to see what *we* would do and were caught off guard that we had taken the offensive. It indicated a bit of caution on their part.

Proceeding with caution, or hesitation, on the streets could be interpreted as fear. I asked myself if they could potentially be scared of us. Was it possible that, rather than them thinking that we mistakenly turned into the wrong neighborhood, like Clark Griswold in *National Lampoon's Vacation*—could they be thinking that we were intentionally roaming this neighborhood looking for trouble as a pair of crazy-ass, mentally disturbed rednecks?

As the situation evolved, I quickly calibrated everyone's movements and behaviors and concluded that our only logical response was to both face our fears *and* conduct an aggressive discussion with them. The fact that they weren't bum-rushing us, even though they had the odds and size on their side, was an indication that there was a slight window, a slight opportunity, for a diplomatic dialogue to recover from this unforced error.

I didn't observe any weapons being pulled, so that was good. I was starting to feel in control of the situation and was going to follow my instincts and calculus to turn this circumstance into a remotely positive outcome. I would rely on my finest, and frankly only God-given weapon—my ability to bullshit and fuck with someone's head. Bullshit was a weapon that unquestionably gave me an advantage. I was sporting ninja-master level bullshit. With that, I told Alan to button up his shirt to the top so that nobody could see the Star of David (I wanted to eliminate potential antisemitism from the equation) around his neck.

I said, "Just shut the fuck up! Got it? Don't say a fucking word! Just nod. I got this."

Alan attentively followed orders as we strutted—with conviction and purpose—toward our potential tormentors. Their body language was now clearly speaking to me in inquisitive, non-adversarial terms. They were a bit surprised to see what they thought were two White boys approaching them in their neighborhood, on their turf, without any regard for their own safety, throwing fear to the wind. It was just the reaction I wanted to achieve to start our interaction.

We had achieved the element of surprise in that their response toward our confident aggression was a clumsily uncertain and hesitant "on their heels" posture.

At this point, our proximity to them was confirmation that they thought we were fucking crazy, which meant that maybe *they* weren't that crazy—or hostile—after all. In the street, whoever has the upper hand on "crazy" has the edge because no one is crazy enough to fuck with a fundamentally assertive crazier motherfucker. Their body language screamed out to me that they thought we were White alien fucking beings who had landed on earth from another fucking solar system.

Within ten feet of the pack I yelled, "Yo, man! What's the fucking problem?"

The little Black guy, apparently the head of this group, looked at me quizzically and was expecting to hear more before he came to a decision about us.

He glared incredulously and asked, "What the fuck are you White motherfuckers doing in my house!?"

Talking instead of attacking, I thought, was a very good sign.

"My man, we're here because Javier (obviously not his real name) from the 7 Immortals is friends with your boy JoJo (also not his real name), with the Ghetto Brothers and he told us we were clear to move through here. Do you know Javier with the 7 Immortals?"

The kid nodded to show that he knew him, which confirmed to me that he was full of shit. He just didn't want to reveal to his pack that he wasn't in the loop with prominent gang leaders. Of course, I was also full of shit, because although I knew of a guy named JoJo being the head of the Ghetto Brothers in the surrounding neighborhoods, I didn't know him from a tee time.

Javier and I had been childhood friends, and although we had gone our different ways, we would still talk and hang out on occasion, but he never provided, nor did I ask for his backup to cross this turf. He was a very smart kid who decided to gang up rather than go down an academic route.

"Javier told me that we would be fine comin' across your turf, man."

Now the Black kid was really curious. The 7 Immortals was one of four predominant gangs in NYC at that time. The four gangs combined controlled roughly 80 percent of the Hispanic and African American neighborhoods. If you weren't a member of one of these gangs in your neighborhood, you certainly knew someone who was.

Javier was the Captain overseeing our neighborhood and was regarded as a management level above the self-appointed, older crew of teenagers that were protecting our block. He was actually a nice guy who was thoughtful and even-tempered and more interested in helping people out rather than doing bad shit. He was not remotely close to being a stereotypical thug and wouldn't strike you as a kid who was "tough" other than the colors and embroidery that he would wear on his sleeveless denim jacket. He was a kid who went to Catholic school with me through eighth grade and was accepted at renowned NYC high schools like Cardinal Spellman, Cardinal Hayes, and Stuyvesant. He hadn't said shit to me about crossing this neighborhood because I hadn't asked him about it. But I still threw his name out there, hoping beyond hope that it would stick and make some kind of impression. I was pissing shit between my legs. That's a combination of shitting and pissing in my pants simultaneously. Like a terror-induced balsamic vinaigrette.

The other three predominant gangs at that time were the Latin Kings, the Black Spades, and the Ghetto Brothers. Back then, the hostility and violence between gangs were not like what exists today. Clearly, the roles of gangs evolved as they transformed their working model from "protecting neighborhoods" to the businesses of trafficking drugs and territory enforcement. Violence was a natural metastasis of these activities in order to assert control, reputation, and business dominance against other gangs.

"You friends with Javier?"

The sense of relief I felt when he directed this question at me was overwhelming. I was surprised, and we were fortunate, that my Hail-Mary pass had seemingly worked. Luckily, Alan was still a stone fucking zombie. He wasn't even sweating. I was pretty sure that during the ten minutes that had elapsed, he had completely dehydrated. Now I was worried that he would pass out.

I nodded and said, "Yeah, man. I told Javier I had to come this way with my friend to go to a party and I guess he's friendly with your guy. He thought it was no big deal and to just use his name if anything came up. He said JoJo was a good guy."

The Black kid affirmed, "Yeah, he's solid, bro."

Bro? The kid called me bro. We continued to exchange some guarded common-ground pleasantries, exchanging names, acting like tough guys, but we were figuratively talking about the weather for the next couple of minutes.

"Cool?" I asked.

"Yeah. We're cool."

"Thanks, man. I'll let Javier know."

After this anguishing Oprah moment, and not wanting to overstay my welcome, cognizant that the longer I talked, the greater the chance that I would somehow fuck this thing up and the guy would wise up to my bullshit, I thanked him and walked away. I didn't even acknowledge his pack when I turned away. Wouldn't give them the respect. By doing that, I elevated the respect of the little Black kid in his sidekicks' eyes. This was the theoretical code of conduct that was recognized as conversational protocol with potential "gang" confrontations in the street, which dictated that first and foremost, you respected the "management hierarchy." During this brief interaction with this gentleman, Alan behaved like the little lap dog that I was hoping he would. All Alan did was stand there with his shirt buttoned up, nodding his head like the little toy dogs on a car dashboard. As we walked away, Alan muttered through the side of his mouth, "What do we do now?"

"Walk. Strut slowly, dude. We can't rush out of here or they'll think we're full of shit. Easy, casual. We can't show any fear."

I looked out of the side of my eyes and noticed movement with these guys talking amongst themselves. I was certain that some of the conversation entailed opinions from some of the guys that we shouldn't have been allowed to walk without a beating. I could tell because there seemed to be an active debate going on where the supposed leader of this pack seemed to be articulating and defending his point of view.

This was all speculation on my part, of course, but I would go with what I felt. Nonetheless, when we turned a corner and were in a position that was completely out of sight of the pack . . . "Run for the train!!" The train was now two blocks away from us, and we ran as fast as we could to get into the subway stop. Only two thoughts ran through my mind in between gasping for air: 1) that a train would be approaching so we could hop on and get the fuck out of here; or 2) that there would be a cop at the station. Fat chance the latter was going to happen, so I had to offset my anxiety with option 1. I had figured, given the debate taking place, that if we didn't see them within five minutes, then we would be safe. There wasn't a cop. The train took about ten minutes, and fortunately the debate must have come and gone, because an attack did not materialize. None of the provocateurs wanted to get hostile and so Alan and I got home safe that night.

CHAPTER SIX

SIX YEARS OF COLLEGE FLY BY, AND NO GOLF IN SIGHT YET

I graduated high school as a moderate B-average student and was accepted to a distinguished engineering school in upstate New York. In retrospect, I recognized this offer as a blatant token selection as I was one of only a handful of Hispanics on campus, and I certainly did not have the grades or SAT scores to be accepted at such a high-level institution. And although my parents were blue-collar, working-class people, they paid the full freight of school costs throughout my cherished six years of undergraduate education. I was fortuitously never burdened with school debt until I decided to pursue a master's degree later in life. My parents culturally felt that education was one of the best investments they could make, and they put their money behind their philosophy and commitment. This was a lifelong lesson, as my wife and I have paid it forward with our children.

I was placed on academic probation after my first year of college because of twenty-four seven frolicking—being either drunk or stoned (usually both), and incessantly fucking around. In an anxious effort to help me find my way, my parents decided to ship me off to a northwest suburb of Chicago to live with my aunt, technically exiling me to another land. I slept in the basement of my aunt's house with strict orders for my aunt to report on my daily activities and to make sure that I enrolled at another college. I neglected to mention that in addition to having been placed on academic probation my freshman year, I had also been kicked off the junior varsity basketball team for arguing with the coach. I thought that was a nice touch. All combined, a recipe for looming disaster was on the menu for me moving forward.

I usually responded decently to adverse events, always thinking of them as moments of opportunity, and I didn't miss a beat when I was exported to Chicago. I started at a community college in Illinois for the fall semester. Acutely aware of there not being a viable national database in existence to vet a student's background, I simply lied about my first year of college attendance. "I took my freshman year off to backpack through Europe," I told the admitting clerk at the junior college. Backpacking through Europe was an exceptionally popular thing to do after graduating high school. Many freshman-bound college students would take what is nowadays considered a "gap year" to unconsciously trundle through Europe by train.

The admitting clerk was very happy to hear that story of exploration and self-realization and felt like she was talking to an enlightened soul, stating, "That's a wonderful experience. I wish more students would take the opportunity to explore the world and learn from different cultures."

Uh, yeah. Whatever. If you grew up on 111th Street in New York City, you wouldn't need to skip around Europe to saturate yourself with different cultures.

"Welcome to Franklin Community College," said the clerk. *Of course, this is not the name of the college. I just don't want them to rebuke my community college degree for lying to get admitted.*

Academically, I did OK there. I also made the cut to play on the varsity basketball team. After my marginal college accomplishments and quick acclimation to Chicago, I elevated my scholastic objectives and researched opportunities to achieve some form of academic credibility.

With one year of college in the trash and two more partially redeeming myself at Franklin, it was now time to get my shit together and begin forming a career path, springboarding on the back of whatever course studies I would dedicate myself to. I decided to apply to an iconic, academic Catholic institution that was, and is still, embedded in Chicago history, lore, and connections: DePaul University. I decided I needed to focus on some type of business curriculum and DePaul was a business-leaning school with strong Chicago linkages. They accepted my application.

I congratulated myself with an "attaboy'" and regarded my renewed efforts to achieve a modicum of academic integrity as a hell of a comeback from being disgracefully suspended from my lackluster first attempt at higher learning. After witnessing my resurgence as a responsible human being, my parents also calmed down—so much so that they also decided to move to Chicago. But not because of me. They decided on the move because, as luck would have it, a house right next door to my aunt's was up for sale. It was the perfect storm. Now I would have two sisters, and two mothers, living right next to each other. Like stereo speakers placed on each side of my room. I had now moved out of my aunt's basement and moved in with my parents right next door, with my own bedroom.

Although I felt redeemed by my acceptance to DePaul and the educational and career opportunities it offered, I was concerned with the academic challenge it presented, especially considering my continued tepid discipline toward enhancing my study skills. Leaning back on my original premise in high school of effectively maximizing my grading opportunities while minimizing my academic sweat equity, I needed to quickly master and consequently employ tactics that optimized my ability to do well academically.

Fuck it. I was smart enough to find a partial workaround as I earnestly wanted to learn something useful that could make me money. My brilliant scheme would be to simply date the most applied—and hopefully prettiest— female student in whatever classes that proved to be daunting. Yup. I did the math and convinced myself that this would be the best approach. *After all, it wasn't brain surgery, right?*

I enrolled in classes and a dating curriculum. My rule of thumb was simple: I would uncharacteristically apply myself to studying for classes that were the core of my selected major, *and* I would compile a dossier of dating candidates to tutor me on supplementary classes that complemented my degree. Unfortunately, my dating theory did contain two troubling flaws. One was that I could conceivably have to endure a false narrative with a woman I didn't have any sincere feelings for under the malicious intent of abusing her emotions solely to serve my selfish needs. The second was that I would grow to care for my unsuspecting accomplice.

Throwing emotional caution to the wind, I committed to a short-term plan that did not include time for any genuine romance or emotionally charged theatrical baggage. Statistics class was a prime example of an academic discipline that represented all kinds of issues for me. My brain was not able to figure out how to process the content. I couldn't just memorize the material because I had to understand how to apply the formulas, and I couldn't retain that shit for longer than a minute. It was my kryptonite but I had to pass. It was a requisite course.

When stats class began, I was fortunate to have crossed paths with Lucy (not her real name). She was on the volleyball team and was an all-American girl who sat two seats directly in front of me. She was an unassuming but very pretty lady and before I could say standard deviation, I started to date the very pretty athlete and consequently, started to do very well in statistics.

Lucy and I had been dating since about midway through the quarter but we hadn't been in a situation where the opportunity presented itself to have sex. Eventually, she asked me to go to her house on a day her mother was going shopping and wouldn't be home. I was excited not only at the opportunity to partake in sexual recreation, but at the realization that Lucy was the one who initiated the invitation and the plan. I went to her house and was greeted at the door by her mom—who was physically a complete contrast to Lucy. Her mom was short, pudgy, with one leg shorter than the other, encouraging a decidedly well-seasoned limp. But that wasn't all; she also had a glass eye that didn't line up with what her other eye was doing. You never knew which eye to line up with when looking at someone with an oscillating glass eye in a discussion. You kind of felt like a boxer avoiding punches by bobbing and weaving to get your bearings and line of sight stabilized. How the fuck Lucy was conceived, pretty as she was, from the DNA of this woman was beyond my comprehension. It had to be some kind of miracle. Maybe that's why they were so devout in their religious beliefs.

We exchanged a short round of mandatory pleasantries, and she went on her way out as Lucy arrived at the door. Let the festivities begin! We pranced down to her family room, which was a converted basement. It had a TV, a pool table, a wet bar, and so on when I took notice of a two-foot wide by three-foot high section on the wall above the floor, directly behind and slightly above the pool table level. It was covered in some kind of bluish, purplish velvet drapery, which was trimmed with a gold-colored material. Lucy got us both beers, we drank a bit and she revealed to my astonishing ears that she was still a virgin. I was dismayed because I had never been with a virgin, didn't know how to respond to that, and immediately felt off-balance. I attempted to recalibrate my mindset to be extra sensitive, cautious, and gentle in my approach. It spoke to her sincere dedication to her faith and religion, but I had never met anyone who still hadn't had sex by twenty-one years of age.

I was exposed early on to sex and had lost my virginity as a freshman in high school.

My Manhattan neighborhood friends were at the forefront of young adolescent promiscuity. In seventh grade, if any one of our friends had engaged in masturbating their girlfriend, they would intentionally not wash their hands until some of us had the infantile perverted opportunity to get a whiff of the scent from their fingers. It was a common, accepted practice. In fact, when I attended a Catholic grade school, two of my classmates, a beautiful Puerto Rican girl and an equally pretty black girl, were pregnant by eighth grade. And they kept the babies. So, it stood to reason that by my freshman year in high school I had begun to engage in full-blown sexual activities. And I actively engaged in this recreation without the benefit of utilizing any birth control tools other than stupidly relying on the technique of exceptional withdrawal timing. I was incredibly lucky not to have accidentally created any human beings that I am aware of.

Lucy and I then started childishly playing with each other, and our passionate wrestling led to my lifting her up onto the pool table, where she enthusiastically discarded her below-the-waist garments. I unbuckled my belt, unzipped my fly, dropped my pants and underwear down to my ankles, and hopped up on the table. What happened next can only be described as divine intervention, a holy revelation akin to getting struck by a lightning bolt while being serenaded by a bevy of baby angels descending from heaven, all strumming harps. To this day, it still unnerves my psyche.

With Lucy on the pool table and me climbing up with my garments lassoing my legs, we clumsily and unseductively bungled ourselves into a faux Kama Sutra position, disruptively scattering the billiard balls. The moving and grooving must have produced pronounced vibrations that reverberated within the immediate surroundings, causing the bluish, purply velvety, drapery with gold-colored trim to fall off the wall. It caught my attention as the drape voluptuously flowed, dropping toward the floor in what appeared to be slow motion. What it revealed was nothing I would have imagined, much less expected in anyone's then moderately appointed home. It revealed the statue of a female saint placed in an embedded rectangle space in the wall that was carved out to accommodate the statue.

It was a religious shrine, complete with dried flowers and dormant candles surrounding the base of the statue. I was on my hands and knees on the pool table, with my pants and underwear wrapped around my ankles, with a hard on, and face to face with a religious symbol. The bluish, purply, velvety drape with gold-colored trim languished on the floor, leaving me to stare directly into the eyes of the saint, which was just above Lucy's head as she lay on her back. I could see Lucy wondering what, other than the sight of her naked flesh from the waist down, was it that captured my attention enough to stop me dead in my tracks? My thoughts quickly whirled back to my initial encounter with Lucy's mother on the steps of the house, trying to figure out which way the glass eye was pointing from her four-foot, seven-inch bulbous frame, and immediately whipped around again to focus my searing eyes on the saint, then recoiled back to Lucy looking at me and still wondering what my problem was.

Lucy was still looking good despite the unveiling of a saint, but I was now spooked out of my wits. I felt my hair standing on end and my legs were shaking. *Was all this a part of a religious ritual?* Amazingly, I still maintained a hard on (for whatever reason, my brain was not communicating with my dick) and without any more thought than to let fear grip my sense of logic *and* lust, I decided to run for my life. I jumped off the pool table and ran up the stairs, pulling my underwear and pants up in whatever manner I could without falling. I didn't want to be the predictable horror-movie equivalent of a girl falling as she runs away from the monster or serial killer. And I certainly could not afford to take a tumble with a hard on. I hurled myself out of that house, buckling up my pants as I hit the sidewalk, never to look back. The last memory I had of Lucy was her lying on the pool table, stupefied by my incoherent actions.

We barely spoke to each other again and I barely survived the stats class due to my unexpectedly breaking up with Lucy just before finals. The timing really sucked. Even though I believe it is absolutely appropriate to follow the values you believe in, the depths of which Lucy and her family were religious was too much for me to digest.

About one month later, just after I had managed to push Lucy and that event out of my consciousness, a priest approached me on campus. He introduced himself, initiated introductory conversational babble, and then bluntly segued into Lucy and our relationship, pointing out that what I had done was not right and that Lucy still cared for me. He then suggested that I give the relationship another chance. It took me about five seconds to respond, "Who the fuck do you think you are, getting in my face about none of your business?" No, I didn't say that, but it was what I was thinking. I politely told him it was not his business and I was sorry he felt that way and that I was not going back to that crazy ass woman! No, I didn't say that either, even though I had thought that. What I actually said was, "I didn't mean to hurt her, Father, but it didn't work out." The priest turned away, frustrated by not having gained any ground with me and not fulfilling his quest, and remarked, "OK, son. Just say ten Hail Marys and ten Our Fathers." No, he didn't say that either. We concluded our conversation and moved on. But I did worry that somehow this priest would try to fuck me in some way at this school like a fucking inquisition retribution.

As far as I was concerned, God was looking out *for me* by clearly preventing me from having sex with Lucy and getting involved with this family.

Not to be deterred, I continued to engage in my ethically questionable dating tactics, including a stint with a female professor of anthropology, all fortunately resulting in favorable outcomes with grades. And although all the degree-inspiring relationships were experienced as short-term episodes that lasted a quarter at a time, I completed my three-year mission (I was working full-time for one year and taking classes at night) at DePaul and was able to graduate with a degree.

CHAPTER SEVEN

ANCHORS AWEIGH, AMIGO. ANCHORS AWEIGH.

The current term is "anchor baby," and I am a living example of it. Prior to the current explosion of overwhelmingly illegal immigration, there was little attention paid to the term as the United States used to do a much better job of managing the influx of immigrants, ensuring that all immigrants coming to the United States adhered to immigration laws that have nowadays become politically inconvenient. The fact that current political rhetoric encourages illegal immigration is insulting to all immigrants who followed the law, as there is no equity placed on the integrity and values associated with being a legal American citizen aspiring to realize the American dream. I want to note, however, that I also know wonderful, hard-working, honorable people and families who are here illegally and who deserve to be supported with every opportunity to become American citizens through legal avenues. The current incentives and pandering provided by current government policies and politicians that look away rather than enforce immigration laws naturally motivates immigrants not to pursue legal citizenship options. Not legally honoring the values and benefits associated with earning the right to be an American citizen is detrimental to our society and demeans the sacrifices made in honor of our freedom.

My father was a very smart man who was involved in the political landscape in Cuba, pre-Castro and during the Castro upheaval. He was fully aware of, and skeptical of, the political instability in Cuba, and he wanted me to be born on American soil, automatically qualifying me to have all the protections afforded to an American citizen. Sometime in the late fall of 1957, our family traveled to New York City and stayed with my mom's sister on 111th Street in Manhattan. I was subsequently born at the then-existing Flower Hospital on Fifth Avenue in February of 1958. My parents decided that being born in the United States, which granted me automatic American citizenship, was worth the tenuous traveling risks.

Fulgencio Batista originally served as Cuba's duly elected president from 1940 until 1944. Just prior to the presidential elections of 1952, Batista staged a military coup ousting the current president, and presided as Cuba's dictator from 1952 until he was overthrown in 1959. My father was not at all confident in the ability of Batista's regime to maintain its power due to the pervasive government corruption, the influence of the mafia (Cuba was regarded as the Latin Las Vegas), and the incessant misery experienced by a robust majority of Cubans. The political stability in Cuba was rapidly deteriorating on multiple levels and he felt these elements all added up to a foreseeable revolutionary clash. Nonetheless, shortly after my birth, we would journey back to Cuba to continue our lives while anticipating Castro's revolution to be successful. Their foresight of having me be an anchor baby turned out to be an intellectually astute decision.

My dad was justifiably concerned about the current state of affairs in Cuba, but also cynical about how the new political realignment would play out.

And he had every reason to be. He was a college friend of Fidel Castro.

My dad, Castro, and another friend were student artists of law and politics at Universidad de La Habana. They often socialized together, passionately exchanging political perspectives and theoretical discussions of civil societal management through government, politics, and business. The three of them were politically conscious and frequently engaged in debating each other, with Castro taking a communist/socialist stance and the other student taking a capitalist stance, while my father, more often than not, remained neutral and acted as a moderator, encouraging further discussion and thought on the themes while respecting both points of view. All three were very intelligent, well-read, and soundly-prepared students. Unwittingly, the gentleman student who always postured the opposing side of Castro's perspective would later come to personally experience a dramatic event, courtesy of Castro, that would impact his ability to continue to live in Cuba.

As Castro was honing his political rhetoric and accumulating vast numbers of followers, he became increasingly aggressive about his socialist perspective and disdain for a capitalist society. However, he was sly enough not to blatantly tip his hand and reveal what his ultimate goal was. Say or feel whatever you want about Castro, but regardless of your personal perspective, regardless of how inherently reprehensible an individual you think he was—and he was— he was also an exceptionally intelligent individual who was well versed in the manipulation of populist rhetoric and who gleefully indulged in the political attention he was garnering between the competing landscapes of two world superpowers—the Soviet Union and the United States of America. This perspective was clearly evident when he daringly thrust Cuba into the theater of war with the Cuban Missile Crisis, performing as the catalyst and architect of a potentially devastating scenario with disastrous consequences for humanity. Fidel was poised to exploit the fear and paranoia that the United States and Russia had for each other for his own political benefit, all in his design to turn Cuba into his own, unique, self-proclaimed political Shangri-La. Cuba was a clean canvas, and he would be its PiCastro.

YOU WOULD THINK THE SUN COMES OUT FOR EVERYONE

Castro's discreet discourse of a Marxist-Leninist type of society embraced the proletarian revolution philosophy of militant tactics, and his tirelessly electric determination, personality, and movement were enthusiastically gaining popularity. However, the Batista regime did not initially view him as a legitimate regime threat. It was a position that would ultimately prove to be a major miscalculation. Complacently ignoring the potential of Castro's appeal, Batista and his ilk naïvely and ignorantly viewed him as an amateur revolutionary romantic with a misguided message that they thought would not resonate with or gather any meaningful support among the populace. Compounding the misguided calculation, the Batista regime also underestimated the resentment of many Cuban people as it related to the glaring class distinctions and abuses conducted by government officials.

Additionally, the blatant and far-reaching environment of corruption of the Batista administration presented a government that was arrogantly insulated, one that embraced an unrealistic perspective of its state of political dominance. Ignorance, the sense of invincibility, and a lack of paranoia led to perilous levels of political stupidity, which contributed to behavior that reflected apathy and disregard toward Castro by the Batista regime. They incorrectly assessed that Castro was nothing more than a diminished bohemian entertainer who did not pose a threat to their authority and control. Moreover, they obnoxiously and continuously ignored the cries of despair echoed by the common laborers while all of Batista's minions reveled in their ordained luxury. Simply, the Batista regime was selfishly unwilling to comprehend the fact that their malicious policies of catering to and upholding the societal elite caste system were at the expense of not enabling similar lifestyle and educational opportunities for the lower socioeconomic segments of the population.

This was a typical Latin American dictatorship management mentality in which there is no such thing as trickle-down economics. It was the common and unpleasantly consistent practice of the elite class in Latin American countries where they would exploit, oppress, and keep the classes exquisitely distinct in order to maintain their social class "purity." This perverse societal manifesto ensured the rigid restriction of any opportunities for the classes to mix in order to preserve the racial and social exclusivity for the ruling class. In fact, if you came from a certain background or were a "campesino," breaking into the ranks of the privileged was nearly impossible because their access to academic specialties and professional opportunities was, at best, a cynical illusion.

I am by no means a socialist or communist by thoughts, actions, or conviction, but I am critical of the persistent dictatorship mentality in Latin American countries where democracy is showcased as perfunctory window dressing when in reality, these dictators are running slave lands where the club elite exclusively enjoy the advantages that ordinary citizens will never come to experience. It is a myopic mentality, as sharing a small portion of the inbred perks of entitlement with the rest of the country's populace would, to a great extent, satisfy the masses—but nothing was ever shared, as greed and the divine right of "inherited" privilege exempted opportunity for anyone else.

There is an old refrain in governance in terms of keeping the majority of the populace happy within the framework of government management: "the sun comes out for everyone." This phrase and working philosophy is a tactic employed by the smarter politicians to keep their populace "satisfied," all the while fundamentally sacrificing a minimum level of perks and power. It is a maliciously smart and functional political ploy whereby deploying "slivers of the pie" to share with the masses will placate and numb them from any internal dissatisfaction and unrest.

In Cuba, where it is sunny most of the time, the sun only came out for chosen Cuban politicians, businessmen, land owners, and Americans as opposed to the Cuban populace. Consequently, the lack of Cuban sun shining on everyone laid the seeds for a revolution whose driving theme was to tame the thirst for societal fairness through the desperate, but misguided, conciliation of the redistribution of wealth. As the passion and temperament of revolution began to metastasize, Castro was intentionally and masterfully displaying two political faces, both of which were seemingly noncommittal toward America or the Soviet Union. However, he was acutely aware that the United States would not support the occupation of a dictator who was a socialist, whereas the Soviet Union would.

The political ignorance of the Batista administration created a susceptible landscape, encouraging an increase in brazenly armed attacks targeting his government, and on July 26, 1953, after Castro unsuccessfully captained an armed coup attempt on the Moncada Cuban military barracks in Santiago de Cuba, he was captured, arrested, and jailed. Unfortunately for Batista, and influenced by a combination of international pressure, his shotgun-riding politicians, advisors, and Cuba's Congress, he released Castro early in 1955 through an amnesty decree and commuted his sentence. Batista regarded Castro as an irreverent but harmless political anarchist, but he also freed him in part to gain sentiment with the people supporting Castro and under the delusional perspective that those people would perceive him, Batista, as a gracious and tolerant leader.

Castro's release from jail by Batista was designed to be a gesture of compassion and goodwill that demonstrated empathy for the plight of the common man while delivering the backhanded insult of delegitimizing and minimizing his status as a potential revolutionary threat. But the freedom from jail allowed Castro to travel to Mexico for approximately eighteen months (until November, 1956) and gave him time to regroup his resources, strategy, and benefactors. During his time in Mexico, Castro also traveled to New York, Miami, Philadelphia, and other cities in the United States in fundraising efforts to support his revolution and another attempt to overthrow Batista. Ironically, the failed attack on the Moncada military barracks on July 26, 1953 inspired the creation of Castro's M-26-7 revolutionary organization (Movimiento 26 de Julio) to commemorate the birthplace of the revolution to overthrow Batista. It was an organization that would ultimately prove to be a key asset in Castro's successful revolutionary efforts.

CHAPTER NINE

FIDELISMO

My father knew about Castro's political and philosophical musings and was cynical enough to confidently assess that Castro was discreetly colluding with the Russians. There was good reason for him to feel that way, as my father witnessed substantial evidence of Castro's political leanings throughout and after college. Castro always considered the American "Yankees" to be an imperialist power no different in form and function than the Batista regime. His thought process would logically lead him to think that if he sided with the imperialist Yankees—in effect a Batista style of politics—then how different would the governance approach be than what currently existed? Furthermore, why would Castro position himself to be a puppet of the American government when his self-induced delusions of being an independent, godlike deity, along with his paranoia, would ultimately not allow him to be controlled by anyone—much less by a government and social paradigm, capitalism, that he deeply detested?

Not to be outsmarted, Castro brilliantly masked his intentions with America so he could leverage the potential dynamics of his political value with a salivating Soviet Union. My father recognized that Castro was a person of superior intellect and speculated that the two world superpowers and others would underestimate Castro on multiple levels. It would be another miscalculation, much like Batista's, but on a global level. Castro counted on being thought of as another country bumpkin looking for his fifteen seconds of back-country revolutionary fame but my father's experience with him revealed a man possessed to achieve his goals. Castro would only sleep around three hours a day and continue to perform with the energy that even Red Bull would be envious of—day in and day out. He was relentless in his ambition and played the world like the bumpkin they thought he was.

As someone who closely followed Castro's political maneuvers and intellectual deliberations on civic governance through his college relationship and beyond, my father would go on to tell me that Castro's commitment and passion were directed at absolute social control and manipulation via government authority—a government authority that he would micromanage and where he would never allow the light of democracy or compromise to prevail. Although Castro came from a very well-to-do family, he abhorred the elite, he hated the capitalist society, and he hated the United States. He used those emotional triggers not only to rationalize his zealous goal of becoming King of Cuba, but also to engage and mobilize a sizable segment of the Cuban population that had been legitimately denied the rewards and recognition of their society for so long. Castro deftly harnessed his personal rage against the United States to advance his true intention of displacing America for him in Cuba.

And as much as Castro hated everything America stood for; he equally did not care about the Cuban people. This wasn't altogether about the United States, the Soviet Union, or providing a better lifestyle and progress for Cuba. This was all about him and his thirst for absolute domination of Cuba and its people. The two superpowers were just his props. In essence, it was a dictatorship that was packaged and sold as a revolution whose messiah would rescue the plight of the working class from the evil clutches of the callous and arrogant rich—which in part was accurate, as a significant portion of the rich in Cuba were selfish pigs. Later, after he gained all-encompassing power, the political term used to describe his narcissistic social control and philosophy would not be communism or socialism. The newly established social and governmental paradigm would come to be known as "Fidelismo" or "Fidelism."

Familiar with Castro's mental and ideological backdrop and suspicious of his grand scheme, my father found it very interesting, but not surprising, to witness the distinct contrast displayed in Castro's public speeches in key metropolitan areas where the international media was present versus speeches he presented in the "backwoods" of Cuba. In the metropolitan areas, he would provide a delicate and discreetly dressed up diplomatic message, attempting to avoid unnecessarily alarming a skeptical American audience about his endgame for the governance of Cuba. However, in the speeches he made to rural, farming communities, he would substantively modify his rhetoric to passionately promote the virtues of a socialist society where wealth would be captured by the government and redistributed to "the people."

The witnessing of the dual representation of Castro's position and the skilled manner in which he crafted his message and manipulated the media alerted my father to naturally become aware of his intentions. It also prompted him to take action, seeking the best avenues and opportunities to protect his family from what he felt would be another repressive regime that contained worse implications and consequences than what had occurred during the Batista era. He hoped for the best but had to be prepared in the event his skepticism, along with what he was witnessing, validated his fears.

Over time, my father's inside access to Castro and his organizations would provide him with valuable behavioral and political insights not otherwise seen by many. He was in the minority in suspecting that Castro would be a disaster for Cuba if he were to gain control. And it wasn't because my father was a Batista sympathizer or was tied in some way to the Batista machine. He intellectually did not accept that a socialist or communist form of government which inflicted magnified, repressive social restrictions curtailing the pursuit of one's freedom for success, progress, and happiness was best suited for a productive society. He did not want the government defining what his freedoms, opportunities, or happiness should be. He felt that communism and socialism prevented a society's progress and its ability to prosper because they vanquished an individual's incentives to invest in their personal efforts to excel, enhance their lifestyle, and realize opportunities for their family.

However, the masses do not really pay attention to inconvenient facts, much less attempt to use those facts to question their perspective of a government that should provide for everything, even when the consequences of their chosen ignorance resulted in the loss of individual independence and freedom of expression. They blindly subscribe to the ideology and unreservedly bequeath their souls to become hostages of the state. Understandably, in their frustration over having experienced the abhorrently selfish components of capitalism, the masses are willingly and delinquently receptive to embracing well-crafted, deceitful messages which are adorned with rhetorically romantic and inspirational social justice nuances. And those frustrated masses never seem to rationally examine the quixotic masquerade that excludes fundamental operational and financial elements that would be realistically necessary to support these daydream initiatives. Once the disenfranchised hear what they want to hear, they don't even want to contemplate the pragmatic facts with which to logically support or disown the consequences of propping up and sustaining a socialist or communist societal framework. They do not want to listen to any reason regarding the type of financial and operational support required to sustain political systems that provide social benefits to everyone. Where would the money come from to support this oasis after the private properties and businesses are kidnapped by government authorities and the revenue streams are at best diminished, or at worst, discontinued?

This type of system wants to replace the population segment of the "prosperous" because they are perceived as capitalizing off of, and failing to respect the struggles of, "regular folk." They do not forecast or acknowledge that the socialist system merely replaces the capitalistic pigs with new socialist control pigs. Facts and truth offer an emotionally jarring and disruptive exercise of reason versus fantasy, of reality versus fiction. In the minds of "campesinos," these eloquent sound bites were akin to a utopian religion, and Castro represented their "Man of La Mancha."

With masterful theatrical oratory (unquestionably one of the most charismatic communicators that ever existed), Castro spoke on behalf of the underprivileged and underrepresented, the insulted and the downtrodden—no one else had ever stood up for them. He was the symbol of an apocalyptic redemption that would right all the historical sins and all the wrongs in Cuba and ensure their seemingly comfortable delusional destiny. Castro would go on to diabolically capitalize on this populist sentiment and its anticipated political conclusion.

The rich and privileged would finally pay for their exploitation and oppression. What the Cuban people failed to understand in their drunken state of revenge, hope, and promise was that Batista would simply be replaced by another oppressive, manipulative, and self-absorbed despot named Fidel Castro. And he would replace the United States' "sugar daddy" role of country partner with the Soviet Union. In doing so, Castro was the driving architect behind the devastation and demise of Cuba—a country whose exciting potential for growth and prosperity in world circles was well known. Castro's ultimate quest was to own and command Cuba down to its smallest detail. The country would be a prop of what he thought himself to be, which was a Shakespearian actor on the world's stage. Castro's revolution was all about himself, not about Cuba or its people. He considered them all his slaves, and he would exploit their despair, hope, and oppression just like the Batista regime had done, except he would trick the population into thinking that they were the actual authors, actors, and heroes starring in the Cuban novela (soap opera) he was producing. The fact is that Cuba did need a change in government, but Castro was not the change it needed.

Castro completely deceived a significant portion of the populace, and to this day, sixty-plus years later, even in death, he never, ever came close to relinquishing the slightest bit of control of the country. Fortunately, as time eroded (erosion also plays an integral part in the decay engulfing Cuba's renowned architectural structures), my father was becoming more aware of the misrepresented romance surrounding the birth of this passionate new coming of Cuba. He also became acutely aware of how Castro's socialist Trojan horse resonated with the overwhelming portion of the population. He concluded he needed to act to salvage whatever he could of his philosophical and political principles for the future of his family but had very few friends he could trust or depend on.

After Castro assumed power, he systematically employed and deployed a legion of local community spies, creating an environment of acute civil paranoia in which you were not able to discern who was a friend. The revolution had no appetite for dissenters. Even generations of established families, rich and middle class, would not stand in the way of this uprising. There were countless stories of beloved, lifelong friends who betrayed each other by secretly providing information, pointing out any given situation that ran afoul of the new rules and guidelines of the revolution: a household had a small, hidden vegetable garden, or they bought extra provisions with dollars sent from the United States, or someone rolled their eyes when the name of Castro was mentioned.

All of these allegations proved treasonous. People had to be very aware of how their words, actions, behavior, and even thoughts were presented or perceived. The sensitivity setting with which to observe, inform on, and turn people in was set very high. Everyone was suspicious of each other and feared unveiling their true sentiments because if Castro's name was not met with a resounding ovation, that person would be considered a heretic and likely face arrest, interrogation, prison, exile, torture, or—at worst, but not unreasonable to expect—execution. It was, and continues to be, somewhat of a version of North Korea in the Caribbean. And this type of spying oversight was not restricted to the boundaries of Cuba. A select minority of Cubans portraying political dissenters immigrated to Cuban communities in the United States to strategically undertake undercover jobs to gather intelligence. Their new job was to infiltrate and spy on friends, family, and exile groups in Cuban American communities for the Cuban government, and report on any real or perceived anti-Castro political activities.

My father was convinced of his assessment regarding the consequences of having Fidel Castro in power and was struggling to establish an exit strategy. He initially wanted to leave my mom in the United States, but they both decided to return to Cuba after my birth. Once on the island, they continued their lives as normally as possible, feigning momentary compliance to reassure those that had claimed allegiance to this new Cuban revolution. This acting continued through Castro's ascension to power, when my father's suspicions of Castro's political direction were disturbingly confirmed. And it wasn't long before my father began to tire of maintaining this fake persona and began to outwardly question Castro's intentions amongst his "friends." In addition, his desire to leave Cuba had once again been revived. He had put himself on the radar when his outspoken gestures made his intentions uncomfortably clear to his friends. Understandably, his name was eventually put on a list with the secret police as an individual who should be investigated. He felt that it would be just a matter of time before they came to arrest him.

As predicted by my father, the special police came to our house to question him in the fall of 1959. He bluntly revealed to them what he felt to be the truth and proceeded to let them know that he could not philosophically live with, or embrace living within, a communist government. It was against his ideology. They thanked him for his honesty and left. They returned a week later, arrested him, and placed him in jail as a political prisoner. No official charge, no due process, and no jury of his peers. But not to worry, because you had a judge presiding over a recently installed revolutionary court almost guaranteeing an arrested person's chances of never getting out of jail alive. Back in those times in Cuba, when you were arrested as a political prisoner, your options were limited. Rarely did they release political prisoners and you were never made aware of your crime, or sentence, or the time you would serve. More often than not, a prisoner was simply executed. In fact, after Castro formally established his authority, over six hundred Batista officials and followers were "tried" in court tribunals, where they received guilty verdicts and were subsequently executed.

As my father told me in reflecting on his ordeal, Castro did not take kindly to what he considered to be 'Castro non conformers,' and it was an efficient, calculated, and necessary action he took to eliminate any real or perceived threats to his rule. Castro would apply the necessary methods to effectively preserve the expectations of a new society in Cuba with dying examples of how dissenters would be treated. My father did not often recant those memories publicly, but just with his family, which was as public as it got. He would tell me that at sunrise on many mornings, he would witness prisoners being escorted in single file to a wall where they were lined up and executed by a firing squad. And every morning, the guards, knowing that he was a new father, would wake him up at sunrise to tell him that today was his day to die.

Post-revolution, Castro would not enlist a compassionate and diplomatic embrace toward his political challengers. In fact, he demonstrated no mercy whatsoever to any real or perceived "political non-conformists" in his efforts to solidify control over his newly established regime, with methods that were brutally more prescriptive and resolute than all the previous Cuban politicians. Castro's philosophy was basically "out of sight, out of mind, out of time." He never wanted a reason to look over his shoulder.

CHAPTER TEN

CAN'T PLAY GOLF IF YOU'RE STUCK IN CUBA

My father's politically motivated incarceration was a particularly distressing situation for my mother on multiple levels, including the concern of execution. She and her family unwrapped multiple attempts at formal diplomatic and informal background channels of communication with the newly anointed Cuban officials to coordinate my father's release from jail. These attempts were difficult and exponentially frustrating because she wasn't sure who, if anyone, could be trusted in Cuba to assist or volunteer to manage the issue. And although my Godfather was also a loyal patriot to Castro, he was unable to sway Cuba's new leader into revoking my father's arrest.

Most of my parents' closest friends had already abandoned Cuba for a new life, primarily relocating to areas like Florida, New York, and New Jersey. Cuban exiles had emigrated to these gateway states as they were primary relocation venues that provided established relationships, resources, and economic opportunities. Most of the Cubans that left in that first wave of immigration were well-trained and educated. They were professionals, academics, intellectuals, and artists—people with admirable skill sets that would undeniably contribute to their new homeland. Nonetheless, their credentials and pedigree were barely recognized when they came to the States, and many were relegated to starting careers or education anew.

To add to that challenging scenario, Cubans were also not allowed to leave Cuba with any valuables, so they arrived in America with nothing except whatever utilitarian items they could carry. What you could carry did not include precious metals or stones, family heirlooms, money, or anything deemed of any value by the newly established communist politburo.

Castro raped and pillaged a society of what they had earned and accomplished over generations without any moral reservations whatsoever. However, the Cuban people, like most immigrants coming to this country, are very resilient, and in spite of the obvious systemic challenges and burdens associated with the recently migrated, Cuban American households have statistically managed to become the Latino sub-segment representing the highest median household income in the United States.

After some time and desperate deliberation, my mother aggressively pursued any attempt to coordinate her husband's release. Even though she was in Cuba, my mom had little hope of realistically accomplishing anything and felt that she would subsequently become a widow under house arrest in Cuba. If that were to be the case, her plan was to send me back to the States to live with my aunt. However, she had one remote glimmer of hope left, one that carried significant risk for the person that would be involved on the Cuban side. My mom had not yet approached this person and was not at all sure if they would be willing to take the risk. Nonetheless, she invested in a leap of faith, hopeful that a noble and sincere individual who was embedded in Castro's inner circle would be sensitive to her circumstance.

My mother's last-ditch effort invoked trusting a family friend, who would presumably have to risk her life to provide substantive guidance, support, influence, and coercion with the right authority—Castro. Incredibly, it paid off, and after a little over six months, my father was released from jail. No one is really certain how this happened because he was released without any explanation or justification. A guard simply approached his cell at sunrise, as the guards always did, to reiterate that today would be the day he would die, except that on that particular day, he was provided with a different message. My father would later tell me that he really thought he was going to be executed that day, but for some unexplained reason, the guard instead said, "You're free to go."

There were obviously very limited theories thrown around as to how my father was able to ultimately acquire his freedom, but one salient theory made this ordeal, and potentially life-altering situation, seem more like a salacious soap opera wrapped in a mystery than a factual trail of evidence leading to a logical conclusion. Unlikely as it may sound, given the intricate and sultry nature of romantic relationships and politics, it seemed to be the theory that made the most sense to my parents, especially to my mother.

The theory had to do with the very good relationship my mother, and her family, had with Castro's newly anointed secretary. This secretary also happened to be one of his favored mistresses. After all formal, governmental attempts to gain my father's freedom were met with passive-aggressive futility, my mother decided to turn to Castro's secretary to plead the circumstances and ask for her help. Everyone's prevailing sense was that my father had now been taking up jail space for too long a period and was at a point where he may have been overstaying his welcome. Our family's anxious consensus was that it was getting close to checkout time for him.

My mother was very conscious of putting this friend in a sensitive position that could be dangerous for her, but felt she had no choice. Castro was exceptionally paranoid of the people that he surrounded himself with, people he "befriended." Only a select few gained his confidence or were given access to his inner circle. And Cubans who were bequeathed that blessing from Castro did not go out of their way to help other Cubans. *Why would they?* If any additional friends who were brought in by his inner circle betrayed a confidence or acted suspiciously in Castro's mind, then both the friend and their sponsor would become suspect of potentially causing harm to him in some way. If Castro misinterpreted any of this, or felt a reason to lose confidence in the relationship he had with an individual, then at best they would be excommunicated from his circle and they would lose all the ancillary benefits that were realized from having gained his confidence. In effect, they would be exiled to the status of prisoner of the state, and redemption would be an unlikely outcome.

At worst they would simply be eliminated from life's equation. The repercussions could, and mostly certainly would, affect their extended families as well. Consequently, people were rather paranoid and extremely cautious of who they would put forward as an endorsement to bring into his circle. It is not unlike when a mob guy brings in an outsider to join the gang who could potentially be an informant. Same deal, comprising deadly results. Adding to the paranoia was the fact that everyone—well, mostly everyone—was also spying on each other, because civilian spies were everywhere. And when you are living in a Gestapo-like society, even "friends" could not resist the slightest temptation to provide credible or fictional perspectives on you or anyone else, if it made them seem more valuable to, and gain favor with, their great leader.

Getting back to the only plausible theory, it seems, on the surface, that maternal sentiments depicted by a recent mother with an effectively fatherless child may have prevailed through the constant pleas coming from my mom to her friend, Castro's secretary and lover. This maternal empathy seemed to have morphed into an act of kindness wherein the secretary is thought to have whispered my parents' case in particularly vulnerable and sensitive moments, strategically delivered prior to an orgasm. (You know, the old "tell me you love me before we go any further" routine.) During those delicate moments, she reminded Castro of the fact that my father was a harmless individual who would never betray or represent an activist position against his movement. No doubt, Castro's reflection of my father's integrity throughout his relationship with him must have also played a significant factor in his decision to ultimately regard him as "harmless" and not a true enemy of his revolution. And those variables must have crystalized Castro's reasoning, particularly since it was the only thing standing between him and getting his tickle on. It was a glimpse of compassion and lust lasting as long as an orgasm—but if that's all it was, it was enough, and my mom gladly embraced the stereotypical results.

All told, my mother's friend never fully laid claim to her efforts facilitating my father's release with anyone, but would later confide to my mother, with a wink and a smile, that Castro "loved" her and that he would always support any requests she made of him. That scenario, coupled with the fact that there was no other rational explanation for my father's inexplicable expulsion, led to the singular conclusion as the reasoning behind my father's release. Simply put, there was no Cuban government official who would not so much as take a crap without Castro's permission, much less take it upon themselves to advocate for the release of my father. The exclusive condition attached to my dad's release was that he was not to leave the country.

Holy shit. Without recognizing it at the time, unless I sprouted wings and learned to fly, we would've been destined to live out the rest of our lives in Cuba.

Just imagine the horror. I would not have been able to join a private country club.

CHAPTER ELEVEN

BLINDSIDED BY THE YIN AND YANG OF GOLF

It was the eighties. I was an account executive at an advertising agency in Chicago, Illinois. To be specific, it was a Hispanic advertising agency that specialized in producing multimedia Spanish-language advertisements for local, regional, and national companies. And although it was regarded primarily as a local agency, it packed some juice and notoriety for two primary reasons: it retained some prominent packaged goods, media, retail, and public utility clients, and the owner of the agency was a colorful, highly-educated, financially-heeled, well-connected Cuban media businessman who represented the elite of the Hispanic community in the windy city, and was a shining example of an immigrant-to-riches story.

Chicago is a city that showcases a bold, beautiful, and commanding landscape; a rich diversity of generational cultures and communities; entrenched sports fanatics; and a fantastic range of hearty, iconic, and cultural foods. Living there provided a sensory-fulfilling experience on multiple levels. Additionally, the people derived from traditional bloodlines of Midwestern graciousness and, even better, the European bloodline ensemble of mostly exotic and beautiful women was giddily—put my head between my hands and thank the Lord—appreciated. Bluntly stated, Chicago is wrapped up as a shitload of elegant and robust all-American living. It's also the place where my enthusiasm for golf originated.

One anchor client of ours, a manager from a utility company by the name of Peoples Gas (still in existence), was a golfer and true fan of the game. So, like any shallow salesman worth his salt, I wanted to develop a relationship with this guy and take up space in his "favorite person" column. Always working the angle, my attempt to learn to play golf was solely intended to get this guy to increase his advertising budget with us—which would lead to a bigger bonus for me. I pushed on toward my end game, educating myself with some serious due diligence, reviewing the history of golf, its origins, its heritage, its evolution, the players, and the almost mystical reverence attributed to the sport, equating it to the mystery and meaning of life.

The sport of golf depicts a fascinating history featuring individuals displaying resolute qualities in their journey to conquer the implausible. It is the discovery of kinetic energy that elucidates how the human spirit intertwines with all the biological organisms, gasses, and chemicals that make up the universe. As it turns out, golf is a defining adventure you embark on to discover the *yin* and *yang* of your soul. There were many aspects of the game that transcended into a spiritual experience of enlightenment. In many ways, the philosophical elements attributed to the sport of golf also resonate with how one addresses, overcomes, and capitalizes on the challenges and opportunities presented by life. *Ok, so I'm overdramatizing a pinch.* But respectfully speaking, the sport has crafted champions and heroes of humble, ordinary men and women who are on a quest to overcome their own challenges, insecurities, and anxieties. In a lot of ways, the game can be much like walking into a dark space without a sense of balance or end in sight, teaching you to compose yourself, harness your fear, and sense your way around until you ultimately emerge into the light.

I found golf to be a mentally complex and exhausting sport that forces you to face and conquer your demons to realize an inspiring and sobering level of survival instinct. Elements of focus, determination, and resolution are required in real time, every time, as you have to constantly adapt to conditions on a playing field that continuously changes—on a daily basis and throughout the day—presenting adversity and opportunities as you attempt to achieve your goals.

My research in the sport of golf taught me that the golf course is a living, breathing thing and that a round of golf would come to represent a reflective and enlightening experience, a journey well worth taking. After taking it all in and embracing the hypnosis, I had one very important thought, a fuck-increasing-the-advertising-budget thought: I needed to play and excel in this sport.

I was ready to be consumed.

CHAPTER TWELVE

IS TWENTY-EIGHT TOO OLD TO TRY A PROFESSIONAL CAREER AT GOLF?

After buying some off-the-rack clubs and practicing as if I were deranged, obsessed, it was time to play. The first time I ever played golf was on a very rainy day. That was done intentionally for several reasons: I wanted to avoid integrating with other players and I also wanted to have the ability to practice by hitting several balls and shots throughout the round. I would walk and not carry an umbrella. Umbrellas are a pain in the ass, and who needs one when you have a baseball hat? My plan was to scour the weather reports, seeking a rainy day. It was another hot and humid summer in Chicago, and I reasoned that given the hot temps, the rain would be refreshing while I played golf. But the driving logic and motivation were that I would have the course to myself. The fact is, I was scared shitless of stepping into this new, dark space, and I didn't want anyone around to see me or help me. It was akin to staring down a triple black diamond run for the first time on a ski slope and saying your prayers after you realize there is only one way to ski down. *Fuck it. Let's go.*

A stormy day finally arrived and I enthusiastically headed out to play a municipal course near me. It was raining so hard that the clubhouse was closed and no one, other than me, was on the property. I played nine holes for free and I do not remember what I shot. I wasn't there to count, thankfully. I do remember practicing quite a bit, hitting multiple shots per hole, relishing some very good shots, and commiserating over the overwhelming number of bad shots I hit. I was drenched but happy. I was wandering around in a windswept rain—alone—with plenty of time to think and talk to myself about many things in my life while juggling the distractions of the weather and the sopping-wet course conditions.

Instead, what transpired—and many golfers will relate to this—was that the adverse conditions and the baggage that had come to define my existence until that very moment did not interfere at any time with my desire to hit the ball and put it in the hole. It was a surreal experience and I loved it right away. Like the first time I discovered pizza. The rain didn't bother me, and reflections of my sordid journey to this point did not surface nor interrupt my focus. I embraced every raindrop, the solitude, and all the action happening between my ears. I could hear every step as I squished through my path and made eye contact with some birds and trees several times over. It was a Carlos Castaneda interlude, where I had found the way of the Yaqui without the mushrooms or peyote. I was truly *in* the moment, and felt attached to the secrets of the universe, inspired by what was taking place—spiritually, mentally, and athletically. The experience unexpectedly filled me with hope as it helped reveal a new world of possibilities to me. This immense revelation to the mystery of life now carried a responsibility to continue to play and practice golf recreationally.

Every free moment I had, irrespective of the weather, would be dedicated to playing this game well. It was a feeling I had never felt before and never wanted to lose.

I was soaked to the bone by the end of the round and the combination of wet gloves and grips was equivalent to holding onto an eel rather than my shitty golf clubs. In hindsight, that was a good thing, because I then had to swing with some type of conscious tempo. Notwithstanding the weather, it may have been one of my most satisfying days on the golf course. Not because I played well or because it was on a beautiful course on a beautiful day. No. It was the solitude and peace I encountered *with* the course. It was my ability to overcome and accomplish my goal against all the challenges I encountered. It was an opportunity to be reflective and have insightful discussions with myself as I thought through and considered my positions around the golf course.

And it was a spirited conversation indeed. I was overwhelmed by the transformation of my perspective for the game of golf after that round. I was moved by the individuality, accountability, and responsibility of this commitment. It struck me that this was actually a blue-collar game requiring a blue-collar play-making attitude—in stark contrast to the "social class" trappings and stigma universally associated with it. This revelation was in direct conflict with my original, demeaning meanderings where I considered golf to be an inferior athletic and mental activity.

I was now hypnotized and this routine in Chicago would endure until I got engaged, married my first wife, and moved to Raritan Bay, New Jersey. In spite of the obvious seasonal weather constraints of the Northeast, I was determined to take my golf into overdrive. After reflection and discussions, my wife agreed to support my ambition to dedicate myself to the sport in the hopes of turning into a professional athlete. Boy, had my perspective ever changed one hundred and eighty degrees from my adolescent view of this sport to now referring to professional golfers as athletes. My family also supported my direction in trying to earn a living as a golf professional even though the only source of income was coming from my wife.

This was the window and if it was going to happen, the time would be now. Which meant that I would be playing golf in New Jersey in the dead of winter. The reality of what I was hoping for was just presented to me, and it was now time to prepare for the ultimate question: *Could I make a living playing competitive, professional golf?* This was going to be a hard road; a true grind. The honeymoon-phase with the game was over. Time to punch in and get to work. I was excited, anxious, and in a serious state of fucking shock. There was no plan "B." I had always been a fan of *The Honeymooners*, so as Ralph Kramden would say, "And away we go!"

CHAPTER THIRTEEN

A DECENT ATHLETE DOESN'T ALWAYS MENTALLY TRANSLATE TO GOLF

I was a decent athlete who had experienced a marginally decorated high school basketball career but a spotty—actually, shitty—collegiate run. In my freshman year, I was thrown off my junior varsity college team for yelling at the coach from midcourt during a game. The fact is, the point guard I was defending against couldn't dribble well with one hand. Naturally, I would overplay his good hand, forcing him to pick up his dribble, resulting in his team starting their offensive series closer to center court, as opposed to letting them start at the top of the key.

My coach didn't think that was a good thing as he wanted me to have the guy drive toward the middle of the free throw line so that our defense would step into the middle to help defend.

That concept was lost on me as their offense was much more interrupted when he would pick up his dribble earlier than planned, resulting in the offense having to move up from the baseline, significantly disrupting the originating sequence of the play. So, he spit-yelled at me when I forced the point guard to pick up his dribble by our bench, just past the half-court line. I was only about ten feet from him when he jumped off the bench and dressed me down. Since the guy had picked up his dribble, I stood straight up and yelled back, citing the insanity of his logic. The next time the whistle blew, which happened to be the next play, I was out of the game—and the team—for good. Forever. The guy was a Bobby Knight impersonator who took himself way too seriously and frankly was a fucking asshole.

However, I, too, have to be accountable for my behavior as a cocky "spic" on an almost all-white JV basketball team. In essence, I too was a bit of an asshole. Of course, the whole experience traumatized me, which is why, to this day, I can specifically recite an elapsed-time reenactment of this incident. It has been over forty-six years since that episode and I still have that bouncing around in my head, sometimes in slow motion. That's fucked up. I still see him jumping off his chair, spit flying as he's almost throwing up yelling in my face, all of it unfolding in slow motion. Yup. That shit is stored in my head to this day, right next to the Kennedy assassination and the Zapruder film. Being on that team was like a scene out of *Hoosiers*. They had one "spic"—me—and they had one black kid, who was more like the Carlton character from *The Fresh Prince of Bel-Air*.

The chemistry was just not there. I was a city kid with an attitude—and this school was in a Whitelandia part of Upstate New York that did not take kindly to city kids of Latino heritage with an NYC basketball attitude. I am not saying I should have been a starter, but I was definitely not worse than sixth man. As a swing guard, I got time like I was the ninth man. I only went in to play for three or four minutes before the half and when the game was decidedly lost, or won. I was honestly astute enough, not blinded by my cockiness, to gauge everyone's abilities, through practices and scrimmages, to determine my spot amongst the players. However, they had their favorite white boys, and being a "spic" with a 'tude did not help me.

I was also fortunate enough to have been a pretty good baseball player and was able to float on a semi-pro team in Chicago, moving around to play all the bases defensively as needed for the team, just to pass the time. However, I do remember I was put in to play third base several times, and that downright scared me silly—for good reason—because even though it was the semi-pros, these guys were good athletes and could hit the shit out of the ball. Especially when a player pulled a hit down the third base line.

Consequently, I always felt my hand-eye coordination to be pretty good and thought that would transfer over easily to golf. After all, it's close to the same fundamentals as they relate to hitting a baseball, and I know how to shift my weight to throw and hit, and—*oh shit, "lightbulb!"*—no one is throwing the ball at you, so how bad could it be? I mean, the ball isn't moving. It's sitting there waiting for you to hit it. In spite of my ignorant approach and perspective, I labored on in my attempt at establishing a new skill set, continuing to disregard any thoughts of taking formal lessons.

CHAPTER FOURTEEN

A CUBAN REVOLUTION IN CORPORATE GOLF OUTINGS

One motivation for this book is to declare my own version of a Cuban revolution targeting the current state of corruption that embodies corporate golf outings. And the primary goal of this Cuban corporate golf outing revolution is to teach you how to successfully subvert, reconstruct, and manipulate the corporate golf outing scoring system better and more diplomatically than all the others who are juicing the system in an otherwise outwardly offensive manner. In short, you will learn how to cheat in corporate golf outings effectively and inconspicuously. At the end of the day, you will have to come to grips with your conscience and rationalize your soon-to-be-winning ways. The savvy methods disclosed within these pages are proven, field-tested techniques, executed in a tactful, gentlemanly, fun, and professional manner. In fact, the techniques are so polished and sublime that even the caddies assigned to your group won't be able to discern if you're cheating. However, part of the new sacred rules revealed in this book is that the caddies also share in the bounty offered by the outing prize trove by treating them to gracious tips, whether or not they suspect you of cheating. Sorry USGA; I know this whole damning exposé is shameful, and I know it hurts. But it's the truth. It's an acknowledged, but never publicly disclosed, dirty little secret hidden in the shadows of an otherwise honorable game.

In fact, golf is such an honorable game that it would be considered dishonorable to openly discuss or even acknowledge the fact that many golfers abuse the handicap system to enhance and secure their ability to win on-course bets, club matches or tournaments, and corporate golf outings. Deceitfully manipulating the handicap system is an endemic problem that has consistently and irritatingly challenged any head or assistant pro that works for any golf club. They all know who the cheaters are, but unfortunately, ninety-nine point nine percent of the time, they are forced to turn a blind eye to maintain their employment. It is such a recognized, under-the-table phenomenon, that a majority of private clubs have been forced to implement prescriptive oversight procedures (forensic audits and colonoscopies) in an attempt to partially mute suspect scoring submissions. Sorry for the meandering narrative, but we are talking about the issue of intentionally juggling your handicap to ensure your winning ways in club matches and tournaments, and corporate outings.

Ironically, and even though I am authoring this essay, I do not have the same perspective on obscuring my real handicap for my personal golf game in order to undeservedly benefit in any form of competition or friendly matches. My personal goal was to get better, thereby reducing my handicap. Lowering my handicap validated my improvement. I did not want to compete with other players on the basis of handicaps offered. I wanted to play against the course and par and I never wanted to give or take strokes. Consequently, I hooked up to play with people who were on the same wavelength, disregarding the crutches offered by the handicap system. These players also wanted to improve and shunned using handicaps when we competed against each other. Think about this for a second. Pros have differing handicaps, but do you think they stand on the first tee of a PGA tournament figuring out who's giving and getting strokes? Some are plus 4s, others are plus 6s, while others are plus 5s.

The answer is no. I felt that ignoring handicaps, many times to my detriment, and playing everyone straight up, facilitated my ability to accomplish my end goal of being a better player, especially under pressure. And that's the difference between very good and also-ran players. (For the record, I am an also-ran player with spots of inspiration throughout my golfing life.) An accomplished player will convert and execute the shot when the opportunity and the situation call for it. Failure to execute at those times leaves you as a marginal player, while the ability to successfully capitalize on those moments elevates your competitive aptitude.

This approach was humiliating and financially painful, as oftentimes I would get taken to the cleaners with bets. Also, having enough money in my pocket for the bet but not a cent more for food that day was a key motivator driving improvement as I could not afford to lose. Who doesn't like to eat? Our group of friends in New Jersey—our "players club"—was a fascinating and eclectic group of mostly men and some women, composed of an odd assortment of different backgrounds and careers. The common bond with all of them was their love for the game of golf.

Hanging around "our" public golf course were white-collar professionals, blue-collar guys, black guys, Jews, Catholics, Italians, Irishmen, younger guys aspiring to get on the tour, and older guys who, the majority of the time, would shoot lower than the young hotshots because all they did was hang around par while the younger guys impatiently tried to shoot the round of a lifetime day in and day out. Temptation is a difficult vice to vanquish when you're young and stupid. Surprisingly, there were no Spanish guys around except for me. For whatever reason, it never occurred to me to take any formal lessons. Instead, I focused on attempting to replicate swings, witnessed through television, that I thought produced exciting, creative, and solid golf shots.

I tried to emulate pros who were favored sources of swing inspiration like Seve Ballesteros, Tom Weiskopf, Sam Snead, and Byron Nelson. There was no way I was going to try to swing like Arnold Palmer, Billy Casper, Chi-Chi Rodriguez, Lee Trevino, or John Mahaffey. Their swings, otherwise considered magical acts of contortion, did not capture my attention as they were too personal, distinct, and ugly to watch. These guys definitely figured this shit out on their own. No one else was trying to emulate these swings. At the end of the day, it didn't matter, because look at what they accomplished in their careers by figuring out their best method to have the club face be square at impact while maximizing their club head speed.

And I thought Ben Hogan's swing—*like I have any right to comment on Hogan's swing (I am kicking myself in the ass and slamming my head on the desk as I write this because I am NOT worthy of applying critical thinking to this legend, much less thinking out loud about my critiquing him as I am a self-proclaimed buffoon)*—looked too technical. It just looked manufactured. Like a robot. It was too perfect. No matter, I still read his lesson books profusely, along with other books by Byron Nelson, Harvey Penick, Jack Nicklaus, and more. I just wanted to understand the dynamics of the swing and the mindset of the golfers who were successful professionally. Additionally, I gained swing secrets from the better guys that I played with, who were always gracious enough to share their philosophy and techniques with players they felt were sincere in their efforts to improve. At that time, there was no technology like the TrackMan or other systems designed to evaluate every fucking aspect of your swing mechanics. It was a trial-and-error baptism followed up by practice, practice, and more practice to develop "feel." And all you had for feedback was whether the ball flight of the shot you just hit concurred with what you had mentally visualized the ball doing.

CHAPTER FIFTEEN

THE MAILMEN

My initial experience with competitive golf and its mental nuances occurred early in my golfing life, while I was playing recreationally. I was just out to challenge myself, learn from mistakes, rejoice in accomplishments, and try to squeeze out some competitive juice with friends. I started to take golf seriously when my disappointments in failing to execute shots properly significantly outweighed my jubilation of a well-executed shot and the corresponding results. If I were to continue playing this game, it would not be for discouragement; rather, it would be for the encouragement that I could better play it. The balance of "negative" versus "positive" was misaligned, and I had to do something about it. I quickly committed to extensive practice. Much more practice than playing. I had heard that pros were hitting a thousand balls a day to practice, and, shit, if they could do it, so could I. It was a unique circumstance of passion that I had discovered in which, unlike my younger immature years, I was determined to commit to a strong work ethic to maximize my ability to achieve positive results.

I was also fortunate to have found and befriended a group of guys who were pretty decent amateurs and started playing with them. I was especially lucky that they let me into their circle to play with them. The league of golfers I had joined all possessed single-digit handicaps so they were pretty good players and fun to play with. They also represented a wide range of ages. I was one of the youngest, with the oldest members going up to about seventy years old. The beauty of this arrangement was that I was able to experience the strengths provided from the different levels of each of these guys. The younger guys obviously hit the ball farther and were more aggressive with their style of play, while the older guys always hit the ball shorter but always straight, were great around the greens, and were solid putters. Most importantly, their management of the golf course was insightful and wickedly results-oriented.

Like they famously say, "You don't draw pictures on a scorecard," and it was great to see some of the older guys consistently wear out the younger ones, including myself, with their deliberate and calculating executions. It was a humbling experience that revealed a new appreciation for learning how to score around a golf course by staying within your limits and exhibiting patience. We referred to the older guys as the "Mailmen" because they always delivered. These "Mailmen" were focused and very competitive, and they provided meaningful mentoring if you had the humility to absorb what they willingly offered as sage advice. Of course, gambling was also involved, and they were never shy about taking my money either—initially. My losing money happened with considerable frequency at the onset as I never took strokes. This was my psychotic methodology to accelerate my learning process.

CHAPTER SIXTEEN

THE MALICIOUS MANIPULATION OF THE HANDICAP SYSTEM

Ultimately, I learned how to survive and play well in an accelerated fashion, otherwise I would have stopped playing. I had found my instructor, my swing coach, and "income" was her name. Sorry, I know that's really cheesy, but I couldn't help it. That sounds like a line delivered by a private dick from a Raymond Chandler movie but I don't believe in giving or accepting strokes, and I certainly do not believe in the handicap system other than to use handicaps to place individuals in brackets and have them go at each other on a "scratch" basis.

The false positive provided by the handicap system lends itself to malicious mockery by a statistically significant portion of golfers who capitalize on intentionally abusing the system as it relates to corporate outings, club matches, and tournaments in which players' handicaps are used to determine the "net" winners. In contrast, there are a limited number of club tournaments where players within four or five strokes of each other are placed in brackets that are referred to as flights, or categories named A, B, C, or 1, 2, 3, or prestigious golf course names. Then they play heads-up, match, or stroke play against each other, just like the way it's played on the PGA tour. I feel the majority of club tournaments should be conducted in this manner because this approach would contribute toward a useful handicap system that would represent a more equitable and credible competitive scoring tool.

I have, and have known, too many friends who deceitfully manipulate the existing handicap system. For example, I won a match play club championship once by shooting two under par in the final round and my competitor and friend, whom I have a great deal of appreciation for, shot one under par in the final round to lose. It was a match worthy of spectators. However, my friend and competitor that day had a registered handicap of eight. I was scratch. To get to the championship round, he had to qualify for the championship and then proceed to run through three layers of players who had much lower handicaps than his, shooting one to two over par for every round during the tournament. This was a "scratch" club tournament where everyone played heads-up without giving strokes. Is it possible to do this? Although remote and highly improbable, this action was not statistically prohibitive. Is it realistic? No.

The weeks following the club championship, he started posting low to mid-eighties scores. And his higher scores were not the result of an injury. Given my experience and constant exposure to golf and playing partners, I would confidently say that at a minimum, twenty five percent of golfers do not maintain an accurate handicap. At a *minimum*. I maintain an accurate handicap and continue to be a low-single-digit handicap player. Many people I have played with post scores that are different from what they actually got, or miss shots or putts on purpose to drive their scores up. The fact is that I can't put my finger on their motivation and rationale for doing this other than their need to gain some level of parity against other golfers who are manipulating the handicap system to help win golf gambling bets, club tournaments, or outings. And as in my previous example, even good players are prone to this.

There was another time when I had just finished playing a round with somebody, also a friend and very good player, with a five-handicap, and he remarked to me, "What did you end up shooting?"

I told him, "One over. Seventy-three."

He continued, "Are you going to put that in?"

I looked at him, caught a little off guard, and asked, "What do you mean?"

He asked again, "What are you going to put down for your score?"

"Dude. What I shot."

"Are you serious? You can't put that in. How are you going to compete with the other guys?"

"Tony. I shoot what I shoot."

"You're crazy. I'm putting in an eighty."

Tony had, in fact, shot a seventy-five. By the way, Tony is not his real name. For the sake of divine respect and to prevent him from garnering contempt or roasting from members at this golf club, I will not divulge the real name of "Tony." However, that attitude toward handicaps represented a robust minority of the active golfing membership at this club, and is demonstrative of the composition at most clubs.

All that said, I will never wrap my head around the motivation for players to run up their scores, despite their rationale to keep up with the other cheaters by maintaining a higher handicap, and I do not agree with it at all. Plus, it pisses me off royally because as a legitimate low-single-digit handicap golfer, I am destined for a slaughter ninety percent of the time. On longer courses that are 6,700 to 6,900 yards long, I have a better chance at equity—but I am fucked on short golf courses, around 6,500 yards, where double-digit and sandbagging high handicappers can hit the green in two with low to mid irons because the holes are not long enough. However, I would be more than happy to play against the player who functionally plays to a ten handicap but is registered as a three.

CHAPTER SEVENTEEN

NINETY MILES TO THE NEAREST PRIVATE COUNTRY CLUB

Over fifteen months had passed since my father was released from a Cuban jail, and he had again reached his philosophical limit with the now-entrenched Cuban system of government and social order. Castro had infamously and easily subdued the bullshit amateur overthrow attempt by the United States at the Bay of Pigs. This fiasco, along with the failed assassination attempts on his life by the United States, further cemented Castro's alignment with the Soviet Union. As the Soviet Union secured its influence and dominance over Cuba, my father decided he would attempt to escape again, knowing that his country was about to be irrevocably damaged by this communist experiment in the Western Hemisphere.

Castro had already begun implementing his policies of nationalizing and seizing lands that were owned by foreign nationals and rich Cuban landowners who had fled Cuba. At this point, my father concluded that he would rather die than live in this paranoid environment of oppression. My mother was understandably concerned and disagreed about disrupting the predictability of a life dictated by government shaping and control, but she supported his efforts. He proceeded to collaborate with underground resources to acquire fake documentation that would facilitate his departure, incognito, not on a raft but on a commercial airliner out of Cuba. Ironically, neither my father nor my mother knew how to swim.

So, on a warm, sublimely tropical day, our family headed out to the airport. They said what they thought would be their final goodbyes to the friend that had transported us to the airport and proceeded to go through the security checkpoints and stand in line on the tarmac. At three years old, I was not aware of the gravity of the circumstances nor the potential consequences that could unfold. I must have thought that we were simply going on a trip. Never would it have occurred to me that it was like "dead man walking" to board some Cuban era airlines. All was quiet and seemed to be moving along splendidly when my father got a tap on the shoulder by an airport security guard along with a request to follow him. He didn't address my father by name. Just a tap, a comment, and a nod to follow him in a certain direction. Although he never described it in detail from an emotional level, he and my mother must have felt the life sucked out of them at that moment. Understandably, we followed the security guard to an office area, where my mother and I were asked to sit in a waiting room while my father was escorted into the main office of the head of airport security.

The door to the office closed, and mom and I were left to ourselves. It must have felt lonely for my mother, but not even close to the feeling of inescapable despair that my father must have felt hearing the door close behind him. However, when all was said and done, our journey wasn't brought to an end that day. Instead, we did leave Cuba on that flight with our family intact to Jamaica.

Jamaica thus became our interim destination for a month before we were granted safe passage to the United States. It wasn't until I was thirty-five years old that my father would describe what happened that eventful day and how fate again played a hand in helping keep our family together. As he walked toward the desk, my father could see only the back of the man who was the head of airport security. As he got closer, my father was shocked to see that it was an old work colleague.

Any of these encounters with colleagues could be considered meaningful in a good or painful way depending on the relationship established prior to Castro's revolution. The end result is that the head of airport security had a somewhat brief conversation, adamantly asking my father to change his mind about what he was doing, to consider the possible consequences, and abandon this hopeless attempt to leave without permission, and embrace the communist system. He also demonstrated a file the secret police had gathered on my dad with information on his movements and almost everything else he did—how he conducted himself—following his release from prison. "After all," he said, *"Mira que bien me va."*—"Look at how well I am doing," as he described how he was enjoying a promising career while working within the new society.

My father appreciated the consideration but insisted he would rather die than live within this type of society. At that point, the head of airport security stood up, said he was sorry about my father's decision, and expressed his sympathy that he would never again see my father. With the last sentence hanging in my father's thoughts and the swirl of emotions surrounding the definitive statement, the man took my father's file and ripped it in half. *"Salte de aqui. Disfruta tu familia y nunca te veré más."*—"Get out of here. Enjoy your family and I will never see you again." At that moment he turned his back, my father was escorted out of his office, and we were chaperoned onto the flight. We ultimately arrived in America on September 20, 1961, and never saw Cuba again.

We were a lot luckier than other families who were on Castro watch lists.

My father never knew what happened, if anything, to the head of airport security for the risk he took in allowing my father to leave Cuba. It took him over thirty years before he felt comfortable enough to speak to me about this episode. He never told me any of his stories about Cuba until I was thirty-five years old. In those days, prior to electronic media, YouTube, Facebook—the age of instant information and gratification—heartfelt and traumatizing experiences were respected in a dignified and private way. Many political prisoners or war veterans do not like to speak of, or share their experiences. In a way, it was a matter of discretion and a sign of character amongst men that they would not burden their loved ones with traumatic, painful, or violent experiences that they had endured or suffered through. It was a matter of honor that they would keep these issues to themselves and absorb the scars associated with them. It is an "old school" characteristic. By contrast, everything today, it seems, has the potential to turn into a reality show. Today, the media feeds a ravenous popular culture that demonstrates little sense of discretion and a great sense of exploitation.

"Fate" was a keystone variable in what happened to my father and our family that day. Fate is comprised of encounters that are life-altering, and it plays a role at critical junctures in a person's life. It is interesting that what people might consider inconsequential occurrences are somehow not considered part of fate's mix. I do not agree with discounting seemingly inconsequential items. I consider fate to be all physical, mental, and spiritual encounters and interactions that intentionally or inadvertently contribute to defining how your story will eventually be written.

CHAPTER EIGHTEEN

IT'S NOT WHO YOU KNOW. IT'S HOW YOU KNOW THEM.

My father would always tell a story by getting to the point first. He would then provide the landscape that would frame the story, the encounter. Of course, it would turn out that the life-altering encounter at the airport was precipitated and shaped by a life-altering encounter with the person who would become the head of airport security, for whom my father played an instrumental, meaningful, and positive role when he was younger. Without my asking the obvious questions, my father described the rest of the story.

Having been a college friend of Castro, he would tell me stories of how he, Castro, and another close friend would debate political issues in articulate and thoughtful ways, often engaged in philosophical, political fencing. You need to understand that debating in Cuba was like a professional sport. As orators, they had the charisma, intellectual depth, and discipline to thoroughly speak on a topic and articulate enough to defend their perspectives in a substantive manner. They were avid readers, consuming exorbitant loads of literature and news with infectious energy. Their idea of a long night's sleep was four or five hours.

Otherwise, they were dedicated to learning, and enthusiastically shared their interpretations of what they had learned. I mean, these guys were on point and always performed as if they were lawyers conducting a high-profile criminal case. They had to be, as it was a very competitive environment laden with big egos and bragging rights. As much disdain as I have for Castro, his early political maneuvers, and his ongoing, systematic destruction of a country that used to be the economic envy of the Caribbean, he is without question one of the greatest political orators of any generation.

My father explained that during the pre-Castro days and after graduating from college, he was working as an administrator in a government office. During his stint there, Castro would often stop by to say hello and shoot the shit. (My father did not describe it as "shooting the shit." That is just my interpretation of it.) He did this with my dad instead of the other college friend because, having witnessed my dad's neutrality on issues, Castro never really felt threatened by him, and this encouraged Castro to foster a more trusting friendship with my father. At that time, Castro was starting to make some political noise and was becoming more of a prominent figure in the political landscape of Cuba, garnering a reputation as a potential start-up political force.

The head of the department where my father worked was a Spaniard executive who was there as a political appointment resulting from Cuba's relationship with Spain at the time. In other words, the head of the office where my father worked was not a Cuban native. However, the Spanish gentleman heading up this department was politically astute and aware of Castro's growing political persona. He would witness Castro occasionally stopping by my father's office and took note of his friendship with my father. One day, the Spaniard decided to terminate a particular employee, and his explanation for terminating this employee was that he felt he was not doing his job, but in reality, it was because he was black. That's it. In those days, even though black and white did get along and interact socially, Cuba was, for the most part, a racist society. You could mingle, but you couldn't mix.

My father and the employee who was fired had enough of an amicable relationship that he approached my father to plead his case in an attempt to recover his job. The terminated employee was also no dummy. He was aware of my father's relationship with Castro and felt it might help in presenting a compelling case to the Spanish executive, if my father agreed to do so. My father liked and respected the man and did not feel his termination was genuinely valid, so he took on the man's dilemma by confronting his boss. He explained that this was a good man who did not warrant this treatment. Moreover, he explained that the employee was a family man with four children to support, and the loss of this job would not allow him to financially provide for his family.

My father sincerely felt that the gentleman's termination was not justified and intentionally malicious. He agreed to help him, but there was one caveat requested by my father in reciprocation for his advocacy. The man unconditionally agreed to the request even though my father would still have followed through in helping him even if he hadn't agreed to my father's terms. After all, it was the right thing to do. My father continued to lobby the Spaniard executive, making his case and requesting that he restore the fired gentleman's job. The Spaniard, wary of my father's relationship with Castro and wanting to avoid any potential political repercussions, ended up not only rehiring but also promoting the man he had recently terminated along with a noteworthy raise in pay. The "newly promoted" man could not find a way to reciprocate or express his appreciation to my dad. But my father did not want reciprocation, as he felt he had made this effort out of honor and justice.

Having fulfilled his side of the promise, the newly rehired man now had to comply with the agreement he had made with my father. The caveat my father was holding over the head of the newly rehired man was that he had to listen to recordings my father possessed of Castro's speeches in the rural areas of Cuba. Areas that were not covered by the national or international press. Areas where his speeches were not sanitized for external consumption. My father played the tapes in a very secluded and protected area so as to avoid attention and allow the man to focus on the facts of the material.

The man reacted in disbelief as he heard, for the first time, Castro passionately vilify the Western, capitalist way of life while rejoicing and promoting the virtues of a socialist, communist system. Even though the man who had lost his job was a Castro follower, my father wanted to infuse this man with a dose of reality versus what most people perceived in a hopeful attempt to bring clarity to his intellect and decision-making process. In my father's mind, this was just as important as recovering this man's job, if not more so. He thought of him as a friend and felt the risk of potentially compromising himself in an attempt to provide him with meaningful insight was worth it.

Ultimately, the man quelled his minor confusion from the contrasting representations provided by my father and replaced his uncertainty with a blind faith commitment as a die-hard Castro disciple. He did, however, greatly appreciate my dad's efforts to protect his family and reassured my father that he would maintain his confidence. He also told my father that he was forever in his debt and that someday, somehow, he would repay him for his kindness. In the end, in a noble display of character and courage, the head of airport security delivered on his promise as he destroyed my father's intelligence file, turned his back on him, and we were escorted away from his airport security office to leave Cuba forever.

CHAPTER NINETEEN

THE CORPORATE GOLF TOUR (CGT) IS ON THE HORIZON

My first exposure to what would turn out to be a distorted, corrupted, and perverted interpretation of the rules of golf as they are applied to corporate outings happened at Fiddler's Elbow Country Club in New Jersey. This experience would unwittingly define my lack of respect for the rules of golf as they were meant to be applied at almost all corporate golf outings. Rules are stubborn things. That is, until you actually experience what it's like to become a victim of the blatant disregard of them at corporate golf outings.

You might think my statements and perspective are those of a blasphemous derelict, but the fact is, through extensive bona fide witnesses and direct onsite field experience, I can confirm that a significant number of people cheat at corporate golf outings. And these people even cheat in their own club events.

They are shameless cheaters, period.

Unfortunately, or fortunately, I do not remember the charitable cause or the purpose of the outing that day, but I clearly recall and can visualize exactly what happened to me. I was a naïve, hopelessly-innocent golfer and this would be a baptism that would chart a destiny of having the most enjoyable and rewarding corporate golf outing tour career that I never thought possible. I have always been a real stickler for the rules of the game as they applied to competitive professional, amateur, and recreational golf, and it was a matter of honor that I conducted myself within the parameters that were developed by the USGA and the Royal and Ancient Golf Club.

For example, even when I played in the winter with the ground frozen solid and the hibernized grass compacted into clumps, I would still insist on playing the ball as it lay. Mulligans? Forget about it. You took the bad with the good, and I theorized the bad lies would contribute to making me a better golfer in the long run. If there was mud on the ball, so what? Play it as it lay. Only when my ball would come to rest on the green would I lift and clean—as it should be. I never improved my lie or my angle, never took an additional drop, would not stand behind another player as they putted to get a read. I was a purist. In fact, sometimes when I was playing a round by myself, I would play a two-ball scramble throughout the round as practice. However, my interpretation of a scramble would be to play the worst shot instead of playing the best shot in the rotation. Resisting the temptation to play the best shot was quite a disciplined exercise, and although labor intensive, it was a very productive exercise because it really forced me to hit consecutively better shots.

To this day, I play the ball down and *do not* play mulligans. In fact, I hate mulligans and re-putting. Hate it. When you employ a mulligan on a tee shot or re-putt, ninety-nine percent of the time, you hit the shot you wanted to hit or you drop the putt. For me, that is more aggravating than initially missing the shot or missing your first putt. In my humble opinion, it only serves to frustrate you more because the inevitable conclusion to this exercise is not "OK, I got the stroke down" or "OK, I just needed to be a little flatter on top." Instead, the conclusion is a heightened level of irritation that left you asking yourself: *Why the fuck didn't I hit the fairway or green or make the putt the first time?*

You are supposed to execute on the first shot. The world is full of single-digit handicappers who play their second ball or attempt second putts. But that's not what counts, right? In legitimate tournaments you don't get to play two balls and take the best shot of the two. So, what's the point?

On this memorable day, I was with three friends at Fiddler's Elbow on the eighteenth hole. It was the first time I played golf in a corporate outing with these guys. It was a par five, and we had reached the green in two shots. My two shots. I was the ringer in the group, but my friends were also respectable golfers (low to mid-eighties shooters). And while my buddies were having a good ol' time drinking, carousing, and fucking around throughout the day, I was taking this somewhat seriously, imagining myself playing in a legitimate competitive event—just one of the little mind games people will play to rationalize this stupid sport. As we read a forty-foot putt that broke about five feet from left to right, we agreed on the line and the putting order for this hole. We were playing a scramble format. The first three guys putted and missed. I was lining up my putt when, for whatever reason, I realized the three of them were standing directly behind the hole, shoulder to shoulder like a continuous blob of flesh. They were not small individuals. They looked like coupled railroad cars in a trainyard. Their positioning was seemingly orchestrated, prescriptive.

I backed off, lined up the putt again, and noticed that there was no direct line of sight between the hole and the clubhouse (where participants were looking out toward the green.) This wall of meat, hair, and cigar smoke had effectively obstructed any view from the clubhouse to the hole. Initially, I was a little annoyed at this, as I was confident in my ability to give the putt a good run for an eagle and do it in front of an onlooking "gallery." These guys were literally standing in my way for a short burst of shallow stardom and fame. Little did I know the real purpose. Thirty feet into my putt, it dawned on me what the hell was going on, as I then experienced these three yahoos jumping up and down, fist pumping (yes, fist pumping existed back then as well; Tiger did not invent the fist pump, he just commercialized it), accompanied by yelps of excitement and "attaboys," because ten feet before the hole, my ball was picked up and I was congratulated for "making the eagle!"

As we walked off the green, I experienced a momentary state of disorientation until I overheard my partners discussing what score they thought we needed to turn in to win. Although the playing format of the outing was a scramble, which occurred roughly twenty-five years ago, the numbers being thrown around were unthinkable: twelve under, thirteen under, "Naahhh, I think we need to be at fifteen under to win." That was fifteen under par for eighteen holes. I knew in actuality that we were nine or ten under for the round.

That's when it hit me. That's when I lost my virginity. We were going to cheat to win. We were going to alter our scorecard. I asked why we needed to do this given the fact that we played very well and it was hard to imagine how any other team could possibly post similar or lower scores.

My teammates responded, "Because everyone else is cheating."

"What!?" I asked, shocked.

They said that people in the field either took putts from eight feet or they took mulligans, and if all that failed, they just altered the scorecard. In fact, they sometimes skipped all the above and just filled out the scorecard before they arrived at the first hole. Someone will have won this outing without ever having teed off on the first hole.

As I said, I was somewhat naïve and found it upsetting that people would deliberately cheat at golf to win. *What was the sense of accomplishment in that? Where was the suffering? Where was the integrity in winning by cheating?* I went along with their plan, still a bit cynical, until I witnessed that we lost to a group that shot twenty under par for this outing. Think about it. *Twenty under par for eighteen holes?!* Not only would they have to birdie sixteen holes, they would also have had to throw in two eagles to boot. *What a day, huh!?* I mean, someone had to post that number, right? Or maybe they parred one hole, birdied fourteen holes, and dropped three eagles? No matter what the configuration, the mathematical probability of producing that kind of score is equivalent to having a St. Bernard, with a little barrel of brandy wrapped around its neck, rescue you after being buried in an avalanche in the Alps.

Uh-huh.

To add insult to injury, I saw the foursome that shot twenty under par. And, by the way, they also won the long drive and closest-to-the-pin skills prizes. These guys unabashedly had no sense of right or wrong and no sense of embarrassment. They were complete pigs in the "greed" sense of the word. They did not look like a foursome that would even come close to sniffing distance of posting one under par much less twenty under. Five over par would probably be more accurate. Yet they walked away with so much in pro shop credits and golf items that they should have declared professional status for accepting all this money—that is, credits. It truly was a breakthrough, *Caddyshack* moment for me, and after I recovered from the shock, this revealing episode inspired my initiative to further study the science of cheating at golf outings. If most of these schmucks were doing it, then I was going to do it better and impart a sense of professionalism in the process. I had just accepted the challenge to engage in a new form of athletic competition and was committed to bringing it to a new level of corruption and contempt.

From here forward, I decreed that all participating groups and contestants in any corporate outing would assuredly accept my group winning golf outings as a plausible outcome, rather than raise speculation about our ability to achieve a victory with very low scores. Keep in mind, that's not an easy task to pull off in front of a pretty cynical audience. In any event, I had lost my virginity and belief in the integrity of corporate golf outings and as a result, things would never be the same again for me and the fortunate partners who would join me in the future. This groundbreaking revelation would also represent the birthplace of a new golfing revolution that would later come to be known as the Corporate Golf Tour.

I truly hope the musings presented in this book will help you achieve a level of accomplishment and success you'd never before thought possible with these outings. It will boost your confidence, it will keep you stocked with the latest and greatest equipment without having to put your hands in your pockets, and maybe most importantly, it will give you the hero platform you have always longed for, because whoever golfs with you from this day forward at corporate outings will always be a winner. No longer will golf outing participants say, "They had to have cheated." No. They will say, "Man, those guys show up at every tournament." You will become the second "most interesting man in the world"—second only because you can't replace the original Dos Equis dude.

CHAPTER TWENTY

INTEGRITY TAKES A MULLIGAN

Corporate golf fundraising outings are generally high-profile events where the notoriety and prestige of winning within executive circles is coupled with substantial gifts or pro shop credits. And the usually lavish "corporate bounty" for coming in first, or at worst second, is not lost on participants. This extravagant, generous, and seemingly well-intentioned fundraising act of humanity is actually a gathering, a convention if you will, of bandits lurking for the opportunity to strike and pillage. High-profile corporate golf outings—excluding pro-ams—represent a quasi-lawless ecosystem resembling a Wild West bastion of cheaters.

And here's the kicker: the caddies are in on it too. They turn their heads and sometimes encourage the activity hoping that they will also be included in a good payday. *Hey, everyone has to make a living, and it ain't killing no one, right?* And think about it: the players will want to cover their tracks, and they do it by effectively buying the caddie's silence with a gag fee on top of their usual tip payout. You do not want the caddie alerting the pro or the starter collecting the scorecards at the end of the outing with an offhand remark like, "You should have seen the antics going on out there with this group." It's golf, but the political adage also pertains to payouts; "the sun comes out for everyone," as the saying goes. So, make sure your caddies are always taken care of.

In some defense of this abuse—not that one can ethically defend cheating—you have to consider that the extravagant price of admission for these events typically lends itself to rationalizing that you have to get some form of return on investment. What am I talking about? For example, these events overwhelmingly take place in exclusive country clubs that the general public does not have access to (unless there is a PGA event there and they can buy tickets to attend as spectators). In fact, corporate outings generally tap into these exclusive properties, on the grounds where PGA professionals play, to add to the allure and justification of the cost to participate. Needless to say, these renowned golf properties charge the organizers of these outings handsomely to rent their venue for a day. The expenses associated with hosting a golf outing at a prestigious country club, which include basic green fees, caddies (excluding tips), and accompanying food and refreshments but does not include prizes for each golfer, represents approximately forty to fifty percent of what the outing organizers would charge per person to participate in the event.

For example, a golf venue may charge the organizers 500–1,000 dollars per golfer—to play golf, eat and drink. The organizers will then charge donors from $1,250–$2,500 for a solo golfer to play in the outing and also include some type of door gift. The outing organizers will then create other sponsorship packages that entail additional costs associated with extra bells and whistles. A simple foursome sponsorship package for a company, with some stupid little course signage, can charge $6,000–$10,000 on the low end to participate in the outing. That's approximately $1,500–$2,500 per person to play eighteen holes. There are also premium types of corporate sponsorships that sell in excess of $20,000, $50,000, or even $100,000 with increased on-site signage and sponsorship of other activities (lunch buffet, reception, putting competitions, etc.) and additional extravagant perks. The pricing structure implemented by organizers for outing sponsorships is undisputedly determined by the fundraising goals of the organization *and* strategies capitalizing on the historical contribution trends of benefactors.

Irrespective of the exorbitant sponsorship fees, ancillary corporate partners, benefactors, and vendors eagerly contribute to the hosting foundation in order to offer and showcase this event to their colleagues and clients, all in an attempt to build or solidify professional relationships. The highest levels of sponsorship will understandably receive special attention and have premium arrangements thrown at them by the golf outing organizers. So, when you invite an important client to participate in this faux competitive activity, losing out on the rewards of winning is not part of the invitation. The clients you are playing with are not used to losing. They are successful captains of industry who play to win. If you lose, it reflects on you, and may inadvertently be considered an indication of your business acumen. "I know you didn't invite me here to lose" was a common welcoming phrase to me by many of these industry titans upon arrival at the outing. Herein lies a high level of pressure to win—unless you have clients who are a bunch of yokels who mistakenly think that "a bad day on the golf course is better than a day at the office." That is a misguided and false expression for sure. A bad day on the golf course sucks.

I rarely entertained or played with the latter type of clients. Thank God. If I didn't plan to deliver these clients a victory, I wouldn't have invited them, or they would not have invited me. I carried with me certain responsibilities as the ringer to certify basic golf scoring legitimacy. As such, I always appreciated a client group where at least one of them had some level of skill to contribute so that the shot making and scoring maneuvers wouldn't have to succumb to complete dependence on the ringer. That was the best-case scenario. Unfortunately, there were a few times when my partners were slugs and smug. They were athletically challenged and mistakenly entitled, with unrealistic expectations of themselves, which made for a very long day for me. And don't think I was the only guy with clients who were harboring the intent to win. No, no, no. I was trying to navigate a busy intersection in Times Square, where almost everyone was a potential pickpocket. But make no mistake: we were going to win, and it would all come down to who would be most deft in their deceit.

The deranged individuals espousing these crusades of corruption were wolves among lambs. Even if the lambs suspected foul play, they never possessed the wool to confront, contest, or expose their predators' malevolent winning results. These wholesome flocks of foursomes were actually just grateful to be at the event, applauding the others who reveled in fleecing them. Moreover, by no strange coincidence, and to add another layer of appalling mockery and hypocrisy to the integrity and ethics of golf, the largest supporters of the foundation and their highly aligned organizations and corresponding partners always seemed to walk away with consecutive and demonstrative wins. Guaranteed. Sometimes, it wasn't a win blatantly displayed to the public, as the organizers would adorn these high-rolling benefactors with lavish, off-menu gifts.

I experienced this system dozens of times firsthand when, as an invited guest of a significant sponsor, I would be offered gifts and prizes in excess of the sponsorship arrangement. This would often happen if I had a relationship with the organizers as well. For example, if a normal participant got to choose one out of five door gifts, I was provided with no choices as all five gifts were given to me and placed in my car so that no one would notice, and if the organizers were giving one gift certificate to the pro shop as the welcoming door gift, I would get three certificates. The system worked great for me.

CHAPTER TWENTY-ONE

A WINNING FORMULA

The formula for me at outings was to entertain and engross my foursome with a snapshot of what it was to play with a "professional" golfer while having everyone walk away well-supplied with gifts and prizes. And because I was a proficient golfer while they weren't, piquing the fascination of clients was a pretty easy lift. To give you an idea, I provided the philanthropic courtesy of sharing course secrets related to swing lessons—including chipping and putting techniques, course management, and sports psychology to simplify the game mentally. I would encourage their progress and ensure they experienced a stress-free, enjoyable, and productive day that they would talk about and share with their friends and colleagues.

Of course, they also expected me to prove the techniques I was talking about by personally demonstrating whatever swing tips I had shared with them. So, if I gave a chipping instruction, it was always ideal that it replicated shots they saw in the commercials and TV demonstrations in which the ball would inevitably land close to, or in, the hole. The difference was that on TV, the shots were recorded for efficacy over time, whereas this was a live demonstration where there was only one take—one shot to execute proficiently and legitimize that what I was telling these guys actually worked.

Anyway, it was personally satisfying because of their stares of wonderment when I was confronted with a difficult shot, whether it was a statistically improbable chip or hitting a line of sight between the trees, and I was able to confidently describe the kind of shot I was going to hit —soft fade, low trajectory, runners, flop shot, intentional snap hook, while accounting for terrain and conditions such as wind direction, course firmness, which way the grass was cut, where the ball lay, whatever—and I would pull the shot off as described. These particular shots and the play-making thinking behind them represented aspects of golf that these guys rarely saw and would never think of attempting. For sound reason.

Oftentimes, I had the client stand behind me as I described and illustrated the optimal statistical outcome of the shot I was attempting to execute. I would predict where the ball should come to rest after it was hit. Then I'd execute the shot as promised. They would just walk away shaking their head, muttering to themselves in disbelief, while I casually restrained my own sense of thrill for pulling off a highly improbable maneuver. In essence, the guests I was playing with expected to win because of these demonstrations.

When we would play a "scramble" format, I was always the fourth guy to hit. That meant I was the "cleanup batter." And that meant that everyone was dependent on me to make up for their bad shots in the rotation—to either hit the green and get close to the hole, or hit the tee shot 280 yards down the fairway. And ninety percent of the time, I did just that. The opportunity to perform hit me in the kneecaps as I was adorned with a wide range of lucrative keepsakes, but the real prize included personal access to the higher echelons and elite leaders of regional industry. It led to the nurturing and galvanization of key relationships that significantly defined my professional success. As such, and moving forward, I realized that one of the reasons for my existence on earth was to provide my guests with a level of fulfillment where their expectations of being on a winning team and playing with a former pro golfer were realized. Unknowingly, I had magically traversed onto a career path that fostered all the thematic qualities I avidly pursued while in high school and college—namely, to have fun while garnering optimum results.

CHAPTER TWENTY-TWO

THE CGT PROVIDES A PLAN B FOR THE "HAVE NOTS"

Let's entertain a small discussion about what plan B options are available for tour-aspiring players as it relates to the corporate golf tour (CGT). During my time, there were many multi-level professional tours in which skilled and aspiring amateurs and professionals could try to play, but no one talks about playing the corporate golf tour while working in a non-golf job. Competing on any level of a professional golf tour is a revered, respected, and closely guarded domain of exclusivity. It is respected because there are many people that understand the sacrifice and commitment directed toward the insane demands of excelling professionally at this game.

These players are like the gladiators of Rome. They must slay or be slayed. They will survive, and hopefully prosper, or unfortunately, be exiled to their "back of mind" plan B option, working as a club pro, or for an insurance company, automotive dealership, corporation, etc. Working-class tour pros have sacrificed almost everything and have all their chips riding on this one bet, this one career choice. But, many with foresight also kept a plan B in the back of their minds.

On occasion, plan B was a position in the family business that was being held for you—just in the highly probable (but never openly expressed) case that plan A does not pan out for the player. This class of pros needn't risk all they have because they have a bloodline crutch—their family's safety net. However, most struggling tour pros who are trying to grind out a nomadic lifestyle in their quest for glory, rewards, and the fulfillment of a spiritual journey, are working-class individuals, the coal miners of the professional golf touring circuit, with minimal external financial family support.

And although they dress nicely on the golf course, mingle with the elite of private clubs in the United States, and surround themselves, by virtue of their profession, with the trappings of wealth and aristocracy, mini-tour pros are distinctly classified in the socioeconomic class of the "have nots." A pro's exposure to these golfing fields of dreams is strictly a brief excursion into the world of the "haves," akin to grandchildren visiting grandparents, to be handed back after a short stay. Basically, pros back then were generally considered only a couple of steps above the working personnel of a private club. This "have not" domain is like a black hole and Groundhog Day combined as it repeats itself every day, containing only momentary glimpses of life with the "haves."

The athletic and emotional absorption of life that this golf exercise entails is only overcome by sheer determination derived from pure survival instinct and an obviously insatiable pursuit of pain and punishment. Generally speaking, pros who embody these essential characteristics also have to develop the mental acrobatics to wrestle with any and all psychological demons challenging their performance. It is the same in every sport, but the condition is enhanced with golf as there are no other teammates on the course to count on other than yourself—and your caddie.

Your caddie is the only one, outside of close friends and family, who is pulling for you. Trust me, no matter how much this is portrayed as a gentleman's game, the other guys are *not* rooting for you. The gentleman shit is reserved for the surface, the cameras, and to pretend that it is okay to lose and learn from the experience.

Mind you, it is appropriate to be a gracious sportsman, but the gentleman shit is overplayed and hypocritical. Every time I played competitively, my competitors and I were cordial with each other but otherwise wanted to run each other into the ground. It was a Michael Jordan type competitive mentality. The pain and sacrifice endured and the blood spilled for this game are distinct elements of suffering only shared by people who enjoy getting a full-body wax. Every day. It is only after you experience the initial adrenalin-fueled illusions, hoping to discover your destiny, that you confront the efficient, faceless tour pyramid as it mercilessly filters the naïve professionals into categories of their respective places within golf's hierarchy. It's the "ah-ha" crossroads moment of crystallization where most pros realize that they don't stand a chance in hell of making a decent career playing on any professional golf tour. These poor slugs—and I say that with the utmost affection and respect—have put everything on the table to survive and break through, but are ultimately deposited into an unforgiving caste system.

Then there is another category of players who never seem to tire of sucking from the family breast and who just want to live the faux life of a professional golfer "trying" to make it on tour. The parents of these particular players are trying to live out their wet dream of at least saying their son or daughter is a professional golfer—irrespective of the costs associated with this recklessly irresponsible exercise. They are the golfing version of ski bums—perineal students of a golfing lifestyle. These players are not inspired, nor are they hungry enough to punctuate themselves in this game. They don't want to face up to the responsibility, commitment, and pride necessary to stand out even though they are afforded the comprehensive environment and resources to do so. Most of them aren't really serious about playing competitive professional golf at the highest levels. They are just going through the motions, relishing the quasi-golf-pro lifestyle and deliberately prolonging the inevitable. The longer their sugar daddies—typically well-heeled parents—can support the delusion of playing a game and escaping the reality of getting a real job in the workplace, the better. I have known players, "professional golfers," who continued to feign they were trying to compete on the pro circuit but were spending more time poolside, than on a range. *I mean, why bother getting a job when they can fake this for as long as possible?* And whether they accomplish anything or not,doesn't matter just as long as they still get a pay day from daddy.

However, some of the mini-tour pros were the envy of most of us. We were envious because this category of pros didn't have to worry so much about expenses or having to struggle to make ends meet as they attempted to play golf for a living. And I'm not referring to the silver-spooned golf pro suckling from a family lineage of wealth or the never-to-grow-up child whose parents blindly supported their parasitic golf lifestyle. During those days, I met a lot of assistant pros in tournaments who had nonchalant attitudes about whether they would succeed in their quest to win a mini-tour event, much less get on the real tour. I was understandably confused about their whole approach and attitude until the background of their adventures was revealed. They had employed another renowned, last-resort option for financial backing. A lot of assistant pros at country clubs were being subsidized or sponsored by members at the clubs where they taught and worked. I mean, sponsoring a golf pro represented a somewhat tantalizing and privileged endeavor as members invested their money in someone they felt had the potential to play on the PGA Tour. Essentially, these members thought they were betting money on a thoroughbred, but the overwhelming amount of time, they were putting money on a mule.

Unfortunately, the fact was that the vast majority of members at country clubs didn't—and still don't—have the faintest of clues about what it takes to be considered a deserving tour pro prospect worthy of praise and investment. And seriously, the last bastion of financial support needed by any really exceptional player who has the onions to possibly make the tour is the backing of a member at a club. Truly exceptional players are already on the radar for top-tier sponsorship support and financial backing. It is the strategic imperative of corporate entities, not to mention an agent's lifeblood, to be on top of all the talent that exists in the golfing universe for sponsorship and investment opportunities. As a result, top-tier golfing talent does not need country club member financial support. Country club member investments in aspiring players who hope to become tour pros are narrowly limited to the players who exist within the club members' proximate golfing bubble and the milieu of country club staff pros with whom they have personal relationships.

The maligned intentions of a certain category of assistant pros combined with the good-faith ignorance of a member with some extra discretionary income ultimately amounts to nothing more than an endeavor for a conversation piece. The odds of realizing a return on the money they invested in an assistant pro trying to compete on a mini-tour was unquestionably less realistic than staking a bet on winning the Publishers Clearing House sweepstakes. Nonetheless, the premium these members received for what they wasted their money on was that even if it didn't work out, they still held onto a dream where they could say they were backing a potential tour pro. It was a super-duper conversation piece, assuming the others in the discussion group were complete morons. The sponsor members at these clubs were staking a much bigger dollar outlay on these assistant pros than the groupies who supported us with unremarkable, but very much appreciated shekels.

Most of us trying to grind out a living on the mini-tour, by whatever means possible, used to deride most of these pros as soft and lazy asses abusing their sponsors' investment and good will. These guys did not have the skills, determination, or work ethic needed to cut it on the mini-tour, much less the

PGA tour. I recall playing with guys who, after nine holes, if they were one or two over par, would call it a day and go to the beach or, better yet, go hit a bar and start drinking early. It would be party time. For some northern pros who had temporarily relocated to Florida, it was their spring break. In part, I felt bad for the members who didn't know they were basically being scammed. The fact is that I felt really bad for myself for not having access to these members because at that time in my life I had never been a member of, or worked at, a private club. I had the rags-to-riches storyline in my head, along the lines of Francis Ouimet when he won the U.S. Open in Brookline. Too bad fantasy golf didn't exist back then. It would have been a much better investment.

I could not escape the fact that I was also under the spell of similar delusions. However, I was not supported by a wealthy family. Not even close. I mean, growing up on 111th Street in NYC reflected, more often than not, economic hardship, not financial security. I was ultimately supported in my golfing ambitions by a wife who was and is a physician. Even so, it was always a financial struggle.

In essence, most of these guys, including myself, were chasing unicorns, yetis, and leprechauns. And most would eventually leave the mini-tour circuit and start fishing for any job opportunity thrown at them. I mean, one way or another, a person has to make money to provide for themselves and potentially others.

However, because America is such a great country, a lot of these formerly aspiring PGA Tour category of "have not" coal miners were able to be born again by fluidly pivoting to the most likely plan B scenario. They converted back to amateur status, affording them the opportunity to configure with an elite band of other golf pro mercenaries that corporations employ, and enjoy showing off to their clients and customers. These tour-aspiring rejects, who couldn't make any substantive dollars on any type of competitive professional tour, found a golden haven of previous professional golfers who succumbed to a prosperous plan B golfing career afterlife. These prior pros who converted back to amateur status were rescued when they were welcomed into a corporate domain that represented financial security versus the professional golf experiment trying to grind out a financially futile mini-tour excursion. Many of the coal miner plan B players, enjoying newly found amateur status as golfing Sicarios, and coupled with a good college background and an affable communication skill set, discovered corporate careers in positions where a considerable amount of their scope of work involved entertaining clients through golf.

These evolved plan B golfers are usually known for their personable, nurturing, enthusiastic demeanor and golfing repertoire and make you feel like they are personally interested in you during a round of golf and beyond. It is professional client golf at its finest. These former pros make someone feel as if they *are* playing with what was once a professional touring golfer. And although it is not on the same scale as playing with the likes of a pro that is inside of the top two thousand official world golf rankings, it is as close to playing in a pro-am as many of these business people would ever experience. The former pro provides ordinary, double-digit handicap golfers with an opportunity to get a glimpse of what it is like to be with a playing professional, enlightening his group with insights, "behind the ropes" stories, comical interludes, swing tips, and an otherwise entertaining time, including cocktails to be had by all at the end of the round. These plan B corporate pros provide an experience that clients will always remember. The former pros will be invited to play with influential and financially well-endowed individuals on the nicest golf properties in the corporate golf tour (CGT).

And even though these former pros have qualified for the plan B nine-to-five workforce, they continue to be surrounded by opulence and wealth in ultra-exclusive clubs adorned with serene, perfectly manicured natural environments and landscapes, otherwise known as first-class golf courses and country clubs. Moreover, they don't have to experience the stress that comes from trying to win money in a bona fide competitive and rule-abiding golf tournament in order to eat. However, an infusion of reality is delivered at the end of the day when the "have not," plan B bodies drift off to modest homes in modest neighborhoods in their modest vehicles. Technically, these now plan B corporate pros have a full-time position, in some executive capacity with a corporation and have accepted the fact that they are now working slobs like everyone else. In my case, this was a situation where I was fortunate to have been provided a niche that involved significant golf time as a dedicated function of my position—with clients as well as senior management. This workday schedule fell under the categories of "relationship building," "team building," and "business development".

The opportunity to create entrepreneurial business niches for yourself is what makes America such a great place. Playing competitive golf as an amateur and a professional provided me with otherwise elusive access to many senior leadership members of corporations. Not to mention, I provided rare insight into an ethnic minority that did not reflect or reinforce the ethnic minority stereotype. I looked as white as the next guy from Iowa, and as a result, it helped make white people feel comfortable about hanging out with a minority. A Cuban American who used to be a professional golfer and played on the mini-tour? *Seriously? You're not a baseball player? You're not cutting sugarcane in the fields? Or were you cutting sugarcane to clear the land to build a golf course and you mistakenly thought that qualified you as a golf professional?*

At my peak, a Hispanic being a professional golfer was comparable to a black dude writing a book about sailing techniques, or an Indian guy being a professional hockey player, or a Puerto Rican guy playing cricket. All would be a compilation of very short stories in which none of these books would be longer than two pages, including the table of contents. I was the embodiment of the Jamaican bobsled team; except I looked like your homogenous white boy next door. And don't think I didn't realize that perspective or capitalize on the benevolence and tolerance of my white mentors.

However, with all due respect, and leaving aside the lazy reference to race baiting, all of my mentors actually always treated me with dignity and afforded me deference and support—personally and professionally—always. I am pretty confident, though, that if I had looked like what they thought a Latino should look like (like I should be picking corn in a field or landscaping yards, or even had a discernible accent) my allure to senior execs, in spite of my golf acumen and brief flirtation with the mini-tour, would have been more constrained, and they would not have promoted me to others as vigorously as they had.

Remember, I grew up on 111th Street in Manhattan. Comically, every white person I have come across that has claimed to have been raised in a "multicultural" neighborhood has been raised in neighborhoods that were predominantly inhabited by white cultural groups. Even throughout the metropolitan tri-state area, where contiguous neighborhoods remained largely delineated by cultural, ethnic, or religious tribes, a white person's exposure to minorities or other darker skinned ethnic cultures and lifestyles was limited. Within urban zip codes, a white person still had to daringly venture outside their prescribed territorial birth nest to experience any kind of true cultural diversity.

I now live in New Jersey, and some of my friends grew up in sections of Hudson County that were considered "tough." Mind you, I give Hudson County a lot of credit as these were rough, blue-collar neighborhoods where kids had to morph into a tough persona to defend their honor. But in that time, New York's inner-city kids represented a different kind of toughness. You see, the Hudson County kids thought that their Hudson County toughness was at least equal to that of the blacks or Hispanics who lived in Harlem or Spanish Harlem. The differences between these contrasting environments were distinct and highlighted by much larger urban real estate swaths of economic disparity and despair that were located in New York City. And Hudson County was not, by any stretch of the imagination, considered an urban, inner-city zone. NYC kids like myself considered Hudson County the suburbs. Unlike Jersey, the inner-city kids in New York not only had to be tough, they had to survive and try in whatever form, to work themselves out of a slum. Our NYC neighborhoods were proliferated by gangs that created, monitored, and enforced their own brand of "street justice" in the community. The New Jersey neighborhoods had community kids disguised as, and pretending to be, members of gangs. At best, they might represent small satellite branches of the gangs from New York. Teens in New York didn't need to pretend to be anything. Kids from Jersey would come into our neighborhood to buy drugs. Nobody from the city ever went to Jersey to buy drugs. Ultimately, New York City kids would get out of our situation either through sports, education, jail, or death. In contrast, a lot of the Jersey guys continued to live in the same communities where they grew up. Why shouldn't they? They were mostly decent neighborhoods.

Nonetheless, no matter the neighborhood background, my strong street smarts, "white chemistry," and golf acumen significantly benefited my ability to get jobs throughout my career that I otherwise would have lost to other candidates who had similar qualifications. This aspect of job security, which I would have never thought of previously, was especially reassuring because I quickly realized after having moved to Tampa and playing in the J.C. Goosie Space Coast mini-tour in North Florida, that I was *not* going to earn enough money to turn this into a profession for myself. Nor was I going to improve to the point where I could experience a competitive, well-compensated, professional-playing lifestyle.

I wanted to enjoy a lifestyle that would provide me with some options where—oh, I don't know—I would not have to eat peanut butter sandwiches and suck down chicken broth for dinner. You know, just have some level of short-and long-term financial stability with enough of a revenue stream to assure necessities like food, utilities, a home, a car, a family, and a couple of pairs of shoes.

CHAPTER TWENTY-THREE

YES. NO MONEY FOR NOTHIN'

M oney was always tight during my professional golfing adventure, and it was directly attributed to me not making any tournament cash because of my playing results. The Space Coast tournaments were essentially big betting parlors as the purse money came from player "entry fees." Everyone would throw their entry fee in a pot, which was then parceled out by way of how you finished in the pack after two days of competition. As I recall, there weren't any sponsors for any of the events, and purses did not pay anything meaningful after fifth place. First and second place would pay for several more tournament fees, related travel expenses, and maybe that month's rent; third place would earn you your entry fee back, pay for your next tournament, and supplement your beer supply; and fourth and fifth place payout would get your entry fee back, subsidize a couple of dinners, and provide you with a coupon for a free large soda with the purchase of two hot dogs at Hank's Hot Dawg Emporium.

I am obviously partially kidding, but that was the simple black and mostly red operational optics of playing on this tour. Ninety percent of all players were in a perpetual sea of red. I am pretty darn sure there were no tournament sponsors back then to help enhance the purses or alleviate the financial pain coming from a sixth to twentieth place and beyond finish. Other than notable pros like Lee Janzen, Marco Dawson, and others who were winning money on the Space Coast tour and other mini-tour events, most of the pros playing on any mini-tour back then had to be creative to find other jobs that would create some form of income.

I used to buy and sell used cars. Hondas were the easiest to find cheap and sell cheap and quick, while still turning a $300–$500 profit. Other guys would work for building contractors doing odd residential or commercial jobs. Some guys had carpentry experience and would get sub-contracts for the private housing developments going up around Tampa, which were numerous. Sometimes they would let me work with them as well, even though I didn't know what the fuck I was doing and needed a lot of hand-holding and direction in cutting and installing simple floor trims. I was fortunate to have benevolent friends who didn't seem to mind my annoying them with my lack of expertise. I even resorted to making clubs to sell to some of the recreational and social golfers, who would follow our mini-tour careers and with whom we would occasionally play.

That's right: I had my own brand of clubs. In addition to Hogan and Wilson there was also a Rojas line of golf clubs. I specialized in making driver and fairway woods made from honey-stained persimmon heads. I would not buy dark brown or cherry-stained wood heads. I would purchase raw heads, shafts, grips, and the other relevant materials from Golfsmith and give the heads a honey stain, which provided for a unique and starkly beautiful club. Unlike today, we rarely bought new golf equipment for ourselves. A new driver was a luxury. There were no tour vans at our events like there are today. I remember how happy I was when Spalding sponsored the Space Coast Tour with their Tour Edition ball because we received a sleeve of balls for every tournament. To give you an idea of how things have changed between then and now, today most junior events supply participants with a dozen balls, hats, towels, shirts, belt buckles, sharpies, and so on. Not then. Back then, we scraped together money to buy club components, mostly from Golfsmith, to directly work on our sticks, adjust our lies and lofts, wrap twine around woods, whatever.

However, one time I was giving somebody a lesson, and as he was using the brand-new five-wood I had just made for him, the head came flying off during a swing. It must have flown 20–30 yards, seemingly in slow motion, with the whole episode feeling like a skeet shoot. I was standing there watching this unfold in a state of shock and embarrassment. I had good quality control ninety-nine percent of the time. Unfortunately for this experience, he was part of the one percent. However, our students and groupies were such nice people that on this one and only occasion where there was a quality control issue, this student took it in stride, and we both laughed about it. We continued the lesson with his other clubs, and I proceeded to fix his club immediately and gave it to him the next day. We enjoyed a long-standing relationship going forward, and he was always very supportive, even fatherly.

Also, for these weekend warriors, playing with us was a thrill and a privilege as they felt like they were playing in an informal pro-am, with the advantage that it was a much more personal, organic experience. In a way, we had a fan base, like dedicated misfit groupies following a bad rock band on a scavenger hunt. I mean, they were hoping that one of us would break through and make it to the big tour so they could say that they used to follow and play with us. These guys were the equivalent to barflies. I guess that made them golf flies. On occasion, they would sign up for lessons from us as well, mostly wanting to find a way to support us without us feeling like they were giving us a handout. We were always grateful for their support and empathy. At least these odd jobs were able to provide a very basic form of income to support a career that I was making absolutely no money in.

CHAPTER TWENTY-FOUR

BRO. SURVIVAL POINTS TO WENDY'S SUPER SALAD BAR

An everyday slice of existence for a traveling mini-tour pro was to eliminate as many expenses as possible and uncover ways where we could s-t-r-e-t-c-h our cash. Many guys would pair or triple up to share gas, hotel rooms, and even food. We would often travel and sleep together in seedy hotels, the cheapest ones we could find—and, trust me, there were plenty of them on the I-4 corridor between Tampa and Orlando—to curtail travel expenses. Our version of dining out was to find area buffets and stuff ourselves to no end. We existed mostly on a diet of Gatorade, peanut butter, sardines, and some white flour product—any product we could put sardines or peanut butter on. Further desperate to save on everything we could, it was not uncommon to go to these restaurants equipped with sandwich bags—large ones—in an attempt to discreetly pack food to take with us for a later meal or early morning sustenance. Sometimes we couldn't find anything open to buy something to eat for our early tee times, so we had to improvise and ingest some kind of nutrients from last night's dinner. And mind you, we had a lot of second-day early tee times.

The hallmark illustration of our lifestyle could best be summed up with Wendy's Super Salad Bar buffet. When I began my short stint as a professional golfer, the Wendy's restaurant chain had launched its Super Salad Bar buffet concept. Although this concept currently does not exist (small wonder), back then you were able to gorge yourself on a buffet that offered at least three culinary sections. One section was a salad station with generous offerings, another was a Mexican spread with everything you needed to make your own tacos, and the other section was Italian, including pasta with sauces, and garlic breadsticks—*and* it was all you could eat. Sometimes we would spend up to an hour and a half eating—nonstop. The first time we ate there, we started to think of ways to extend the bar buffet to include takeaway items for ourselves. Naturally, that wasn't the ethical idea of the buffet concept. You could eat whatever you wanted, as long as the food stayed within the confines of the restaurant.

Therefore, our task was clear. We had to free the nourishment from the restraints presented by the walls of the restaurant. We would eat our fill and continue to put outrageous amounts of food on our plates, taking items that would be easy to pack in a large sandwich bag. We would bring back tacos, chili, garlic bread and pasta to our table, eat two or three tacos, some chili and pasta then pack the remaining tacos and garlic bread, providing us with dinner later that day, and breakfast the next morning. This was one of our methods of survival. We may have looked the part as golfers, all pretty and dignified and shit, but we were struggling in every capacity for the opportunity to pursue, and compete in, the game we loved.

It was a precarious time in my life as I was going through a separation from my first wife, and we had a child I wanted to, and needed to, help support. At this point, I was very disillusioned about my ability to play on the mini-tour. Although my handicap at that time was a plus two, if I remember correctly, I was constantly getting run over by most of the guys in the tournaments I played in. I was competitive against the assistant pros who were down there killing time with no real aspiration to actually play for a living, and that was as far as it went. The other guys who were winning the tournaments were at least three or four distinct levels above me. I wasn't cashing any checks on this tour, and between my travel expenses and tournament fees, I was losing quite a bit of money.

Like actors who wait on tables while they attend multiple auditions in hopes of getting their big break, most of us on the mini-tour back then were scraping together money by doing other jobs and making time for practice. In addition to flipping Hondas, making clubs, giving lessons, and trying my hand at carpentry, I also landed a gig as a writer for a golf publication out of Tampa that was distributed throughout the northern tier of the state. Writing for the publication was a huge benefit as I was able to play and review private golf courses throughout our area, and my columns became a featured section of the publication—right next to the ad solicited by me from the country club. Most of the mini-tour pros had access to play for free at most courses because the head pros at these clubs were sympathetic to the mini-tour journey and would grant us courtesies at their clubs. However, as a writer, I had one additional unique asset that the other players did not have. I had a press pass. What was the significance of this benefit? Was it the access you gained to watch tour events? Yes, but no. I didn't really want to spend my time watching guys play when I should have been playing or practicing. No, it had to do with being resourceful in getting more access to premium courses and mingling with the golfing establishment, which helped increase my awareness of the golfing bubble in north-central Florida.

So why did the "press card" prove to be so valuable? The Senior PGA tour (now the Champions Tour) was scheduled for a first-time appearance—a tour stop at a brand-new golf course in Tampa. A touring buddy and I went to cover the event. It was a very sunny, humid Friday afternoon with temperatures in the high eighties. As we walked with the gallery adjacent to the driving range where the pros were hitting balls, something caught my eye. My hearing then chimed in for confirmation. Pros were hitting drivers into a roped-off section of the woods. I looked back and realized that the driving range was about 225 yards long and that was way too short a distance for a shot with a driver. And there was nothing but bush and shit beyond the back of the range. I shared this observation with my friend, and we immediately confirmed that these guys were blowing balls into the woods with their drivers and there was no way the club was going to be able to recover these balls in this thick "you're fucked" brush. One shot and these balls were gone. For them.

We walked back to where the pros were hitting and observed the types of balls that were flying into the woods. They were spanking brand-new, unblemished Titleist balata balls. The king's jewels of balls at that time. Nothing else was even close. These balls were expensive even back then. When we would buy these balls, we would strictly use them for tournament rounds because they had such a soft outer cover that after one round, the cover on the ball would tear from the grooves on your club, or they would be knocked out of round. Simply, the balls provided a superior feel and spin but at the cost of being very fragile. These balls were precious, revered. A sacred item that was never taken for granted. They were our version of a Fabergé egg. Our eyes lit up at the thought of the opportunity that was developing. Our goal was to trespass, and invisibly make our way into these woods, in order to retrieve as many balls as humanly possible.

But how would we collect the balls and get them out without being noticed or worse, get caught and arrested—and subsequently fired from the golf publication? We devised a plan: go home and get jackets with waist drawstrings; return to the course; and, as inconspicuous as possible, work our way through the bushes to the area where the balls were landing. We were looking forward to experiencing a balata version of Wendy's Super Salad Bar buffet. And this had to happen at peak times, as we strategized that the more people there were at the range, the less likely it was that we would be noticed. Hiding in plain sight was our master plan.

The land used by this golf course was expansive, so once we were in the woods, no one would notice us meandering through them. We also had to make sure that no one would notice us from the range, so the jackets and our clothing all had to blend in with the foliage. Hopefully, no one would become suspicious that we were wearing jackets in the sweltering heat and high humidity. We also hoped no rattlesnakes or cottonmouths would also be looking for balls. As we walked back and forth along the entry point, waiting for an opportunity to descend into this jungle, a lapse in foot traffic occurred, and we dove into the woods, squatting, shuffling, and sliding to get closer to our target destination.

We were doing the Titleist balata conga in the dense vegetation without the benefit of machetes. We didn't have a good sense of the range of flight until we started hearing balls whiz by us, landing by our feet—like gunfire I supposed, not that I knew what that was like except for what I'd seen in the movies. It was obvious that we were too close and in danger of getting killed. We backed up and waited. And waited. And waited. And sweated. I must have lost five pounds in the sweltering heat crouching there for over an hour. Finally, after all the players had finished working on the range, we went to collect our treasure.

We were scrounging around putting handfuls of balls in the space we created with our jackets—not just in the pockets but between the inner jacket lining and our body. Essentially, we had transformed our bodies into garbage bags with legs and arms. We zipped up our sweat-soaked jackets, tightly secured the drawstrings at the waist, and seamlessly eased back to the spectator walking path, now resembling seriously overweight people—like Fat Bastard from the Austin Powers movies. We walked off the grounds, maneuvered into my friend's car, and drove back to my place to review our trove of treasure. Surprisingly, no one even said "boo" to us. They must have thought we were in the woods taking a leak or having sex or something.

At my house, we laid out what seemed to be a couple hundred balls and separated them into three categories: tournament-grade balls (perfect or near perfect condition), practice round balls (good balls that you can rely on to fly correctly, but not ones you would use in a tournament), and practice balls (whichever balls did not fall into the other two categories). In one day, we had gathered enough balls for an entire season. What a success story! It saved us a ton of money since we bled with every penny we spent on professionally representing ourselves to the public and to the game by looking the part—wearing nice clothing, shoes, and having decent equipment. In reality, ninety percent of the guys on the mini-tour were hurting financially.

Pictured from left to right: My father, Fidel Castro, Arnaldo Goenaga Barron with his son, Arnaldo Jr., in New York City in 1955.

Eduardo Chibas and my father in New York City.

Written dedication from Fidel Castro to my father: "To my brother, Eurice B. Rojas in whom I see as an exponent of new virtues contained in the generation that will definitely liberate Cuba. New York, Nov. 3, 1955. Fidel."

Left to right arrows depict my father, Arnaldo Goenaga Barron, and Fidel Castro attending an M-26-7 meeting in New York City in 1955. Portraits hanging in front of the table are Calixto Garcia Iñiguez, José Martí, and, José Antonio Maceo y Grajales

Fidel Castro and my father over Castro's left shoulder in New York City.

Pictured from left to right: My father, Eduardo Chibas.

Fidel Castro, middle, with my dad, far right, in New York City, 1955.

My Aunt and Godmother, Oneida Alvarez, holding me standing alongside my Godfather, Arnaldo Goenaga Barron, during the Baptism ceremony in April of 1958.

Pictured from left to right: Fidel Castro, Arnaldo Goenaga Barron and my father hosting a fundraiser in New York City in 1955 to support replacing the current Batista regime with a new Cuban government.

Arnaldo G. Barron (in the middle with sunglasses) alongside his wife and son (to his right) being welcomed in New York City by a group of M-26-7 members. They were celebrating his release from jail following his arrest in Texas for attempting to smuggle weapons to Cuba. My father is pictured present on the right wearing a hat and wool overcoat. The reference to "Orion" on the hand-held boards is in recognition of the boat Barron had commissioned to smuggle the arms.

Written dedication from Eduardo Chibas to my father. "To Eurice B. Rojas,
A Cuban that will honor our homeland. Your fraternal companion/partner/colleague, Eduardo
R. Chibas"

My father on left side of picture. Men and women on a hunger strike in support of the Cubans imprisoned in a Brownsville, Texas jail who were arrested by U.S Coast Guard for attempting to smuggle arms to Cuba.

Arnaldo G. Barron, my mother holding me, and my dad and aunt (all behind the Cuban flag) after my Baptism.

Eduardo Chibas and my father in New York City.

Arnaldo G. Barron and my dad walking the streets of New York City.

Eduardo Chibas at the microphone during one of his live Sunday broadcasts in Cuba.

Arnaldo Goenaga Barron and his wife Gloria.

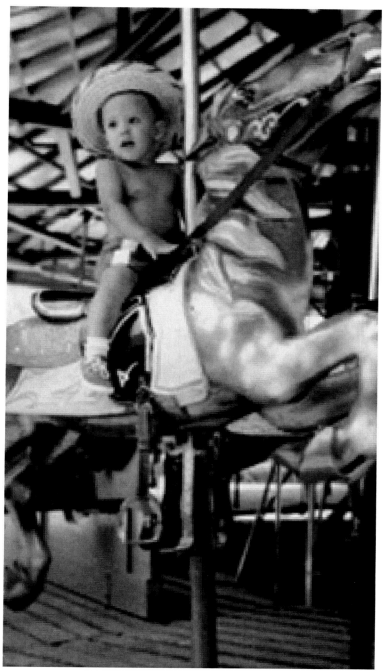

"Ride 'em cowboy!" Me on a carousel in Cuba.

My mother, father and me in a family portrait after several years settled in NYC.

CHAPTER TWENTY-FIVE

CUBAN TWO-STEP

Initially, my father gave Castro's ideology and goals the benefit of the doubt. He originally felt Castro was figuratively, literally, and symbolically following the script of another infamous Cuban revolutionary from the city of Santiago de Cuba by the name of Eduardo Chibas. Widely recognized as an activist politician, Chibas preceded Castro with his ideology for an independent, corruption-free Cuba. He was considered by many, including Castro, to be the inspiration behind the Cuban revolution undertaken by Castro. Castro would symbolically quote Chibas during many public gatherings and also cited him in a speech to motivate the rebels prior to the military's infamous Attack on the Moncada Barracks in 1953. Moreover, after Castro seized power, he delivered a passionate endorsement of Chibas at his gravesite, thanking Chibas for the influence he had provided the revolution.

Ironically, they each had unforgivingly contrasting political views as Chibas was fervently anti-communist while Castro was cuddling up to communism. Chibas became a member of the initially influential Autenticos party in 1938, and although he went on to establish his own political party, called Partido del Pueblo Cubano (Ortodoxo) in 1947, he was also appointed the head of the Autenticos party in 1948. The Ortodoxo party he founded was considered a very liberal faction, but the staunchly anti-communist group was devout in its beliefs that Cuba could experience governmental change through constitutional reformatting rather than military upheaval. Chibas's popularity and appeal derived from the passionate, bordering on theatrical, oratory skills he used in his attempts to expose corruption in the Cuban government and, most importantly, his foresight and deftness in effectively utilizing the mass reach of a new communication tool—radio.

The radio phenomenon was beginning to gain audience momentum in Cuba (approximately twenty percent of the Cuban population had household radios in the 1950s, representing the largest radio audience in the Caribbean), and the potential of reaching a national audience to communicate his positions and perspectives through radio was not lost on Chibas. Airing every Sunday evening at 8 p.m., he successfully produced and hosted a live, weekly radio broadcast that captivated a significant segment of the Cuban population with programming content highlighting a congruent combination of themes, including nationalistic overtones, dramatic political testimony, and cynical proclamations of distrust and corruption targeting current government leaders. Tragically, Chibas ultimately used his radio platform to essentially commit suicide. He shot himself in the stomach with a .38 handgun during one of his live broadcasts to symbolically preserve his honor and integrity when his promised evidence of embezzlement of a government official (he was expected to unveil evidence against the education minister during his live show) failed to materialize. He died eleven days later on August 16, 1951, from the gunshot wound. My father was greatly influenced by Chibas, whom he believed to be an intelligent, thoughtful, and dedicated political leader whose approach to government reform in Cuba was the most meaningful and civilized. In fact, my father was so inspired by Chibas that my middle name, Eduardo, was a testament to his affinity for Chibas. However, I haven't the slightest idea of where my first name, Eurice, came from other than him handing his name down to me. I wish he would have explained the origins of the name "Eurice." And for some inexplicable reason, I was never compelled to ask.

Arnaldo Goenaga Barron was another instrumental figure of the Castro revolution and a close friend and trusted colleague of my father. That friendship ensured my dad's allegiance and motivation to engage in the activities of the M-26-7 organization. My father was an active participant in the M-26-7 (Movimiento de Julio 26) organization that was developed by Arnaldo Barron and Castro as a symbolic tribute to the failed Attack on the Moncada Barracks on July 26, 1953. Of particular significance, the failure of the attack was turned into a rallying propaganda tool, primarily through M-26-7, for the Cuban people as the event was considered by many to be the birthplace of Castro's revolution. As a tangible perspective of my father's close relationship with Barron (all his close friends called him Barron and not Arnaldo), Barron accepted my parents' request for him to be my godfather.

So, my middle name is in honor of Chibas, and a prominent leader of the Cuban revolution with Castro became my godfather. Barron was also a trusted confidant of Castro. He not only fought alongside Castro at the failed Moncada attack, but was also arrested and imprisoned with Castro after that failed attack. His contributions and activism for the revolution were both courageous and well-documented. Following his release from jail for the Moncada attack, Castro fled to Mexico to reorganize his revolution. He was later invited by Barron to stay at his apartment when he came to New York City for fifteen days in October of 1955. During those fifteen days, Castro committed all his efforts toward organizing and galvanizing all the Cuban revolutionary organizations under M-26-7, and formally recognized Barron as a founding member and leader of M-26-7.

Approximately two and a half years later, in March of 1958, Barron chartered an eighty-three-foot boat named *El Orion* of Nicaraguan registry to lead a group of thirty-six other revolutionaries in an attempt to smuggle a substantial cache of military arms into Cuba. However, the U.S. Coast Guard intercepted *El Orion* on the Gulf Coast off the shores of Padre Island and arrested all onboard. They were put in a Brownsville jail in Texas and charged with violating the U.S. Neutrality Act. Pressure to release these jailed Cuban revolutionaries was highlighted by compelling acts of protest throughout Cuban enclaves in the United States, including hunger strikes coordinated by the M-26-7 organization. In May of that year, all the activists were freed on bond and placed on three to five years of probation. Following the *El Orion* incident, Barron was also indicted on another charge in November 1958 for violating the Foreign Agents Registration Act of 1938 where he failed to legally file the required paperwork identifying himself as a person acting on the behalf of a political organization. In March of 1959, he ultimately pleaded "no contest" and submitted the required paperwork. In April 1959, Barron received a suspended sentence and five years of probation.

My dad wanted a system of government for Cuba that was better than the repressive, corrupt regime that Batista imposed on most Cubans. But he wanted that new government structure to be aligned with the democratic and capitalist values represented in the United States. In its origins, Castro continued to attempt to conceal the true political alignment of his movement toward the Soviet Union until the latter stages of the revolution, and my father mistakenly felt that the "new" Cuban revolution spearheaded by Castro was following in the anti-corrupt, anti-communist footsteps framed by Chibas.

My father's faith in what he originally thought to have been a pathway to a relationship with the United States was eroding, and he correctly assessed that Castro was also just in it for himself and his delusional version of what he thought was best for Cuba. His disappointment in Castro, and in himself for allowing himself to be duped by the false narrative, had cemented his decision to leave Cuba, whatever the cost would be. He felt that he had been betrayed and that Castro had deceived the Cuban people and the world.

CHAPTER TWENTY-SIX

THE ART OF REVOLUTION: KEEP YOUR ENEMIES DEAD AND YOUR FRIENDS DEAD

It was a day in Havana that Ernest Hemmingway would have been proud of. The weather and landscape were a beautiful tapestry of colors, sunshine, and gentle trade winds gracefully persuading palm leaves to dance—a setting befitting paradise. January of 1959 marked an historical milestone for the island. Castro had just come to power and was celebrating with his first parade down the streets of Havana. It was a flotilla of then-current Chevrolets, Buicks, and Cadillacs rolling down the avenues with key players of the revolution along for the ride, enjoying the fruits of their labor to avenge and govern Cuba. The adoring crowds that embraced, collaborated, and promoted the revolution lined the streets at least twenty bodies deep, enthusiastically celebrating the anticipation of a new chapter for Cuba, one which they felt they had been instrumental in authoring.

It was a day that motivated one of the three college colleagues who had always engaged in the philosophical and political student tug-of-war debates with Castro and my father to go to the parade. This college friend was curious to witness the victory lap of an authentic uprising, and the friend who was responsible for it, firsthand. And even though he opposed the new regime and its projected political trajectory, he wanted to see his collegiate compadre. After all, as a firsthand witness to history, he knew this revolution would go on to have profound implications and consequences not only for Cuba but for the world.

It was a revolution that would forever transform the social and political structure of a nation that was once regarded as the most successful economic engine in the Caribbean. It was a revolution that would embrace a new form of communism—"Fidelismo," as it would later be referred to. A revolution that would enthusiastically embrace the rapid deterioration of once revered architectural treasures, along with the incessant maintenance of vintage model 1957 and 1958 American automobiles that are forced into service today as current-year models—sixty-plus years later. The college friend remembered his interactions with my father and Castro in a favorable and sentimental way, recalling the lively conversations, the passionate banter, and the satisfied feeling he got knowing that each of them had pushed each other to their intellectual limits. The three had always succeeded in overachieving in every one of their debates.

It was like performing a strong workout, striving to be a better athlete, while deploying the exhausting and requisite mental discipline that goes into playing competitive chess at the masters level.

This type of relationship, forged over time and composed of mutual respect and affection, was a rare and unique friendship that most people would never experience in their lifetime. These were relationships that were highly regarded and should have been appreciated forever. Afterward, like most competitive athletes, they would leave those differences on the battlefield, lower their intellectual guard, and just hang out, wanting to simply bullshit and roast each other. It was kind of like Muhammad Ali, Joe Frazier, and George Foreman in the ring at the same time, hugging each other after a bout. The college friend remembered those days fondly as they undoubtedly represented good times and good days. After all, each of the three amigos contributed to making the other stronger and better in positioning and communicating their perspectives.

But let's not forget that this college friend happened to always propose the opposing point of view against Castro in their debates. And it wasn't because he was role-playing or simply taking up space as the devil's advocate. They were both fundamentally and philosophically different and looked at the world from diametrically opposite political points of view. This wasn't supposed to be—and it shouldn't have been—a big deal because at the end of the day, they were friends no matter what and appreciated each other's company. At the time, the three friends were young and carefree, and the pointed tension usually associated with discussions about perceived social injustices and governmental corruption was recognized as nothing more than substantive fodder for discussions that were passionate but largely rhetorical in nature.

Growing up, Castro was a front-row spectator to the criticism of a capitalist system. His father, Angel Castro, was a prominent businessman who initially experienced hard labor in Cuban nickel mines and later worked for a subsidiary of the United Fruit Company. He was reputed to be a strong worker who eventually saved enough money to start his own entrepreneurial ventures by pimping immigrant laborers (largely Haitian) for fees to the United Fruit Company. Ultimately, with the accumulated monies, he invested in property, eventually becoming a bit of a land baron and managing hundreds of employees whom he used to cultivate his farming products and maintain his livestock. And although Castro's father enjoyed the benefits of capitalism, he nonetheless held deep animus toward the shining knight of capitalism—America—and its colonization efforts toward Cuba. Notably, Angel Castro did not spare sharing his hostility toward America with any of his children. Whatever the case, Castro came from a financially well-endowed family, by Cuban standards, did not suffer from any perceived social injustices, and was exposed to anti-American vitriol in his household throughout his most impressionable years.

Political differences aside, and secure in feeling their friendship transcended politics, the college friend naïvely decided to attend the parade to see his old friend. And just like the historical, well-intentioned, good sport gesture to hang out after one of their bruising debates, he wanted to acknowledge his friend for his accomplishment, however misguided he felt it to be.

The crowd was stifling—like Brazil during Carnival or the Macy's Thanksgiving Day parade in New York City. The college friend had never seen or experienced anything like this in Cuba. The parade route echoed with a distinct exuberance of cheers, pulsating music, honking cars, and the rhythm of bouncing bodies drizzling with sweat. Lines of parade cars were passing this particular area, and in spite of the overwhelming energy that surrounded him, he calmly waited for a possible glimpse of his school buddy. He noticed the excitement and noise reaching what he thought to be a crescendo and figured Castro to be close at hand. Finally, beyond the jumping bodies and waving arms, he could make out Castro standing saintly in his convertible, waving to the crowds. As Castro got closer, the college friend pushed toward the front so that Castro would hopefully see and recognize him. He was overcome with anxiety and suspense about what could transpire. And although he was generally anticipating a brief but welcoming interaction, he had no idea how making eye contact with Castro would be received and interpreted. In fact, the passing eye contact would quickly and clearly define this man's destiny.

He managed to get closer to the front and was encouraged that Castro's ability to acknowledge his presence was as optimal as it would get. He was on Castro's left-hand side and as Castro turned to span the hypnotized legions of fans from his right to his left, their eyes locked for what seemed to be a lifetime as memories of college were surely resurrected. Castro momentarily paused his right-to-left movement to seemingly embrace their collegiate history with fondness. A warm and welcoming smile began to manifest on Castro's face. However, it would turn out to be nothing more than a momentary neurological, autonomic reaction as his head movement immediately stopped and the warm and developing welcoming smile quickly transformed into a stern squint of contempt.

The seemingly nostalgic and sentimental gaze abruptly morphed into a "gotcha" sneer. Castro then promptly discarded the visual connection and coldly shifted his attention straight ahead toward the convoy of cars. The car passed, and the college reunion was over. The college friend had maintained his arm elevated but had stopped waving. Shaken, he slowly lowered his arm as he tried to interpret what the seemingly distressed stare from Castro symbolized. Having known Castro like he thought he did, he was initially inclined to minimize the curt exchange as any type of prognostication signaling malintent. However, the initial reaction and subsequent contrast, within seconds of acknowledging each other, was too extreme. Too disproportionate for the moment.

Could Castro have inadvertently forecasted a warning? Was it a threat? Rather than latching onto the good memories, did Castro discount them because he was captivated by what he recalled as differing political points of view? The college friend could not fathom that Castro would consider him a political threat as he had no current financial or political footing to rationally lead to that conclusion. Nonetheless, he had personally witnessed unreasonably crazier things that had happened to anti-Castro people during this historic uprising and felt the need to heed his own presumed paranoia. And although the college friend wanted to extend his former classmate the benefit of benevolence, he could not ignore the instinctual bad feeling he felt after their very brief eye contact.

He aggressively pushed his way back through the parade revelers and proceeded to the nearest phone to call his Cuban domicile. To the dismay of his family, he informed them that he was going to gas up his boat, leave for Miami, and contact them upon his arrival there. He communicated to them that they were not to worry, but he had to move immediately and would explain later. Fortunately for the college friend, the weather and seas were favorable, resulting in an uneventful voyage to Miami.

Upon arriving in Miami, he called home, only to have his family confirm what he had suspected and feared would happen. The college friend's family told him he should thank God he was calling safely from Miami because following the conclusion of the revolutionary parade, Castro's special police had gone to his house looking for him. In a rare display of carelessness, Castro had underestimated his colleague's discerning interpretation of their very brief special encounter. Shortly after having gained his footing in Miami, the college friend courageously coordinated a nighttime rendezvous to Cuba in his boat to escape with his family, resigned to the fact that he would never see his homeland again. One quick, telling look was all it took for him to sacrifice his homeland for his life.

CHAPTER TWENTY-SEVEN

PING, PING, CHING, CHING!

While sweating through my professional golfing episode, getting any cash I could to support myself through the mini-tour mill was greatly appreciated. I used to have a Ping Anser putter that apparently was a collectible and worth a considerable amount of money, at least by my standards of wealth at that time. These were the first Ping Anser putters Karsten Solheim made, and there was a stamp in the backside cavity identifying their origins as a Scottsdale-produced product, even though they were actually from Phoenix. I didn't know this shit, but I had been putting with it, and another mini-tour pro told me about it. I really didn't care or pay attention to him, but fortunately for me, he turned out to be correct.

One day, I happened to be with a group of guys playing in a quickly assembled, pro-am-style gathering of twelve on a Thursday morning at the Claw golf course in Tampa. It was six pros and six individuals who followed what most of us were doing on the mini-tour, paired up as two pros and two individuals per group. The guest players each threw a hundred bucks on the table, and the pros didn't contribute anything. The winning team would take the top prize of six hundred dollars to split amongst that group, with the two winning pros getting two hundred bucks each and the two guests getting their hundred bucks back. My partner and I did not win the loosely assembled outing. But I did walk away with five hundred dollars. One of the gentlemen in my group was a Japanese guy, who turned out to be a golf club collector, and he apparently was familiar with Ping putters.

He asked to see my putter during the round and proceeded to ask me all sorts of questions about the club, including where and when I had gotten it and how often I played with it. At the end of the round, after some small talk, he offered me five hundred bucks for the stick on the spot. I was in such a state of shock and in such need of a cash infusion that I didn't even negotiate. That five hundred represented a lot of money for me at that moment in time. I agreed, and the next day he picked up the putter and handed me the cash, which was good enough for me to get another putter and offset some of the expenses associated with signing up and playing in another tournament.

Several weeks had passed and I was playing in a foursome at Rogers Park, also in Tampa, with a couple of regular, off-the-street guys and one of my tour buddies. One of the guys, wearing jeans in ninety-plus degree weather and sporting a chain wallet—a real down and dirty blue-collar guy—was putting with a Ping Anser strikingly similar to the one I had just sold for five hundred dollars weeks earlier. These two guys quickly assessed that my friend and I were mini-tour players and established a bit of deference to our level of golf. They were very happy to have stumbled upon a golfer's best-case scenario that they would later talk about with all their friends. On the third hole, I asked the guy with the Anser if I could see his putter. He happily obliged, and upon inspection, I found it to be the exact same putter I had unloaded a couple of weeks back. I restrained my excitement and acted nonchalantly while trying to figure out how to get that putter in my hands without this guy suspecting what the putter was worth. And whatever I cooked up to get that putter, it had to be a plan where he willingly gave me or sold me the putter for next to nothing.

I handed him back his putter, commenting, "Nice stick." I quickly figured out a plan that would seem so innocent and unsuspecting that, at worst, this guy would either sell me this stick for fifty bucks max, or end up just giving it to me. I wasn't even going to tell my pal what I was up to. The plan went into action and I started putting like shit.

I three-putted from ten, twelve, fifteen, and twenty feet, missed multiple three-to five-footers, all the while lamenting how I hadn't cut any checks, was in a difficult financial position, and was contemplating just quitting the mini-tour circuit and getting a nine-to-five job. And the blame for all of my depressing lack of results was attributed to—guess what? My putting woes. The baited line was cast, and all I could do was wait for a nibble. "Would you like to try my putter?"

It was as if I had just hooked a marlin. Now, I had to reel him in. "Sure. I'll give it a shot. Thanks." We traded putters for the remaining holes, and guess what happened? I started to putt as if I had a magic wand in my hands. It was the opposite of the putting demonstration that had occurred in the previous holes. No more three-putts. I didn't miss any five-footers and dropped a couple of one-putt birdies from ten and twenty feet. We finished the round, and I stated, "Wow! That was great! I haven't putted like that in a while. Thank you so much for letting me use your putter. Man, if I had a putter like that in my bag, I could do some damage in tournaments."

I thanked him again, wished him well, and started to slowly walk away with my eyes closed, mentally willing him to say, "Hold on a sec."

"Hold on there a sec, chief." I opened my eyes. "When's your next tournament?"

Jackpot, I whispered to myself. I turned, anticipating the next gesture, and responded, "Next week."

He said, "Why don't you take this putter for your tournament? If it works, you can keep it. If it doesn't, just give it back."

"Are you serious? I can't take your putter, my man. I appreciate it, but I can't take your putter from you." I was just verbally dancing with him, as I knew the conclusion to this act. This guy was going to be like the guy you go to dinner with and is insistent on picking up the tab.

"No, no. I insist. Just promise me you'll win with my stick."

What a nice guy, I thought. *I mean, really nice. He is just giving away something that is his and wants nothing in return other than to hope his generous and sincere gesture would contribute to my success.* His thoughtfulness hit me in the nuts.

At that moment, I realized that I couldn't fleece this guy. I absolutely could not take advantage of his good nature. I changed my mind and decided to be honest and contribute to his knowledge. I figured karma would be kind to me as a result, and golfers are big in believing in karma.

"Hey. I appreciate it my friend, but I can't take the putter. Do you know what you have in that putter?"

He looked at me quizzically and so I proceeded to explain the background of the Ping Anser and why the putter that was in his possession was worth at least five hundred bucks.

He reacted like someone had just told him he was a new father. I saw a new chain wallet in his future. He thanked me profusely and we parted ways. I did not offer to buy the putter, and I never knew what happened to him, or that putter, because I never ran into him again. And karma? Karma did not do shit for me. Karma never accompanied me to a tournament.

I should have stuck to my original plan. At least I would have made some money.

ROGER DODGER IN TAMPA

Another source of income, albeit an unreliable one, was from playing for bets with other players. This was a form of cannibalism because either you were taking money out of some other pro's pocket, or they were taking money out of yours. That said, it was usually a friendly, not-too-painful wager, except when you got into a money game with professional gamblers. A noted betting parlor for golf was Rogers Park golf course in Tampa. I recently looked up Rogers Park and was amazed by the renovation and transformation of the course, management, and clubhouse since I last played there. They really have stepped it up and made it an inviting place for individuals and families to enjoy. This transformation is in complete contrast to what Rogers Park was like when we were playing on the Space Coast tour.

Back in the day, Rogers Park was a fascinating collection of gamblers and golfers, in that order. In essence, it was a well-known and respected breeding ground for a wolf pack of professional golf gamblers who ruled the money games. Rogers Park was also blessed with the largest collection of skilled black golfers I had ever experienced, largely due to its history and heritage. A lot of famous black sports personalities played extensively at the course— prominent athletes like Jackie Robinson and Joe Louis played there, along with professional golfers who had established themselves in the annals of the PGA, like Charlie Sifford, Lee Elder, and Charles Owens, amongst others. It was evident that Rogers Park was the anointed golf course for all the "brothers" in the area, and I say that with nothing but heartfelt affection and respect.

The fact is, Rogers Park, before it was partially transformed into a golf course, and during Southern segregation, was the only park area in Tampa that provided access to African Americans for picnics and other outdoor recreational activities. It also became the only public golf course that welcomed black residents to play golf with no restrictions.

Willie Black was an African American gentleman who served as the architect of Rogers Park golf course and was its original head pro. Mr. Black designed the course, and its construction entailed enlisting a large group of African American caddies and volunteers that helped clear the land to establish the initial nine-hole course in 1952, which was later expanded to eighteen holes in 1961. The course would later become part of "The Chitlin' Circuit" by hosting an African American professional golfing tournament titled "The Mid Winter Classic." Because of these milestones, Rogers Park is deservedly recognized in the *National Register of Historic Places*.

For a bunch of guys, this place was as close to a second home as it could possibly be. On most days, these dudes would just go home to sleep and return to the golf course to hang out for the rest of the day, smoking, talking, smoking, playing golf, playing cards, smoking, and having a good time. They basically had informal membership rights to the club and got serious preferential treatment over others who were not frequent visitors. And if you were a player and wanted to gamble on your game, you just had to make sure you brought the cash to Rogers Park. Betting by players and spectators (golf flies) was a constant, and the money gambled represented big numbers in those times. Betting on matches oftentimes hovered around thousands of dollars—*back then!* And if a player didn't have the money, they could get backers to pony up the cash—with a very short-term, high "vig" loan. The attuned golfer demographics of the club were predominantly occupied by players and gamblers who were all local residents, along with a sprinkling of mini-tour white boys. This served as a true test of nerves for any competitive golfer, and the games were not for the squeamish. In need of cash to live for another week, many mini-tour guys would go there with the hope of landing a quick infusion of dollars. Most of these guys underestimated their black colleagues and, most often, would lose their bets.

A lot of the mini-tour boys did not appreciate how good the Rogers Park guys were. Even worse, they disrespected the black players' home course familiarity, assuming their mini-tour golfing pedigree would overcome those obstacles. They quickly learned, however, as the game and the bet were over before the white guys had a chance to reconcile their disbelief. And trust me, the black golfers anticipated and counted on the overconfidence of the white guys.

The clubhouse and the pro shop were a run-down, mostly dilapidated structure—which I would romantically describe as a trailer park housing a campground trailer. However, I thought it had a familiar feel, one that I was comfortable with having come from a public golf background. I remember the pro shop was famous for offering slightly defective FootJoy classic golf shoes at great prices. It was where I would purchase all my FJ shoes. I mean, no one cared or could tell the difference, and since they were half the price of what they sold for in golf stores, it was a no-brainer.

Nonetheless, it was a great environment with entertainingly eccentric characters who, when it came down to it, mostly respected good golf. It was sort of a fond homecoming for me because it felt similar to trying to earn my stripes on a basketball court in NYC. You had to take your licks and pay the price before you were accepted. Since then, Rogers Park seems to have transformed itself into more of a family type of environment. Back then, I never saw any families or kids coming to play golf at Rogers Park.

I still remember the bittersweet and possibly limb-saving decision I made to run away from and never play at Rogers Park again. Fortunately, or unfortunately, I got into a pretty big game (by my standards, being that I never had an extra cent in my pocket): five hundred dollars was on the line for eighteen holes of stroke play. I needed the money desperately but didn't have enough to pay up in the event that I didn't win. Naïvely, I thought I could owe my opponent the money if I lost or, strangely enough, that he would be alright with keeping a running tab. Obviously, that was the wrong competitive mindset if I wanted to win this match. I knew the black guy I was playing against thought I would be a relatively easy mark to win. This guy was known to be a good player, and although I played at Rogers Park several times a week, the regulars knew me to be a grinding mini-tour guy who did not demonstrate much low-scoring potential. I was already starting on my heels as they knew I could shoot par, and some under, but not light up the course on a regular basis. The regulars here scouted everyone and had the lowdown on all the golfers who were supposed to be players and gamblers at Rogers. It was part of their scope of work. My other obvious disadvantage was that the regulars probably knew the course better than they knew anything else in their lives. And did I mention they were legit players?

To put it in perspective, all these guys were sandbaggers. Pool hustlers with scratch handicaps. In reality, a lot of these guys would shoot under par while yawning. I, on the other hand, would every once in a while, throw in red numbers but not crazy red—one, two, or three under on good days, while sniffing at four or five under during lunar eclipses. But not on this day. On this day I would post one of the lowest rounds of my life, and it would not serve me well. On the front side, I went a couple under par. I was obviously pressing this guy's game, because he wasn't expecting this. He was also two under on the front.

As we started on the back side, I birdied ten and eleven to go four under while this guy made pars. He subsequently birdied two more holes to match me at four under through sixteen holes. By this time, word had gotten out that this was a closer match than anyone had expected, and people had come out to watch. We both birdied seventeen to go five under. Side bets were flying, and frankly, I was shitting in my pants and ready to throw up. It was like a scene from the main *Caddyshack* match during the climax of the movie. But unlike *Caddyshack*, there were minimal trees or brush on the course, making the gallery anything but discreet.

On the eighteenth hole, my opponent knocked his approach shot to about four feet from the hole for a birdie. He kept looking at me and was waiting for me to tell him to pick up the ball, giving him the putt, but I didn't say shit. I had hit my shot into the green to about twelve feet. I now had to drop my putt for a birdie to offset a seemingly kick-in birdie putt from him, and not lose this match. As I looked over my putt, time seemed to have stopped. I could hear myself breathing and I couldn't feel my arms from the elbow down. The line of my putt to the hole was a straight line. Shit. It was a straight putt. "Really? A straight fucking putt"? I muttered.

Before I could consciously acknowledge my body moving, I drew the putter back and hit the ball. And even though the putt took only a couple of seconds to roll toward the hole, it was like watching grass grow. The ball magically disappeared into the cup, and I marked my score at six under. My opponent casually swiped at his birdie putt (which would have tied him at six under with me) and missed. He looked at me dismissively and said, "That was good, right?" Three seconds of a maelstrom of thoughts compelled me to unconsciously respond, "No. I didn't give you that." He proceeded to take a full swing at his ball, batted the ball toward the clubhouse, and huffed off, walking toward the cafeteria, showing his displeasure at the lack of respect I afforded him. Some in the gallery just nodded their heads, seemingly disappointed at my decision not to have given him the putt, while a scattered few were happy to have collected their bets. None of the two or three guys who had won their bets on me hung around to witness me collecting my five-hundred-dollar purse.

I stood around the eighteenth hole for a couple of minutes, making believe I was rummaging through my bag and putting stuff away. In reality, I was stalling and thinking mostly negative thoughts. I was absorbed in what had just transpired, including interpreting the reactions from my opponent and the others that had watched our match. Everyone that had followed the match was my competitor's entourage and not friends of mine. I was anxiously trying to figure out how this was going to play out and was trying to make assessments on how to proceed given the circumstances that were quickly unfolding before my eyes.

To this day, I thank God for my upbringing in the streets of New York City. It gave me the skills to correctly interpret and respond to confrontational situations. You definitely didn't learn this shit from schoolbooks. I sensed that these guys were not going to emulate the Bobby Jones school of golf etiquette and sportsmanship, and felt like I was in a pool hall with guys feeling that I had just out-scammed them, even though I hadn't meant to. They were all scowling and angrily jabbering back and forth under their breath. My answer to what I thought was unfolding was to escape, to run for the proverbial hills—"I have to get the fuck out of here!" was my initial, knee-jerk thought to this potentially prickly predicament.

I time-traveled back to the situation that Alan and I encountered during high school, frantically contemplating his blasphemous suggestion of running away. I also remembered the St. John the Divine and the Dominican gang debacle, where I hid under my bed while my dad bailed me out. *Where are you now, papi?!* Holy shit! My life was now flashing before my eyes, and I took that to have been a sign that my death was imminent! I was mentally spiraling out of control. "Get a grip, Rojas," I muttered to myself. Thank God, I hadn't lost the bet. I simply would have committed suicide by impaling myself with a sand wedge.

I truly felt an ass-kicking was on the agenda. Their agenda and my ass. Maybe I was being paranoid, and the guys were going to simply hand over the money without any questions and say, "Thank you. Nice round." Nope. I wasn't betting on that scenario playing out. I collected my senses and discounted running away as an option. But now the question was, *how would I get out of here without setting off any alarms?* As everyone withdrew to the clubhouse, I followed them, lagging slightly behind, and stopping by my Honda to deposit my golf clubs in the trunk. As I walked into the clubhouse, I saw that everyone had gone to a corner of the room where there were a couple of small tables. It was the spot where bets were squared up after matches.

I sat down across from my competitor and pondered my fate.

He stared at me and growled, "So, what do you want to do with the bet?"

What the fuck kind of question was that? I thought. That's the kind of question wherein you have to entertain a lightning-fast discussion with yourself to: 1) assess the illogical perspective of that question along with the disposition of all of this motherfucker's friends who were hanging around this stage waiting to see how this shit played out; and 2) determine the best option with which to proceed using a very deliberate, congenial tone of delivery. I mean, fundamentally, what the fuck did this asshole think I wanted to do with the bet he lost to me? I wanted my money, please. So what if I didn't have the money to pay him. He didn't know that. Wait—what if he didn't have the money to pay me? Should I have been a gracious sportsman and given him a credit? Offered a payment plan? What would that do for me? I think that's what he was looking for. I don't think he had the money either and went into this match thinking I was his bitch and it was going to be easy pickin's. I mean, him asking that question of me was like asking me if his last putt was good. What the fuck should I do?

Then the light bulb went off. *I didn't need this bullshit.* If I gave him credit, this shit was going to continue to go back and forth playing matches until he came out on top. I had noticed that when he asked me that question, people who had followed us on the course watching the match, and who were now inside, inched closer. I didn't take that to be in anticipation of a warm and fuzzy huddle cuddle because I was a nice guy. The walls were closing in, and no doubt they were sending a deliberate message. I could feel their eyes on me and it was making my skin itch. What was I going to say? I didn't actually think they were going to harm me—much—but I still decided I needed to get the fuck out of here, and I needed to do it in an unassuming, discreet way that did not reflect the fact that I was basically going to skip out on this situation like a fucking coward. What was the downside? Fuck dignity. I would still be in one piece and be able to continue playing, but not at Rogers Park as I was about to enact another Cuban embargo modeled after the 109th street situation.

I had won and he was at my mercy. Or was I at his mercy? I didn't want anything to do with this, but I needed to convey an indifferent attitude with my body language—especially given the fact that I had just decided to abandon ship and forgo collecting my money. I was going to hit the eject button, but I couldn't let them know I was running away. Long ago, I had made a lifelong commitment to never *run* away from a fight. I would now rationalize abiding by that doctrine by simply adjusting the pace of my retreat to a meandering *stroll*.

I casually moved my chair to the side where I slowly took my shoes off and stretched out as if I were planning to stay for a while. Seemingly unperturbed by the tension they were attempting to impose on me, I asked, "How do you want to settle this, my man? I'm going to get my Marlboro's." I had just effectuated my escape plan. I sauntered, *not ran*, to the car in my socks, without my shoes, presumably to get my Marlboro's, got in and drove off, never to revisit Rogers Park Golf Course or its Pro Shop again. I figured they wouldn't possibly think I would have left without wearing my shoes, and as a result, no one was going to be suspicious that this was a getaway maneuver for me. I had just donated a classic pair of FootJoys. Oh well, they were only half-price anyway.

CHAPTER TWENTY-NINE

WELCOME, PLAN B!

A fter a deep drive, I stood on the fairway of the seventeenth hole at a course nicknamed "The Claw" in Tampa, Florida. The Claw was the course where the University of South Florida golf team played and practiced. It was a well-respected test of golf. The track was long, and a lot of the greens were turtleback mound greens like those you would find on courses designed by Donald Ross. The Claw was designed by William F. Mitchell. Mr. Mitchell was a golf course architect who began his career as a greenskeeper and from 1948 to 1974 went on to design or remodel about two hundred courses in the United States.

Not only was The Claw a fundamentally well-designed and challenging golf course, but it was also kept in decent condition for a public track. A lot of aspiring mini-tour players would play there because everyone felt it was a great training ground that forced your game to wisely manage your way through eighteen holes. The greens were challenging in the sense that they were "position" greens. In other words, the available pin positions gave you very limited options on where to hit the ball on the green with your approaches to enable scoring opportunities. Only half the green was ever realistically available for you to get into a position to comfortably two-putt or provide you with an opportunity for a birdie. If you were out of position on the green, you knew you were already on your heels. It also meant that if you were going to miss the green on your approach, you absolutely had to miss it on the correct side for any chance of redemption to save par.

Bluntly stated, you had better be armed with a deft sense of feel for your short game even if you did miss a green with the angle in your favor. But missing short-sided on these greens would never allow you to improve on par. Even worse, you could get brutally, I'm going to say it, "mauled" by The Claw. The main motivation for playing this course was that if you went low at The Claw, you could be fairly confident that you could go low anywhere. The golf course staff was also very receptive to the mini-tour players. The greenskeeper and the head pro supported the mini-tour guys as much as they could and welcomed their presence by significantly discounting or comping their rounds. That support was a meaningful, gracious gesture and deeply appreciated by the players.

On this noteworthy day at The Claw, I was playing in a foursome composed of three other mini-tour guys and myself. And there was money on the line. Not big bucks, but enough to treat yourself to dinner. It was another beautiful day in Florida. I was playing well—swinging better than I was scoring—and was keeping loose and casual by entertaining the irreverent musings between us.

However, as I stood by myself on the fairway of the seventeenth hole, I thought about my approach shot, which was about 120 yards away, with a slight breeze blowing left to right and a deep, left-side pin position on the green. At that time, I played a slight draw, so I would be fighting the wind to get the ball close to the hole. I didn't want to be long or left and short-sided and decided to play the odds and hit the middle of the green and comfort myself with a better-attended stat of looking at a long putt for birdie and relatively easy par, rather than a wish and a prayer for a par if I missed the green on the short side. It's a conservative play, but an odds-on one.

I pulled a sand wedge from my bag and waited for another player to hit. At that time, I was bouncing the round around in my mind and decanting the fact that I was currently even for the round. I thought, even if I birdied one or two of the last two holes coming in—which was a statistically difficult feat to accomplish due to the demanding layout of the last two holes—I could finish at one or two under par at best. *What would that do for me?* Two guys were already two under, and another guy was even with me. Coming in third out of four guys wasn't going to do shit for me. And if this were a mini-tour event, I would be looking at an early starting time the following day as well, because the way the course was set up today, at least several players would go six or maybe seven under par. In fact, there would be a clusterfuck at two or three under, guaranteeing "dew sweeper" tee times on the following day for anyone shooting around par.

"Dew sweeper," was the deservedly insulting moniker for the first groups that teed off in the early morning on the second day of a tournament. The purpose of "dew sweepers" was to get the worst-scoring players out of the way by having these early morning groups "mop" up the course from the early morning dew for the players that were to follow, who had a good first-round score. Being referred to as a "dew sweeper" was not considered an encouraging label for a player. I thought about having "dew sweeper" embroidered on the side of my bag, and that suddenly led me to a moment of clarity. Like I had been hit by a lightning bolt. I bent over, picked up my ball, put my bag on my back, and started to walk. As I walked away, I yelled over to the other guys I was with, "Guys, have a nice life. I'm done!" They looked at me and nonchalantly waved, not suspecting at all what I was doing. As far as they were concerned, I was just leaving for the day. I would never see those fine men ever again. To this day, I am not aware of what became of their lives or careers.

I went home, threw my bag into a dark corner of the garage, hugged my typewriter, and started to piece together my resume. I did not leave that desk until I had something good enough to review. I had reached the point of no return in my golf career. It was a lucid moment in which I accepted what I had been postponing. I had been mentally wrapped up by this romantic illusion but prudently confronted this new reality, humbly accepting the fact that I was not going to be a professional golfer. However, I had to somehow think of this in a positive way and learn from it. Although disillusioned and disappointed, I did not interpret this reality in a defeatist manner. I realized this new exercise was no less mentally disruptive than having originally decided to pursue a professional golf career.

For the first time in a long time, I felt relieved as I thought that no matter how much effort I had to put in towards totally restructuring my life and career again, it was the absolute right decision. In retrospect, I thought, *participating and competing in the business world could not possibly be as demanding and draining as trying to eke out a living on the mini-tour*. If I had been able to try my hand at the mini-tour and it had not devastated me, then surely I would have a decent shot in the corporate world. To this day, I am grateful for the experience and the ability to build and establish my character while attempting to play professional golf. And there is no doubt whatsoever that attempting to play competitive professional golf is a true test of character. You find yourself in a truly lonely place with no one to depend on but yourself.

Thankfully, this new breakthrough realization came rather swiftly. It had become evident that my flirtation with the professional golf tour was very much like a well-intentioned but hopelessly futile effort trying to maintain a meaningful, long-distance romantic relationship. Fortunately, this long-distance relationship analogy lasted for just over one season, making it a bit easier to take the step of breaking off the relationship to reprioritize my goals. I also recognized that I had to commit to a whole new level of determination to make up for lost time in my business career. The fact is that I had interrupted my original career, foregoing career-ascending job opportunities in the advertising world, so I could start playing serious golf for several years.

At that time, and before I had decided to pursue golf full time, I was being recruited by headhunters across the country. I was in my career wheelhouse with options abounding and was at a point where I was so overconfident, I felt I could conquer whatever would confront me. I was bulletproof. Golf? Shit. I would make money and have fun as well. Not quite, as it turned out. At least I was smart enough to quickly realize the limits of my athletic contributions and the poor financial return for the time and energy expended. What the fuck was I thinking? As if I could disrespect professional golfers by just walking into and competing against their income base?

However, most importantly, I had zero regrets about this fanciful golfing pursuit and instead was exceptionally grateful for the learning, the humility, the frailty, and the adventure that helped shape my life. It was my decision, and I held myself completely accountable.

But what was awaiting me now? I was certainly determined to change my trajectory no matter what and my first obvious look would be to fall back on my previous skill set in the ad agency industry. It was undoubtedly time to move to the next chapter. I would never be a professional golfer, but hey—it would still be fun to play golf. Little did I know, at that moment, how much fun and how professionally rewarding the golfing world would come to be for me. Little did I know how significantly the intersections of golf would ultimately continue to impact my future.

CHAPTER THIRTY

MIND IF I PLAY THROUGH?

"We'd like to fly you up again to go through another round of interviews with the director of marketing and also meet with the vice president." After my separation and divorce from my first wife, I moved to Miami Beach. I had no money to speak of and ended up moving in with my parents who, along with my neighboring aunt from Chicago, had relocated from Chicago to Miami Beach to be closer to other Cuban friends and relatives living there. The resume I had assembled apparently was attractive and interesting enough for me to get interviews, and I was able to quickly garner an upper-management position at a prominent ad agency located next to Miami in Coral Gables, Florida. For whatever reason, I made it a point to include my time on the mini-tour in my resume. At that time, the ad agency office in Coral Gables was primarily functioning to service Latin American and large domestic packaged goods clients in the United States that were targeting a rapidly growing, Spanish-language-dominant Hispanic market. Given the stature of the agency and my position, a headhunter had contacted me about eight months after I started at the ad agency for a position in a Fortune 300 corporation. As the industry would describe it, I had an opportunity to move to the "client side" of the business versus working on the "agency side."

Let me explain that there is a world of difference in one's approach to lifestyle, work, and career between the "agency side" and the "client side" of the marketing industry. The client side has all the money and, by default, all the power. They are the orchestra leaders because they control the budgets for marketing, media, promotions, and advertising. As a result, clients are always praised for making "brilliant" business decisions (the exception being if you have a real moron as a client and you try to save them from themselves and their own very stupid mistakes, potentially jeopardizing their budgets), and they pass most of the demands, deadlines, and stress of their job performance onto agency people. Agency people are little more than farm hands pretending to be strategic partners with the client. Exceptionally skilled agency people are master purveyors of bullshit, consisting of nothing more than ornately packaged data-driven fish food. They are professional magicians who have evolved the technique of ass-kissing to levels of shameless depravity that should be featured as a societal documentary on the Smithsonian Channel.

If you deal with large budgets (tens or even hundreds of millions of dollars), then it is the agency's foremost responsibility to treat clients like the royal descendants they pretend to be, catering to their slightest whims.

This level of relationship building—or, if you will, "motivational" sales techniques targeting clients with free high-end meals, trips, activities, gifts, and things along those lines, —are usually frowned upon because of their proximity to real or perceived kickbacks that are regulated by corporate ethics-compliance policies. However, the tactic most often used by vendors to feign compliance with corporate policies includes cleverly disguised exercises, technically referred to as "team building activities." Team building workshops are a prevalent way of conducting business with the best of clients, and vendors are particularly astute at knowing which switches to flip to ingratiate themselves with clients in never-ending attempts to secure and increase their overall budgets. I was looking forward to having an agency kiss my ass for a change.

This was my second trip up to Greenwich, Connecticut, after my initial meeting with the director of marketing. I wondered if this was how athletes felt when their contract came up and they were in the free agency market. However, with my immediate and successful corporate world reentry upon leaving the mini-tour, my confidence began to gain momentum again with this new job opportunity. It felt good because I was just being myself, and my enthusiastic, athletic identity seemed to strike a positive chord—a "good fit," as they refer to it in the corporate world—with this company. It was a process that evolved with a very welcoming and organic flow.

I was being recruited for the position of manager of special markets for a tobacco company. It was similar to being a brand manager for a packaged goods company. However, this scope of work placed a strong emphasis on promotional activities targeting minority populations, with a particular focus on Hispanic segments of the population in the United States, to support brand volume growth strategies. I also very well understood and was not deterred by the fact that there were considerable anti-tobacco efforts against marketing activities targeting minority segments of the population, categorizing these legitimate business tactics as a demonically inspired business model. The media and the anti-tobacco groups had established pretty effective campaigns assailing tobacco use and deploying a wide net to portray *all* tobacco companies as morally corrupt culprits. And whether you agree with the political theater or not, those efforts did provide a valuable counterbalance for overt marketing and business efforts from some of the other tobacco companies.

I just had a problem with attempts to frame the narrative as a demonic strategy exercised by these companies. The tobacco company I ultimately worked for could not have been more conservative and responsible in abiding by the legal and regulatory framework for the industry, and they were definitely not fans of engaging in any efforts that entailed marketing to teens like some other companies were accused of doing. It is a fact that a tobacco company has every right to market a product that is legal for adults to purchase. In one of my interviews with this company, I was asked if I would have any ethical or moral issues with selling tobacco to adult consumers. I confirmed that I would not have any issues with these efforts as adults should be held accountable when they freely make educated, responsible decisions on what they choose to buy and put in their body in an open marketplace—especially if it's *a legal product*. No one was forcing these purchase decisions upon them. Frankly, I understood the consequences of consuming this product, and the consequences of consuming other such products in excess, like alcohol or fast foods.

The fact is, consumers don't have any logical basis to pretend not to know, or act ignorant of the consequences associated with what they are putting in their bodies. To begin with, I assure you that there is not one healthcare professional who would advocate the overindulgence of any of the product lines that I just mentioned. And this is not to mention all the conduits available that provide a person with information and educational materials with options that contribute to a healthier lifestyle. More than an abundant supply of statistically meaningful information exists on these topics at our electronic fingertips. None of this information includes supporting the excessive consumption of fast foods followed by an alcohol chaser and a smoke. A person doesn't have a justifiable basis to act stupid and play the victim like it's someone else's fault that they've experienced a disease that correlates with the increased health risk associated with their lifestyle and dietary choices. It's your decision, so you own it. Everyone knows, *or should know*, that the more you consume any of these products, the more bullets you put in a gun while playing Russian roulette. If you pretend not to know about the consequences, then you are either disingenuous or simply a fucking idiot.

Ironically, following the tobacco sector, I worked in the hospital industry in the tri-state area of the northeast. It was a senior management position in which I learned that this industry was more challenging, by far, to deal with from a moral and ethical perspective. I had almost unfettered access to entire realms of highly valued, granular, and proprietary health and financial data (regional and national) focusing on population segments, disease and treatment protocol and outcome data, financial performance indicators for healthcare services, physician performance formulas (financial and clinical), key financial drivers of profitable diseases, insurance reimbursement coding techniques, operational service delivery models, legislative forecasting, competitive activity, and other data sets required to develop a "strategic" business portfolio that delivered profitable outcomes. From what I saw, my functional experience with the hospital ecosystem, unfortunately, revealed that it is an industry captivated by the management of medical operational processes and billing procedures that are designed to optimize profits.

In my opinion, there is still a large body of excellent physicians and related caregivers, but their work ethic is significantly stifled by the money-manufacturing business model that defines the current U.S. healthcare framework. It seems as if it represents one of the most insincere, calculating environments a consumer could be exposed to. It made my history of pushing tobacco products feel akin to selling Girl Scout cookies. If you were to apply the same moral or ethical question posed to me by the tobacco company during my interview but apply it to the healthcare industry, I would say that it is the healthcare industry that is ethically corrupt. I felt much better about selling tobacco products to adults than about strategizing how to develop profit-centered healthcare service business models directed at an unsuspecting and naïve public.

But isn't convenient ignorance and hypocrisy rampant in our society?

As manager of special markets for the tobacco company, my responsibility was to primarily target Hispanic consumers and raise their levels of awareness and education about the products that we sold, with the goal being that a percentage of them would be motivated enough to purchase the product, and most importantly, become a loyal consumer of our brands. The media and "woke" mob would define this as the exploitation of a seemingly ignorant and uneducated franchise of the population. The premise of this assumption presents a dehumanizing and insulting gesture toward the intended audience it is supposedly advocating for. But the media theme sensationalizing corporate "colonization" sells well for all the wrong reasons. It reads bad and wrong, right?

The tactics of targeting, profiling, and segmenting are all perfectly legitimate exercises to help a company optimize its sales efforts. Most products or services sold to consumers are customized and tailored for segments of the population. If it's not tobacco, it's cereal, body creams, clothing, organic foods, movies, or cars. Pick any product. Just look at AI and how many solicitations you receive from companies when anyone electronically expresses interest in particular subjects or items. Exploitation is a seemingly harsh description for trying to provide a product that represents value to a particular consumer. "Exploit" is an insulting term gratuitously deployed by social justice monkeys. Just refer to it for what it really is—marketing, which is another word for "exploit," but not as social justice-monkey reprehensible.

It turned out that I would also meet the CEO on this trip, in addition to my direct report and the vice president of marketing. It was going to be a longer day, but a welcome addition to the itinerary. I did a bit of research on the CEO and found out that he served our country as a marine (once a marine, always a marine) *and* was a member of the Winged Foot Country Club in Mamaroneck, New York. I was inspired by this find. Winged Foot. It is legendary in the golfing world from any respected perspective and is one of a handful of golf courses that are regarded as revered holy golfing grounds. I should have been nervous, but I was not and wanted to talk to him about Winged Foot. My meeting with the CEO ultimately occurred during the latter part of the day, and as I entered his office, he impressed me as a laid-back gentleman, who was slightly tilted back in his chair, gently holding a cigarette between his fingers, with his legs crossed. He got up to greet me—a tall, polished man measuring a little over six feet—and then floated back down into his seat.

We met for an hour. Our discussion began with an account of my skills and experience, along with some casual talk. That took all of ten minutes. And it wasn't because I only had ten minutes worth of skills to discuss.

Unexpectedly, the conversation quickly shifted, and the next fifty minutes were spent enthusiastically talking about my golf career—my short golf career—and what it was like to play on the mini-tour. He went on to tell me that this position would be a great opportunity for me and that one of the things I would be *obligated* to do, on a frequent basis, would be to take out and entertain their distributors by playing golf. He specifically told me that I *had to* go out and play golf as much as possible with these distributors. I would be expected to coordinate first-class golf junkets and take them out to play at the most exclusive golf courses in the country. And make no mistake, all activities related to these junkets would be happily expensed.

Of course, I didn't have any reservations about this being part of my job. We thanked each other for the meeting, and I was excused. I left that meeting filled with spectacular anticipation. Holy shit! I would be paid, in part, to travel to great locations and play golf. I would be getting paid to travel and stay at some of the best resorts and play golf at some of the best courses in the country. As I digested this information, I had trouble maintaining a professional demeanor.

At the beginning of this book, I said that America is the greatest country in the world. I was not kidding. I LOVE AMERICA! Shit! My mindset shifted because the opportunity was sinking in, and I was now nervous that I might not get the job.

One week had passed without any updates from the headhunter. My arrogance—I mean confidence—was diminishing quickly. The second week in, I contacted the headhunter. "Hey, John. What's the delay?" The headhunter told me that they were evaluating me and another candidate. "John. With all due respect, I need a decision now. My place has made a counteroffer, and I need to make a decision."

John told me that I was the guy and that he'd get them to move on a decision. "And by the way, John, they increased the counteroffer for the position by $5,000."

It was a head fake, and right or wrong, I was writing this script as I went along. I was being rash and wasn't cognizant of the potential consequences. Luckily, the play worked in my favor. John got back to me in a couple of days and told me that the company would contact me to offer me the position by the following day—and by the way, incredibly, they had agreed to the additional $5,000. I was beyond orgasmic. Sperm was coming out of my ears and nose. I had made the cut. I had gotten my "tour" card and my career on the corporate golf tour was about to begin.

CHAPTER THIRTY-ONE

WHEREVER HUGO, I GO IN A HURRY

It was the fall of 1989, and hurricane Hugo was bearing down on the East Coast, taking aim at South Carolina. It was standing between me and a new start in life. I was leaving one experience behind and starting another adventure. Hugo was now an intrusive and unwelcome partner barging into my new journey. I had a hard date to begin my relocation in Greenwich, Connecticut, and the timing would get me past my boy Hugo with only a day to spare. I had packed my Honda Civic hatchback to the point where there wasn't an inch of daylight or field of vision in the rear. Everything I owned was in that vehicle. In my haste to get on the road, I did not bother to think through a single backup plan in the event I got caught up in traffic on roads that would be used to evacuate any of the foreseeable hurricane-affected areas. My only thought was to drive west and try to outrun the storm in that direction. Thankfully, the winds favored me, and it was a clean ride all the way to the Hyatt in Old Greenwich.

I must have looked like a real Jethro, who had obviously lost his way and was stumbling around a northeastern legion of wealthy, white Anglo-Saxon protestant enclaves. Nonetheless, my relocation to Greenwich was consummated. I had left the land of "Miami Vice" and entered the world of Plymouth Rock. Quite the cultural transition. Could I pull it off? Hey, it was no different than a good ol' boy snuff company landing their corporate headquarters in Greenwich, Connecticut like the Mayflower. I was now cued up to spend a lot of time in key Hispanic hot spots of demographic density—New York metro areas, Texas, California, Chicago, and Miami. I would have to do my homework and map out all the top hundred courses in every one of those markets. My first swing through these states would consist of a meet-and-greet playbook with all the distributors, our sales force, and sales management teams. We were a fully vertically integrated company that saw the product from start to finish. In other words, we produced it, we marketed it, and we sold it.

CHAPTER THIRTY-TWO

MIAMI VICE AND LITTLE HAVANA

My first assignment in my new job happened to be back in Miami. We were producing a full-on Latin rock concert in an outdoor venue on the waterfront. We were the show's executive producers and were working with a top national concert promoter. The concert would go live just two days after I hit the Miami tarmac and so I prepared backup plans on top of backup plans to cover any potential catastrophes related to weather, travel, production issues, talent issues, security, etc. Acutely aware of the fact that I was partially hired for my golf background, I had to make the best use of my time so I could also perform on the golf course without any concert-related mental baggage on my shoulders. I mean, that skill set was what gave me the edge over the other candidates for this position, and my boss was flying down to tee it up with me and attend the concert. So not only did this concert have to be a resounding success on multiple levels, but I had to put in a strong round to get this career off to a roaring start. And you can't play well if you have all kinds of job shit floating between your ears.

The pressure was on to pull off three distinct objectives: a great concert, great golf, and, of course, great dinners, partially to speak about the status of the concert but mostly to speak about the day golfing. After landing, I picked up my car rental. I was told it had to be a sports car and I ended up selecting a white Toyota Supra convertible. It didn't matter if our sticks wouldn't fit in the trunk. We would just put them in the back seat, and driving around in a white convertible Supra in Miami Beach and Little Havana was a much better look than a Ford or Chevy sedan. Kind of a carefree and reckless, hip look—replicating background scenes in a Miami Vice episode. My last-minute meetings and review of all the concert items pointed to a flawless execution of the event, inclusive of the musical artists, ticket sales, weather, on-site venue and production checks, and confirmation of dinners at the best restaurants

On the second day, another beautiful Florida day, I picked up my boss, accompanied by my golf bag with the top down in the rental. My boss was the director of marketing and happened to be a golf fanatic. He was a young guy, athletic, and a no-nonsense businessperson who also took his golf seriously. I had set up a tee time at the Links at Key Biscayne, which is now known as Crandon Golf at Key Biscayne. It is a well-respected public golf course that used to host a senior PGA tour event and was once regarded as one of the top one hundred public golf courses in the United States. It has always been considered a "player's" course, with significant length, blustery winds (most of the time), and many aesthetically rewarding holes carved out along protected mangroves. Although I've had the opportunity to play many great courses, I would still go there to play at the drop of a hat. It is a true test of your golfing skills, with well-designed, memorable holes in a drop-dead beautiful setting.

Pulling the bags out of the back seats at the club drop-off was a deliciously obnoxious and cocky move. By the third hole, we were both in the fairway (we were playing by ourselves as a twosome) when my boss turned to me and said, "I am going to do something now, and I want you to know that if what I do ever leaks out, or I find that you inadvertently told someone, I will fire you on the spot." I looked at him, smiled, and said by way of bonding, "C'mon. Your secret is safe with me." He went on to pull out a bag with some weed and a pipe in it. He stuffed the pipe, and we proceeded to toke up at the Links of Key Biscayne.

I happened to have played a good round that day, reinforcing that their decision to hire me was the correct one from a golfing perspective. But I still had to demonstrate my competence with the successful execution of the concert.

Despite all the peripheral noise, I took a moment to appreciate the fact that it was a beautiful sunny day to play golf in South Miami, which would be followed by a great dinner at a fabulous, trendy restaurant while riding around in a convertible sports car and staying at the Hyatt in Coral Gables. Wow! What a way to start my career on the client side.

But I didn't want to get caught up in the trappings of my good fortune that day, as the concert still needed to be a success. This day was a litmus test of what my work with this new company and my new boss would be moving forward. It wasn't a test that I wanted to fail.

The next day at the concert, I learned a valuable, often overlooked, real-time expression of basic wisdom that should serve as a key foundation of the values and perspective one should be aware of toward one's work ethic and employment responsibilities. We were halfway through a sold-out concert, and at that point, I felt 99.9 percent confident that the results pointed to an unmitigated success. I went from the highest levels of anxiety and insecurity to euphoria and job security. With all the positive feelings consuming the oxygen, I couldn't help but replace my humility and replace it with cockiness.

My boss and I were next to each other, leaning on a railing, absorbing all the high energy emanating from the pulsating crowd, when I enthusiastically turned to him and said, "Pretty good, eh? Am I a badass or what?!"

My new boss paused for a moment, looked at me, and plainly stated, "I didn't hire you to fuck things up."

It was like being shot between the eyes with a nail hammer. With that, we both turned back to gaze upon our production and enjoyed the rest of the concert. A fine welcome aboard, indeed!

MY PLAN B: TOP HUNDRED PRIVATE CLUBS AND GULFSTREAM IVs

It was soon confirmed that I had made the right career change at the right time. I was making more money in one month than I had earned in a year playing, selling Hondas, making clubs, and giving lessons. True to management's word, a significant part of my new job, in addition to the marketing due diligence, was to host and entertain distribution clients with golf activities throughout the U.S. In addition to the company supporting this exercise, we also had vendors at our disposal who were more than happy to procure invites to some of the country's most exclusive golf courses when we were traveling and had free time on our hands. And we always calculated free time into our schedule.

Some of the most memorable courses that our vendors set up for us included Bel-Air Country Club; TPC's in Scottsdale, San Antonio, Sawgrass; Pelican Hill Golf Club; Riviera Country Club; Shinnecock Hills; Baltusrol (Upper and Lower); Somerset Hills Country Club; Sleepy Hollow Country Club; Plainfield Country Club; Quacker Ridge Golf Course; Merion Golf Club. And it didn't stop there. The executives at the company were members of several extraordinary country clubs in the tri-state area. When I wasn't traveling, I would play these tracks with members at least twice a month. They were, in no

OUT OF THE ROUGH

particular order: Winged Foot Country Club, Westchester Country Club, Brae Burn Country Club, Century Country Club, Old Oaks Country Club, Tamarack Country Club, St. Andrews Golf Club, Whippoorwill Club, Shorehaven Golf Club, Greenwich Country Club, and the Stanwich Club. Work, in one form or another, was magically intertwined with these extravagant golf escapades.

Margins in the tobacco industry were pushing an 80 percent gross margin. In case you're wondering, those are *huge* margins. The net overall profit, after all expenses, contributed to a stock market–appreciative bottom line and a shit ton of revenue enabling significant discretionary company excesses. The executives aligned those profits with a lot of corporate perks designed to continue business-building efforts with clients, politicians, and team members. Compensation for team members represented the top-tier classification of a particular salary category, including stock options, which happened to split at least twice in the five years I was with the company. And after two years of having proven my value to the company, I was promoted to director of international marketing in a new division that carried the exciting responsibilities of opening global sales markets for the company. It was a ton of work getting this new venture off the ground, but although we put in the hours, we were unquestionably pampered throughout the process.

In fact, we were spoiled.

When we conducted business travel (no Zoom shit back then; you had to physically interact with people), company policy was to book first-class accommodations for any commercial flight over three hours and all international flights. If we weren't flying first class, we would be forced to fly private Gulfstream IV aircraft, otherwise known as "G4s." The company had three G4s and several other jets that were based at Westchester County Airport. *How spoiled do you have to be to complain about flying a fully-loaded-with-amenities G4?* You go to Westchester Airport and walk right into a gourmet catered plane, stocked with any liquor you want, in which you are welcomed by your own private attendant, before being seated in a supremely comfortable seat that is exquisitely appointed with soft as a baby's ass Italian leather. *Why would we complain?*

"What are we flying to Mexico, or Puerto Rico, or Honduras, or Canada, or anywhere in the United States?"

"We're flying the G4."

"Fuck, man! C'mon!"

The issue with our frequent use of the G4s was that it significantly muted our ability to take advantage of, and redeem, highly valuable commercial air miles and benefits. Incredibly, we tried to fend off flying in the G4s as much as we could so as to hoard as many customer travel awards as possible. For example, for several years, I was able to treat my wife and myself to a two-week, first-class-from-start-to-finish vacation in an exotic location with just food and entertainment money coming out of my pocket. It was an extraordinary change in lifestyle where, several years earlier, I had been stuffing my pockets with sandwich bags full of food from a fast-food joint so I would have something to eat later for dinner or breakfast the following day.

Most often, the giveaway as to what we would be flying to our destination was determined by whether senior guys were flying with us because they rarely flew commercial. The G4s were also mandated travel equipment if they weren't being used. Reassuringly, all the pilots were marine pilots. As a marine, the CEO would have no one else taking out these G4s. And make no mistake, these marine pilots were some tough-ass motherfuckers, and it was an honor and a fucking incredible experience to fly with them. Unsurprisingly, they would all wear their marine hats and dipped tobacco.

One time, our team was scheduled to fly into Los Angeles for a business meeting. It was snowing so heavily that commercial traffic at the surrounding airports in the tri-state area was significantly backed up. So, they pulled a G4 out of the hangar for us to fly, seemingly oblivious to the weather. When we arrived at Westchester Airport, there was an appreciable amount of snow on the runway and the snow was falling so quickly and thickly that the airport was having a tough time keeping up with clearing the snowfall. I was, to say the least, a little concerned when I entered the plane. I wandered into the cockpit and stupidly asked the pilot if we were actually going to fly in this soup.

He looked at me and said, "Son, I eat this shit for breakfast! Get back there and buckle up, 'cause we're outta here!"

His confidence immediately hypnotized me. The plane ripped down the runway, forcefully lifted up in a seemingly vertical ascent, and quickly got above and over the storm, and we arrived fresh in L.A.

The CEO's honorable devotion to and support for the United States Marine Corps was inspiring. In fact, during my tenure there, the *Wall Street Journal* published an article highlighting how the company, during Operation Desert Storm, was sending marine troops, in addition to other goods and staples, smokeless tobacco shipments. It was further reported that marine snipers were using smokeless tobacco to help them stay awake during their missions by dropping a pinch of the product inside of their eyelids. When we read that article, all of us tried it. Just once because it burned like hell. It was like doing an eyewash with lemon juice. God bless our troops.

I was traveling for the equivalent of six months annually to destinations all over the world conducting meetings with in-country political officials, legal firms, distributors, tobacco growers, and sales teams. A range of countries including Canada, Taiwan, South Korea, Puerto Rico, Mexico, Argentina, Chile, Honduras, Costa Rica, and Kyrgyzstan, were all ordained stops for our newly established international division. And there were complex logistics that went into the planning for these trips. Prior to these trips, we had security briefings by former FBI officials, along with cultural appropriateness training for each country. Made sense. Each country had different levels of security risks and cultures, so we put effort into learning about the local etiquette in order to avoid making simple gestures that could be mistaken as an insult.

In one incident, I was on the G4 flying to Tegucigalpa, Honduras, accompanying the CEO, two presidents of the company's subsidiaries, the vice chairman of the company's board, and a security attaché, who was a former FBI agent. The agent was also packing a firearm. From the airport in Tegucigalpa, we were going to a tobacco farm that required a two-hour ride through a mountain highway that, we were advised, was besieged with bandits that were engaged in kidnappings. The total worth of the executives on this flight was approximately fifty to seventy-five million dollars. That was a lot of money for that time and would have been quite a tempting little prize for any bandit in Honduras. A bandit gang could probably buy Honduras with the ransom they would be able to procure for the safe return of these American corporate executives. I figured there was some potential, however ridiculously remote, that some gang was going to attempt some crazy shit on the mountain highway, and I wanted no part of it.

When we landed and parked the plane in Tegucigalpa, I looked out the window and noticed a squad of soldiers taking positions surrounding the plane. I asked the marine pilot what was going on, and he informed me that they were there to protect the plane. I saw no other G4s at the airport. We gave our security attaché all our passports, and he disappeared into the terminal, escorted by some of the armed guards.

As we waited outside the plane, I asked one of the pilots if they were staying at the same hotel as we were, and he said "Oh no. We're staying on the plane."

"What?" I thought I'd heard him wrong.

He explained, "We're not leaving this plane alone here. We don't trust these fucking soldiers." Those marines were tough motherfuckers.

Within a half hour, the security attaché returned with the passports and told us we were good to go. We stepped outside the airport to find two Sprinter-like vans waiting to give us a ride. One van was for the passengers, and the other was for our baggage and two additional Honduran escorts. Thinking about getting into that van with the executives made me feel queasy because I continued to worry that we were targets. I pivoted to helping the two escorts loading the bags onto their van and began speaking to them in Spanish.

As the executives were getting into their van, the CEO, the guy with whom I had interviewed, waved to me and said, "C'mon Eurice!" to get into their van.

Holding a bag that I was getting ready to toss into the van, I looked at him and the other execs, turned to look at the baggage van and the two Honduran escorts, and said, "That's all right, Mr. B. I'm going to ride with these guys! Thanks!"

As Mr. B climbed into the van, I overheard him say, "That Eurice. He gets along with everyone!"

God bless Mr. B., but my only thought was that there was no fucking way I was getting into that van and driving through the mountains where bandits were lurking. I fucking hitched a ride with the two Honduran escorts because if we got stopped by bandits, I would've taken the opportunity to convert myself into a taller version of a Honduran, disregarding any English language and purely communicating in Spanish. Additionally, I would have disavowed any connection to the executives. The wits I developed on the streets of New York were at play again, and I didn't want to write about my experience as a hostage. I wanted to keep playing golf. The trip was ultimately uneventful, but I had no choice but to bet on my incoherent risk assessment. It was nothing personal. Just survival. For the record, the safety of senior executives and middle management when traveling abroad was of paramount concern not only for our company but for the international companies we were conducting business with. That was especially the case when we traveled to Mexico and South America.

Mexico lived up to all the hype exploited in the finest narco-trafficking cinema. At a business meeting in Monterrey that I attended with the president of our international division (plus a couple of lawyers, and several other extraneous executives), we experienced firsthand how the Mexican elite safeguarded themselves from the famed nefarious cartel members who use mayhem and violence as tactics to conduct business. We were meeting with the CEO of a Mexican conglomerate and his team to celebrate our American and Mexican business union. It was our first time meeting him so the unveiling of security and related safety measures were on full display at his office. We were asked to wait in the lobby, where two gentlemen in suits and sunglasses stood guard and advised us that we would be escorted to the CEO's office one at a time. As the door opened, another man in a suit and sunglasses stepped out and directed us into the elevator, one at a time. The elevator was only big enough to accommodate two people, one of whom was always a security guard.

After ten minutes of shuffling our folks upstairs and conducting a successful meeting, our team was invited by the CEO to dine at his ranch house in the countryside just outside of Monterrey. His ranch house also happened to be an equestrian training center where this gentleman trained horses for equestrian competitions, including horses that participated in the Olympics representing Mexico. Strangely enough, observing the exceptionally manicured grounds and stylish home wasn't the most interesting part of the evening. Worthy of an espionage or drug cartel dreamscape, we were picked up by two black Chevy Suburbans driven by guys donning suits, sunglasses, and earpieces with automatic military rifles positioned in the front seat. Dust enveloped our vehicles as we drove down a dirt road leading to a fenced gateway, where we could see the house and compound. The entryway gate was opened by a pair of guards wearing suits, sunglasses, and earpieces (in the pitch dark of night) carrying military rifles over their shoulders. When we reached the end of the driveway, the host welcomed us, accompanied by another pair of guys dressed in suits, sunglasses, earpieces, and carrying military rifles that were slung over their shoulders.

The CEO proudly guided us through the main living area to the dining room, which was framed with floor-to-ceiling (fifteen-foot ceiling) windows. He enthusiastically flipped a switch that turned on floodlights, showcasing his expansive equestrian training compound. The lighting also revealed a comprehensive view of several more guys wearing suits, sunglasses, earpieces, and carrying military rifles, methodically intersecting each other throughout the perimeter of the dining area. We chatted uncomfortably and sat for a fabulous dinner in a highly unusual dining setting. Not one comment was made or question posed about the security measures we were experiencing. But there was no need to ask about the elephant in the room when the reasons were evident.

The evening progressed without any fanfare, and we were returned to our hotels in the same thrilling movie sequence that had begun the evening. After a nightcap in the lobby bar, we numbly acknowledged that we had witnessed the unimaginable circumstances of the constant state of unease that accompanies a life of privilege, if you can refer to it as such, in Mexico. We acknowledged that we were vulnerable strangers in a very different world order than we were used to, without the normal safeguards we take for granted in the United States. The realization of vulnerability was a recurring theme that resonated on every international business trip I undertook.

This was a period in my life where my earlier, seemingly reckless behavior of pursuing a golf career was undergoing a corrective episode. My current career path led me to my now-wife. We first met in a business meeting and married quickly after I started the new job in Greenwich. Although she initially enjoyed most of the perks associated with my business traveling lifestyle, the uniqueness and excitement of the constant travel eventually wore thin. We both traveled frequently on trips on the G4 with other executive couples and experienced the full complement of private flights. My wife and I once flew in the G4 to Canada to pick up several of the top executives and their wives of a chocolate company in Eastern Canada that our company was interested in purchasing. We then flew to Palm Beach to one of the compounds owned by the company where we were joined by my boss and his wife.

The sprawling Palm Beach property included a total of nineteen rooms, eight of which were cabanas by the pool. It had a massive three-thousand-square foot dining and entertainment area with a fully stocked premium bar, service staff, a top chef, and a concierge. We wanted to team-build and impress our potential chocolate company friends. The men golfed and went deep-sea fishing while the women went to spas and shopped in exclusive stores neighboring the property. After several days of team-building frolic, my wife and I hopped back aboard the G4 and escorted the chocolate company couples back to Canada. This was just one of many trips we took throughout the years where my wife accompanied me on the company's private planes, including flights to Puerto Rico, Vegas, Palm Beach, Palm Springs, and Banff. Whenever the topic of starting a family arose, the constant travel from home proved to be an obstacle to any reasonable thought of equitably sharing in the responsibilities of raising children.

The demands of my job required extensive travel and entertaining. That, coupled with the resulting loneliness and the functional inability to reasonably develop a family, came to a flashpoint on my fifth business trip to South Korea and Taiwan. We would always couple South Korea and Taiwan on our trips, dedicating a week of business activities to each country. My first week in South Korea was completed. I had just finished meeting with distributors and training a Korean sales team on the appropriate techniques of using our products so that they would know how to demonstrate safe product usage to retailers and customers. During the training session, we were forced to invoke an injury time-out because the manager of the sales force had ingested the saliva juice emitting from the tobacco in his mouth, and he needed to go throw up.

Fucking idiot.

We had just finished demonstrating how to place and maintain a portion of tobacco between your cheek and gums in your mouth, but when I turned to him for a public endorsement of the process, I noticed the complexion on his face had turned into a washed-out, algae hue.

"You fucking swallowed this shit, didn't you?" I asked, knowing the answer. He was barely able to tilt his head to confirm that was the case. I think the stupid fucker was dizzy as well.

I turned to the group and said, "We're going to take a twenty-minute break, everyone." I wanted to avoid having this shithead puke on me or in front of the sales team. That would have made for bad optics and probably would have scared people. Of course, simple mistakes like this were to be expected when trying to introduce a consumable product to a foreign nation that has no historical usage point of reference—particularly when it is a product that you must learn how to use so that you don't become ill.

There is a thirteen- to fourteen-hour time difference between the U.S. East Coast and many countries in the East Asia region. That's a pretty big window to acclimate to. I mean, it's not like having to spend four weeks at a Mount Everest expedition base camp, but it's a fucking grind for your body and mind to compensate for. The other grind is the process of cultural acclimation.

The business guys in East Asia may appear rigidly orthodox on the surface while at work, but when the sun goes down, they undergo a transformation.

They would whip out their lamp shades, boom boxes and confetti and drive us into the ground with nightly partying. As most international business people know, cultural sensitivities and business hierarchies are always on the radar. Thus, you would never, ever, intentionally (or unintentionally) insult the host of the company and country in which you are the guest. That, along with the time difference, presented a monumental challenge. The Asian hosts would, every night, take us out to—as they referred to them—piano bars. A piano bar is a cocktail lounge housing dedicated private karaoke booths and staffed, I shit you not, with female hostesses. The president of the distribution company, and host of the dinner, would then personally select and assign a hostess to each man attending every dinner soirée.

The piano bar was strictly for men. No females allowed. This was a culturally accepted phenomenon in South Korea and other parts of East Asia. The host and dinner guests would constantly toast each other, drinking scotch (these guys loved their scotch) that would be brought into the room from the host's private scotch collection held at that piano bar, while simultaneously gorging on the cuisine. Karaoke would never be sung, but the hostesses would feed us by hand and then massage our shoulders while we chewed our food. We only raised our hands to toast, but never to eat our food. We just had to drink and chew. I was truly experiencing a unique cultural event. At the conclusion of each evening, our host insisted that we take our hostess back to our hotel room with us. You heard right.

Where the fuck was I? I was now an official Twilight Zone member. We would drink and drink until practically paralyzed, then saunter off with our hostess to the hotel lobby, where we over-tipped the hostess and delicately explained (so as not to insult them or the host) why we wouldn't be indulging in anything else that evening. They would always reluctantly take the tip and, thankfully depart, experiencing minimal humiliation over the rejection. This happened every night without exception. The next day, with meetings starting at 7:30 a.m., our team would painfully trundle into an office only to find the same motherfuckers we had gone out with the night before sitting church-like, straight up, like they had just come out of a panini press. I mean, these bastards were fucking starched up and ready to unleash hell as if they had only indulged in milk and cookies the night before. We, on the other hand, looked like we had slept on the street in our clothes. We gave them a lot of credit. These were some tough dudes, but at that time, South Korea also had one of the highest rates of liver cancer in the world.

One night I declared, "Just one more week in Taiwan and I'm out of here."

I was looking forward to enjoying two weeks of uninterrupted home time. I'd been working at a strenuous pace, only getting home for only one week out of five. Prior to the East Asian swing and a week at home, I had been in Argentina and Chile for two weeks. At this point, and having traveled domestically and internationally like this for five years, I was running on fumes. I was wiped out, to say the least, and I was facing another week of golfing, heavy drinking, eating, and politely telling hostesses to go back to their house. My physical and mental state were broken. This week I traveled by myself to Taiwan as my colleagues headed back to the States after completing their assignments in South Korea. I stayed in Taipei for a day and then was chauffeured out to another city, Taichung, about two hours away from the capital. I was looking at another week of rinse-and-repeat overindulging in my quest to be a respectful guest.

The first night in Taichung turned out to be a low-key night with just the distributor and me hanging out. However, we still went through the motions with libations and assigned women. The distributor told me he was going to be like an American cowboy and ride his female companion bareback that night. I diplomatically ejected my host, returned to my hotel, politely dispensed with the hostess, and went on to blankly stare at my luggage in my room for half an hour. Without thinking, I picked up the phone, called my distributor, and proceeded to inform him that I had an emergency back home and had to get to the airport and catch the first available flight out of Taipei to Los Angeles.

I couldn't believe I had just done that. I strongly believe it was an innate reactive moment from my body and mind to save myself from cascading into a bewildering abyss of a mindless existence. I thought about company repercussions for failing to fulfill my business mission but would simply tell my boss that I felt like I had reached the final stages of Jack Nicholson in *The Shining*. I didn't know what the consequences would be, but I could not have cared less. I was convinced the personal consequences would be worse. In addition, I had even begun to develop a phobia of flying because I had flown so many hundreds of thousands of miles that I felt the statistical odds of being in an air disaster were gaining on me. My mind had gone *Full Metal Jacket*.

The distributor, in his broken English, said he understood and advised me that there was a Singapore Airlines flight to Los Angeles at around 1 a.m. and that he would send a driver to pick me up by 10:30 p.m. to take me to Taipei.

"Thank you, my friend. I will get on that flight and contact you soon to reschedule," I told him, diligently. *Yeah. Get the fuck out of here. You won't see my ass anytime soon, dude.* I called Singapore Airlines, and they indeed had a flight just past 1 a.m., and proceeded to book my ticket to salvation with them. I would have just enough time to get there and get the fuck on board. TSA and security clearance did not exist back then, so there was no two-hour advance timing required to pass security screenings. All one had to do was just show up, get one's ticket, and go. As promised, the chauffeur was knocking on my door by ten thirty. I had already packed my shit twice. I thought repeated packing would cosmically bring me closer to home.

Mentally, I was fucked up, but spiritually I was relieved to begin my long trip back home. The driver came into my room to pick up my bags, and I found myself babbling, attempting to engage in some sort of conversation. But the motherfucker didn't speak English except for "yes, sir" and "no, sir." He had a total of three English words in his vocabulary. We loaded the vehicle and took off. I had just short of two hours to get to the airport, and the driver was aware of the time constraints because the distributor had informed him of what time my flight was scheduled to leave.

The weather was unfavorable, with pea soup fog enveloping the whole area. The road was especially thick, with visibility limited to about twenty to thirty yards. The driver got up to eighty miles an hour, and if anything occurred on the road that was outside of his narrow visual radius, the presumed accident would turn us into a Jell-O mold of unrecognizable human flesh. My bowels were a rumbling indication of my nervousness. Cars, and more noticeably trucks, started passing us as if we were going backwards. I transcended beyond merely shitting in my pants to introducing myself to the grim reaper and death. I felt like I was in the Bataan Death March. Now I knew I was all in, as I was participating in a suicide mission to *get the fuck back home*.

I was convinced I would perish on this road, and my wife wouldn't be notified for three days or so, if they would be even able to identify my charred body or burned-up passport and identification documents by then. However, during this anxiety-driven dystopia, my three-English-words driver provided me with a sense of tranquility and serenity. No, don't speculate; it had nothing to do with his driving acumen. The man had an eight-track system, and, as unbelievable as it sounds, appeared to be an Elvis fan because that's the music he was playing. I found myself singing along to a medley of *Hound Dog,*

Jailhouse Rock, Viva Las Vegas and more while driving in pea soup fog at eighty miles an hour somewhere in Taiwan with the blurry images of cars and trucks as they continued to fly by us. He got me to the airport and immediately established himself as an honorary family member. I got on my plane and journeyed back to the States, relishing the fact that I had survived my episode in the twilight zone.

However, new priorities had clearly surfaced. My wife and I decided to dedicate this time toward creating a family. It was time to change career paths again. I needed to dramatically increase my presence at home. I didn't anticipate encountering landing another job that offered a fortuitous golfing platform like the tobacco company had.

Incredibly, I was proven wrong.

My search for a balanced lifestyle with minimal travel led me to join a hospital that was five minutes away from my house as a senior executive. Coincidentally, the guy who hired me, the president of the hospital, was a golfing crackhead, and the position of vice president of marketing and public affairs was offered to me containing the same conditions that were provided to me by the tobacco company: to dedicate a significant portion of my scope of work engaging in fanciful golfing experiences with our top physicians, board members, and any other friends of the hospital administration.

Additionally, the key hospital vendors, the big contract guys, were equally invested in golf as a means to engage in team building with the hospital executive suite.

I was in a state of shock... How was it possible that fate would again intervene, helping contribute to a new career path that would continue to nurture an affinity with business golf? I happened to have played golf (and played very well) a couple of times with the president of the hospital prior to him offering me the job. In fact, I questioned his offer as someone else was already occupying that position, and he simply stated, "No worries. I'll fire him in a couple of months." Remarkably, he did just that. This new opportunity would serve to launch an unprecedented, twenty-one-year corporate golf outing and CGT hall of fame championship playing record.

CHAPTER THIRTY-FOUR

THE SPORTSMAN, THE GENTLEMAN, AND THE BODY CHECK

Golf etiquette is framed by pillars of honor, honesty, integrity, sportsmanship, and basic courtesies derived from being a gentleman. Historically, of course, being labeled as a gentleman was also a way to distinguish one's class in society. This was particularly evident in the early days of golf, when only the wealthy were defined as "gentlemen." Originally, golf was not intended to be a sport for the masses, as the only individuals able to indulge in the game were the elite and entitled. Everyone else was simply there to support the upper class in their newly established hobby.

Golf is one of the very few amateur or professional sports that is largely self-officiated. I can't think of any other competitive sport where an athlete would call a penalty on themselves, thereby having to suffer the consequences. Can you? It's where honor, honesty, sportsmanship, and integrity are supposed to guide how you play the game. In addition to performing as a player, you also must play a role as an umpire, referee, and judge. A tournament official does not officiate play and is only called upon when the player has a question for the clarification of a rule and how it applies to their circumstance. That's it. Tournament officials explain the rules; confirm infractions cited by players;

approve where you can drop a ball, with or without a penalty stroke; and oh, that's right, they can also issue warnings and penalties for pace of play.

There have, however, been rare instances in which golfers have been disqualified after a tournament. Even rarer (like a meteor striking the earth), situations where a golfer is told to hit the showers *during* a tournament. There are no penalty boxes anywhere on a golf course.

Professional golfers and their corresponding fans represent the ultimate example of sportsmanlike behavior. In other professional sports, the fans curse and try to mentally project the force of ill will against the home team opponent and the officials. In golf, there is literally no home team, no player opponents, or officials to defile, with the only exceptions occurring at the Ryder Cup and the Presidents Cup. The opponent is the golf course. And as a fan, how could you curse or mentally project ill will at something as inanimate as a golf course? How can the passion of animosity toward a nemesis be directed at the field where golfers play? It can't. If a player hits an errant tee shot or misses a putt, people don't scream *Fuck you, Medinah! You suck, Riveria!* or *You blow, Bethpage!*

For the most part, golf fans are rather reserved, sublime, and all-encouraging toward the players. You *rarely, if ever,* hear any boos. *Can you believe that? A professional sport where fans almost never boo a player?* You never see any fans doing "waves," and you never hear a crowd in unison singing "na, na, na, na—na, na, na, na—hey, hey, hey, goodbye!" The sixteenth hole at the Waste Management tournament and the Ryder Cup are distinct and welcome exceptions, as the President's Cup is a more restrained team event.

Additionally, golf is the only sport where the athlete has to make a Herculean effort to check his or her emotions and adrenalin at the door— no matter how intense the moment is in a tournament. In every team sport, athletes experience a defining moment of success or failure that is determined by what that athlete *and* the team do. In individual sports like golf you cannot rely on your teammates to contribute. You do have a partner in the form of a caddie—a Sherpa of sorts, but otherwise a golfer is on their own ascension to the mountaintop. You are the master of your destiny. *Holy shit.* That can translate into a lot of pressure.

So, what does a professional athlete—a professional golfer—do to manage this pressure? Unlike any other professional sport, with the exception of possibly curling (is that even a professional sport?), golf does not allow the athlete to experience any rush of body action or movement to release their adrenalin.

So how does a professional golfer manage the stress and anxiety associated with those moments of pressure that decide whether they are a hero or a slug? In other sports, both team-oriented and individual ones, you can run, skate, slide, hit someone, swim, jump, bike, blah, blah, blah—all exercises and actions that are associated with helping to *release* anxiety, adrenalin, and stress. None of these actions that release endorphins apply to professional golfers at any level of competition.

Golfers can't tackle another player when they are about to swing or putt. They don't run up and down fairways to improve the pace of play. They don't box out the other players once they are on the green. They don't take out the pins and start fencing. They don't jump into a water hazard and swim a hundred-meter butterfly to get rid of their butterflies. And they don't jump into sand bunkers to measure their long jump—as if golfers are able to jump any appreciable distances anyway. *They don't even really trash talk!*

So how does a professional golfer manage the pressure of success in crucial moments when substantial dollars are on the line, or more importantly, when winning a tournament represents the launch of a career from almost complete obscurity to radar-worthy significance and editorial chatter? A declaration to the world exclaiming, "I have arrived!" No golfer, at any level, is exempt from these traumatizing pressure cooker situations. Even amateur golfers experience the same sweat-bubbling, palm-moisturizing, nausea-producing, sphincter-tightening, dust-ball-gathering-in-your-throat anxieties during pivotal moments of a match or a round—moments that are also usually accompanied by rapid breathing, diarrhea, and, in extreme cases, dizziness.

What is a golfer to do? Pop another beta blocker? Valium? Xanax? All the above? No, no, no.

To reduce the stress and anxiety, golfers are relegated to more intellectual and meditative exercises like eating a banana or protein bar, drinking water or an energy drink (not containing vodka), and then continuing to feign dominance over their unease by engaging in a lovely conversation with their playing partner. That's right, a delightful conversation about the kids, family, caddie, weather, favorite foods, ice cream, and so on. Any topic that is controversial, or confrontational, anything that could be considered distracting to your opponent enough to disrupt their mental perspective, would be considered unsportsmanlike or ungentlemanly.

For example, a golfer would never share a porn video with their playing partner during a tournament round. Unfortunately, that would eliminate another productive and meaningful tactic to reduce stress: masturbation. Million-dollar putt on the line? No big deal. Major amateur championship? So what. Club championship? Yawner. $5 Nassau? Make it $10, with presses on every hole.

Again, what's a golfer to do, seriously? Squealing like a pig may help, but it would be considered bad form. Throwing up on your playing partner is not an option, but it may merit consideration depending on how you feel about the person you are playing with. Anything? Nope. Golfers can't do shit. They suck it up and try to get into the hypnosis of every shot. And that hypnosis excludes the consequences of what that shot represents, casting them as a winner or loser of the tournament because if they allow that aspect to flaw their hypnotic exercise, they won't be able to execute optimally. Strong players compose themselves mentally to accept their fate irrespective of the rewards or consequences and stabilize their thoughts to focus on the shot they are about to hit. No more, no less.

No good player would allow themselves to get lost in the stress-driven swill of what the shot could represent outside of the shot they actually have to play. The shot hasn't been hit, so it doesn't make sense for them to get ahead of it. They only acknowledge the accolades or repercussions *after* they have completed playing the hole.

Golf is like fishing. It requires patience.

Golf is also like poker. You must learn not to reveal your hand—to yourself! Poker players don't yell fucking "whoopee!" when they are dealt a good hand. They realize it's just one hand, and there are a lot of hands yet to be dealt. And as unlikely as it may sound, golf is also like college football in that it is mostly a running game, not a passing game. You advance two or three yards at a time, and you grind to score. Six out of ten times, you run for par, and you try to pass the other four times for eagles and birdies to gain some meaningful advantages.

And although the new breed of professional golfers are athletes that have significantly contributed toward elevating the excitement factor of the game with long drives, precise iron shots, short game magic acts, and low scoring, golf is still not accepted as an exciting sport to the masses of sports fans. Making an eagle is not quite equivalent to hitting a grand slam in the bottom of the ninth, or a player leaping into the stands to rob a hitter of a home run. It's not like keeping your toes in bounds as you stretch to catch a pass in the end zone for a touchdown in the final seconds to win a playoff game. And it's not like skying above the rim to slam dunk a basketball on a fast break or witnessing a record-breaking hundred-meter dash.

Even getting a hole-in-one is overrated, in my humble opinion. It is a bit disappointing because after you achieve something as statistically implausible as a hole in one, you expect a bit more exuberance and lingering aftereffects. But it is essentially underwhelming afterward, as you realize how quickly the elation disappears, coupled with the ensuing disappointment that you'll probably never see another one again. I'd rather witness a lightning strike than get a hole-in-one. I'll talk about the lightning strike to a much greater degree than my holing out on a three par.

And it's not like winning the lottery, where you still maintain the excitement related to actually picking up the money and ultimately buying material shit with it. They probably have similar odds, but winning the lottery is the gift that keeps on giving. Substantively, a hole-in-one is a fleeting feeling that functionally needs to count toward a good score. That's really the point, isn't it? In fact, you come to the realization that you still have more work to do to capitalize on two strokes on one hole, because unless the hole in one occurred on a finishing-round three-par, you now have to tee it up on the next hole to hit the next shot—and now there's pressure to not relinquish the strokes you gained on your miraculous conversion of the hole in one. And just for the record, I speak from experience as I have had a hole in one. Just one.

Irrespective of other sports, the bottom line, simply put, is that golf can be as calming or nerve-racking as you allow it to be. Every golf shot addresses an adverse situation; an opportunity, a gamble, an experience that obligates the player to commit to executing every shot they are presented with. You do your best to realistically align your expectations for the excitement, pleasure, frustration, and education the game is going to provide you. So, take a deep breath, relax, maintain your composure, and swing away.

CORPORATE GOLF TOUR Q-SCHOOL

You don't go through the normal PGA-established channels to get your playing card for the corporate golf tour. Plan B players have to go through another type of Q-school or Korn Ferry tour machination for their right to play professional corporate golf. It's called a J-O-B interview! Now, please, you are not going to get on the corporate golf tour by working in the mailroom—or in purchasing, clerical, etc. You need to shoot for, and move into at least a middle-management position. When you do get a position as a middle manager, you'd better have "game," because that will provide you with significant exposure to all the golfaholics in the executive suite. And before you even get close to holing out your first putt, be prepared to lick a lot of assholes as your primary scope of work to secure your invite. If you are a minority, you can subtly play the underserved, underrepresented, and "token" population card and accept that you need to lick a great many more assholes than your white colleagues. The other white guys on your management level are not pulling for you, and while you are all playing the same ass-licking game, you're not really on the same team.

Lastly, and probably most importantly, conduct the due diligence to identify a suitable corporate environment that considers golf as an expected lifestyle and business development choice for executives. You have to be very discerning when you are selecting a company in which the corporate culture in the executive suite is religiously dedicated to conducting golf as a key business-building tool for their important clients. High-ranking executives will typically bestow their exalted business lifestyle perks, which include privileged access to America's most exclusive clubs, to a select legion of eager clients expecting lavish overtures. It is the desired environment where you can further prove your worth to a company through your golf performance.

Understandably, this passionate golfing obsession by senior-level executives would also feature prominent access, as a fundamental business extension, to *prestigious corporate golf outings*. Sponsorship support for these golf outing fundraisers is secured from national and local corporations and companies that have some level of business relationship or link that one of the senior executives has with the organization conducting the outing. As a result, the senior executive poo-bahs of these corporate entities have created dedicated budgets to support a kaleidoscope of proprietary, ancillary, or external golf outings that celebrate good causes. For example, someone on the senior management team of a particular corporation may also have a seat on the board of a not-for-profit charity, where that membership would carry an obligation to support the not-for-profit organization on a personal and business level, representing the company he or she works for.

However, another significant and sometimes infinitely more valuable connection for golf-related activities features a backdoor slide to corporate golf outings outside of the sometimes-hopeless anticipation of a C-suite invite. All sizable corporations with substantial operation budgets have to contract with *vendors*! Vendors can be an excellent option as a gateway into prime, luxurious, high-return outings. Why? Because vendors subscribe to the very best outings as they often must reciprocate with a corporation to maintain a "good vendor" standing.

Most importantly, vendors use outings as a business and relationship-building tool for their best, and potentially best, clients. If they are aware that a key client has a passionate interest in the game of golf, then the relationship-building or bonding entertainment strategy to solidify or enhance their sales or service contracts with the client immediately switches to a greater weight dedicated to golf-related activities. These golf activities would involve playing at the vendor's private club, taking the client to top 100 rated golf courses, going on golf junkets (in Southern parts of U.S. during winter months and that were just dressed up as professional educational seminars), providing clients with VIP tickets to PGA events, gifting them with the latest golf equipment, and lastly, offering invitations to participate in extravagant golf outings. The fact is, when a vendor invites a client as a guest to an extravagant corporate outing, that guest can expect a rousing and rewarding experience. Well-contracted vendors prescriptively participate in significant golf sponsorship levels, ensuring they are able to give their clients an experience worthy of royalty.

Most often, when a vendor "wins" a major contract servicing a multinational corporation, other aspects of "value" are provided by the vendor in addition to the expected criteria of proven credibility, quality, price, and service of the product the vendor is peddling. That added value item, which is often the key difference between winning and losing a contract bid, is usually tied to an arms-length collegial or familial connection, or an affinity shared by the vendor and the corporate decision maker on a common theme or activity. Oftentimes, that added value theme is reliable access to exceptional golfing experiences. And trust me, any astute vendor worth keeping is well contracted for good reason. These are high-altitude levels of executive bonding that forge iron-clad business relationships. I happened to be fortunate enough to often "qualify" for a playing spot as the tip of the "you're in for a great day" spear, whether for senior executives, clients, or vendors, providing the pixie dust for a complete outing extravaganza featuring guaranteed gifts.

It's important to recognize that the criteria utilized by the group's sponsor in selecting, or "qualifying," participants for an outing aren't completely driven by frivolous and juvenile inclinations toward solely winning golf prizes. The sponsor of an outing foursome, whether vendor or senior exec, lays out the criteria for each outing invite, and it is a process designed as a highly selective draft. Included as key criteria for the sponsor forming the group are legitimate business reasons and obligations, and the selection process requires sifting through a traffic jam of noteworthy people representing valuable relationships, all lobbying to fill up the foursome slots for premiere outings.

The wide range of valuable candidates—potential players which includes clients and team members along with golf-loving board members (and their friends) who request to play in a particular outing because of the noteworthy golf course. The selection of players encompasses layers of complicated political, professional, and self-serving motivations that address the potential of closing an important deal or fostering a relationship that will advance a business or personal agenda. As a result, the open spots for a four-person invitation get quickly liquidated as spaces are taken up with substantial priorities decided by whomever is sponsoring the foursome and carrying the tab for the outing.

Another key consideration for the sponsor is the ultimate chemistry and interactions of the group throughout the day on the course and at the reception following the round. Therefore, the sponsor must ensure that everyone does more than just engage in polite jabbering—this is where the elite player has leverage in securing a playing "exemption" within the foursome. The astute sponsor assembling the team for the outing recognizes that they need the following: 1) a ringer; 2) a ringer who is highly social, engaging, and generates excitement and enthusiasm; 3) a ringer who is selfless and turns their focus of attention to everyone else in the group rather than themselves during the round; 4) a ringer who productively manages the scorecard and the playing format; 5) a ringer who can put down cocktails, tell entertaining stories, and provide unwavering reinforcement of progress made by members of the group with the on-course swing instructions provided that day; and lastly 6) a ringer who dutifully abides by the sponsors' objectives to further a specific agenda or help close a deal.

Gaining a playing spot as an invited guest to an exclusive corporate golf outing by a senior executive or key vendor is as revered an occasion as winning a Willy Wonka golden ticket. The guests would be giddily welcomed with ornate door gifts of the highest order, all delivered with the delicate and personal attention of dedicated representatives from the fundraising organization. On this day, everyone would experience a good time on the golf course, complemented by inebriation, gifts, lessons, storytelling, and bonding. And this is how you earn your tour card on the CGT.

CHAPTER THIRTY-SIX

THE ROUND MAY BE OVER, BUT YOU'RE STILL PREPPING FOR YOUR NEXT INVITE

Those six characteristics are important and meaningful enough for me to dedicate a brief chapter to them for emphasis. After the round and during the flow of cocktails, never, ever talk about your round or the spectacular shots that you hit. Let your group wax on about them. You have to unshackle graciousness to levels that know no bounds—without being kiss-ass obvious. It is a deftly executed espionage maneuver to be able to pull that off in an unassuming, yet deliberate manner.

You should always start by talking about and complimenting your group's round; strictly speaking, camaraderie and teamwork are the themes. By this time, you have already strategically checked with the club pro handling the outing's scorecard to get your group's status amongst the winner's circle and provide all with a status update. I mean, there is nothing more enjoyable than coming back to your table and espousing that your group is coming in first. It really sets the tone for the rest of the evening. Then continue to talk about their better shots as well as their bad shots, delicately masking the bad shots under the guise of a learning experience of what not to do.

You are professionally obligated to be a reservoir of encouragement and positivity for your guests. And when guests finally get around to asking you about your round, you nonchalantly remark that you shot par or one or two over and shrug it off as if it were no big deal. You have now become an exception, a prize to be with, as you have provided a level of exposure to golf that they are not accustomed to. As planned by you, the members of your group willingly volunteer to become your voice box—join your fan club—and gleefully promote their experience with you to other key executives. What an eye-opener that was for me.

There are also other aspects that you must posture with your group. You need to slightly dampen any overt displays and loud banter regarding the outing performance of your group. Your advice for them is to engage in behavior that is humble and unassuming, even feigning shock over their performance, and perform what they might consider uncharacteristically politely reserved behavior. And this perspective is not limited solely to the awards dinner table. No, the conversation of the behavior protocol starts when you have finished your round and are organizing and collecting your things, from the point where the golf carts assemble after the round all the way through the cleanup and refresh activity in the locker room.

The guests in your foursome should be warned not to loudly or obnoxiously brag about your group's score, all the mulligans you took, the putts that were picked up from ten feet, and so on. Comments should be limited to "that was the best round of my life" or "man, you should have seen some of the shots we hit out there" or "He was dropping everything. I think he shot three under just on his ball." You often hear groups coming in and talking shit from their carts and through the locker room, reaching a premature crescendo, mistakenly celebrating their anticipated win during the cocktail reception period when the alcohol is flowing and fueling their illusory exuberance.

The bottom line is this: maintain a friendly, discreet, and professional demeanor throughout the evening, extending into the pro shop. Especially avoid gloating in the pro shop while you collect your rewards. Humility must be maintained while mingling and deliberating your selection of items in the pro shop. Everyone can celebrate once you leave the premises on your cell phones or in the office the next day as you reenact the glorious day.

Lastly, before the day is complete, there are three final must-do items that must be checked off to ensure your return trip invitation to this or any other outing: First, give any skill contest awards that you earn to someone else in the group to augment their winnings—without hesitation. Don't be greedy for the fifty, seventy-five, or hundred bucks that you can snipe. You have to think and invest in the long game, and keeping fifty bucks for yourself, even though you're the one responsible for the victory, makes you look petty and cheap. Fifty bucks doesn't mean shit for you in the pro shop, but it buys you much more value in goodwill with your neediest group partner. And be especially creamy with your generosity. For example, chances are high that your partner will initially refuse to accept your gesture. That is generally the knee-jerk reaction to this situation. But be resolute in your attempt to ease their conscience by suggesting they use the extra credit to purchase something for their wife or kid as a memento of the day. It makes your partner a hero to their family, and you, the underpinning to their knighthood status.

Second, arrange follow-up lessons with the members of your group. Offer up personal lessons focusing on the elements that you feel would help their game given what you witnessed on the course that day. And you will offer up this valuable one-on-one time at their convenience and at the place of their choosing. If you happen to belong to a private country club, invite them to your facilities. This gesture goes a long way in the bonding and relationship-building category.

And finally, without question, stay for the duration of the evening's festivities to represent your team and be the conduit for collecting the rewards. If any of the members of your group do not attend the cocktail, dinner, and awards ceremony because of pre-existing commitments, you will collect the winnings and ensure the appropriate and equitable distribution to whoever did not stay.

Now you can capitalize on an opportunity to coordinate the winnings handoff with a lesson and accomplish two objectives at the same time. What's more, your partner will experience another winning day. All in all, being gracious pays dividends. After all, it is a gentleman's game.

CHAPTER THIRTY-SEVEN

THE DEVIL IS IN THE DECEPTION

Making up its fundamental philosophy, the guidelines of corporate golf tour rules and etiquette presented in this book are conceived around the elementary fact that clients playing in an outing want to win pretty much under any circumstances. As a result, all subsequent guidelines that relate to the corporate golf tour revolve around a simple premise: if clients or your boss want to win in a corporate golf outing, particularly a prestigious one, then you must find a way to secure a victorious outcome, which in turn ensures the corresponding rewards (dressed up as hefty pro shop credits), allowing your boss or clients to buy golf shit that they don't need and already have the money to buy ten times over.

And don't confuse these issues as conflicting interests—it's not about already having the money to buy whatever golf shit they don't need ten times over, or winning for the twentieth time. It's about winning and receiving prizes just because they exist and because they think they're worth it and deserve it. I mean, someone is going to win, so better them than anyone else. The corporate golf tour redefines the bedrock of the founding fathers of golf, as those formally established rules and guidelines are unequivocally realigned into an artfully constructed deceitful and cheating framework that is applied at corporate golf outings.

To ensure a victory through cheating, several key tactics must be employed to overcome seemingly complicated factors.

First and foremost, *you must secure the scorecard* at the onset of the round. You are the guardian of the gate. You are the scorekeeper. No one else should be allowed to manage the card. And—this is very important—if someone other than you insists on keeping the scorecard, then you also keep score on your own card, even if it's not the official outing card, and submit *your* card at the end of play. But how do you keep the other guy from submitting the "official" card? As you wrap up play and everyone is collecting and coordinating their shit—car keys, cell phones, whatever other shit—you volunteer to take the "official" card to the pro to submit. However, you destroy the "official" scorecard, submit the card you have been keeping score with, and advise the assistant pro that Canadian geese ate the "official" scorecard. The assistant pro is already busy and isn't going to give a shit and will take your card. Moreover, historically, there are a bunch of groups who lose their cards or don't even bother handing cards in at all. This happens every time without exception at outings.

Second, and of particular importance, you need to mentally overcome your traditional mindset of the sportsmanlike and integrity-oriented DNA associated with the sport of golf and descend into the dark and opaque world of cheating. But rest assured; there are meaningful benefits to be gained through cheating, not the least of which is the adrenaline rush associated with honestly winning through cheating. I point out the adrenaline rush because at corporate golf outings, your group is competing among nests of cheating assassins. Their skills are exquisite and not to be underestimated. Their records of achievements are considerable and are considered mythical. Like Greek Gods.

You would think the legitimate rush would come from striping an iron from two hundred yards to three feet to set up a birdie for a win or eagling the last hole to qualify for a significant golf tournament. But it's not. This is a different type of adrenaline rush. It's like the excitement you feel when you star in your own magic show for a party of your closest friends. And this rush also delightfully relates to the inevitable shit-eating grin you have as you walk out of the pro shop with substantial gifts that you knowingly did not pay for while faking yourself and everyone else out by establishing a modicum of plausible cheating deniability with your conscience. You earnestly have to believe and accept that your self-deception is forthright and justified. It is, in fact, the truth in your parallel universe. And maintaining the sanctity of a clean conscience is what makes this next tactic so significant.

The third essential tactic is to create a mirage of truth and honesty. You accomplish this by setting the table in a manner that dilutes the act of cheating by creating an impression with your boss, guests, and clients that they are in the acceptable realm of "barely cheating." Trust me; it is much easier than it sounds as long as you have deviousness in your DNA. You have to make everyone feel comfortable in their own skin, without having to overtly confront the moral and ethical crossroads of being a cheater at golf. Your group has to be convinced that cheating is actually a normal expectation and an integral part of the rule of play and format of the outing, like a shamble, Callaway, scramble, or best ball. In fact, the ultimate accomplishment is being able to convince your guests or clients that if they *don't* apply cheating maneuvers, they would be doing something contrary to the spirit of the format and unnecessarily placing your group at a serious disadvantage compared to the rest of the groups that cheat. This aberration of logic can only be permitted by a complete suspension of reality by members of your group—a suspension of reality that you have to gracefully author, orchestrate, and implement.

The practical application of this seemingly counterintuitive, twisted, and contradictory logic of sports psychology is to fundamentally convince your group that, by combining just a little cheating with a little forgiveness while embracing that perspective as standard operating behavior for the field, they are not relinquishing 100 percent of their integrity. Even though you are taking the art of subliminal cheating to extravagant levels, the players in your group can't feel like they're cheating extravagantly.

As an example of reinforcing the "not cheating much" sentiment, you apply the following simple methodology and discourse: continue reinforcing the context that most everyone else in the field is cheating that day. You can continue to compound the storyline by reciting the entertaining and legendary achievements of some of the hall-of-fame cheaters gracing the outing on that or any other day.

"Rudy, man, that guy over there [pointing to a golfer that could be Rudy or some other unsuspecting schmuck] is the guy I learned from and who possesses an unmatched winning record. I played with him a couple of times, and I was lucky enough to have him take me under his wings. It was part tutorial and part bragging, but I picked up most of his secret techniques for cheating at outings."

"Rudy" is an alias for an otherwise very real, middle-aged, unassuming, and highly successful lawyer who was actually a decent golfer but got his kicks from punking everyone at a golf outing by flagrantly defacing the game in plain sight. He was an inspiring gentleman who jumped in with both feet with no regrets, no fear, never thinking twice about cheating, and always looked straight ahead. And, despite his cheating, Rudy was also a lot of fun to be around. But Rudy didn't have my golfing pedigree and couldn't lay claim to being an accomplished competitive golfer. Rudy was also astutely aware that this distinction provided me the unambiguous advantage I needed to relieve him of his crown. Guys like Rudy had their run, and competition for the top cheating spots requires an ever-evolving, ever-transitioning effort to constantly improve techniques and consistency. Please note that you don't have to give a monologue about an actual, real-life Rudy. You could just pick a guy out of the crowd and make up some cheating shit about that person to reinforce your narrative. I never encountered or knew of a woman that cheated. It was all men.

And the deception isn't solely focused on a conscience-cleaning exorcism disregarding meaningful interaction and dynamics between everyone in your group. The point is to provide a captivating, flowing choreography of sights, sounds, and scents, all adding up to provide your partners with an out-of-body, highlight-film day. The beauty of this masquerading romp is that your group is not really keeping track of what is going on. Fortunately, and as intentionally drawn up, they are fucking around, drinking, hitting occasional decent shots, enjoying full camaraderie while inhaling the scenery, the aesthetic design of the holes—I mean, you are playing in some of the finest private golf clubs in the country—and everyone is really caught up in the moment as you continue to hit good, sometimes phenomenal shots on a seemingly consistent basis so that they essentially have no pressure to perform and can carry on with their stroll of golf bliss.

Since the group is being distracted and entertained by the ongoing activities, including a happy level of inebriation while witnessing very good playmaking, they will only be able to selectively relive and celebrate the highlights, quickly dismiss their car wrecks, and fail to recall exactly what the team shot. So, when you state the team's score, they will genuinely think the score is pretty close to where they legitimately felt they were. And all of that thinking is largely because most of what they remember will be the good stuff. In fact, at the conclusion of the round, you reinforce to the group—or to the alpha person you have identified as the key influencer of the pack—that you only resorted to shaving two or three strokes off the final score rather than the ten to fifteen strokes you did in reality. You continue to emphatically point to statistics and ego, saying, for example, "You would have made those putts nine out of ten times anyway, so why should you penalize yourself now? Think about it, we only took a stroke on a couple of putts and took a mulligan on the second shot on a par five."

The reality is that your group has taken so many mulligans and second putts (by design and with very little necessary cajoling), that they have lost count of strokes and don't know what's real or not. If the diversion has gone according to plan, they have lost count because they fundamentally don't give a rat's ass, making it easier to accept these maligned meanderings as normal behavior. You have created a state of intentional confusion, which has effectively translated into an alternate reality in which rampant cheating is perceived as an incidental indiscretion.

The whole point of this narrative is that cheating at these events was not supposed to play like a brash lie. It is not supposed to make anyone feel uncomfortable. I mean, there is an ethical line that most people don't want to cross, and you certainly do not want to challenge anyone's intrinsic values for the sake of winning. Not in golf. Not when you want to enjoy your winnings and the experience of the day as opposed to carrying a bad conscience about the whole thing. It's not altogether like the business industry, where you strive to win no matter the blood, cost, or bodies you leave in your wake.

So, with tempered frequency, you even pen in a real score on a hole, disregarding encouragement by the group to pencil in a lower score with comments like, "No, no, no. We can't put a birdie down for that. That's too off the charts. We weren't even close to a birdie. Let's do the right thing and take par." Just to be crystal clear, this last gesture is specifically meant as a subliminal, manipulative, sleight-of-hand tactic to distract your partners and suspend any lingering beliefs that what you are orchestrating is morally objectionable. It is impeccably designed to keep your group off balance. It reaps the intended reward of reassuring your playing partners in crime that you, as the leader of this adventure, demonstrate a partial ethical conscience and are not the bastard spawn of a devil named corruption. This maneuver ensures that your playing partners will be swayed to think that they are just putting their toes into the cheating waters rather than yelling "cannonball!"

before jumping into a pool where people are comfortably and serenely tanning or reading poolside.

Not to worry. You still have more than ample opportunity before the round is over to contradict your earlier publicly displayed ethical epiphany and circle back with yourself to execute two dishonest scoring options: 1) put down a birdie anyway without your group seeing what you are doing, and advise them that you are putting down a par; or 2) atone for it on another hole where you parred, but you write down a birdie. Either way, you have got to make up for that stroke that you disingenuously endorsed as an attempt at fair play. This ploy is an organically engineered theatre performance that integrates a precise gymnastics routine with shrewd political playmaking. The whole script needs to be played delicately, like a flower swaying back-and-forth in a slight breeze. And who gets hurt by a little flower swaying gently in the breeze as you perform a reverse two-and-a-half-somersault with a two-and-a-half-twist diving routine while you sink a putt.

CHAPTER THIRTY-EIGHT

THREE OR MORE WRONGS MAKE RIGHT ON THE RIGHT HOLES

When you do make up for a stroke on a hole, you must demonstrate your Corporate Golf Tour knowledge for the amateurishly overlooked, but highly significant, nuance of intentionally filling in low scores on low-handicap holes. This key tactic is paramount to a winning strategy. Of all the birdies or eagles you apply on the scorecard, you have to ensure that some birdies or an eagle have been reserved for the top two, three, or four low-handicap holes. The logic behind this scoring methodology is profound as it greatly increases your chances for success. Why? Because when multiple groups have submitted cheating scores that are tied, the pro will likely choose to conduct a "match of cards" of the low handicap holes between groups that are tied to determine the winner of the outing. When the pro performs a match of cards to determine a winner resulting from tied scores, they will rely on who scored lowest on the toughest holes on the course.

Statistically speaking, this "tie-breaking" methodology may not be decided on the first or second low-handicap "playoff holes" tie-breaker, causing the deadlock to expand to the third or fourth low-handicap holes to determine the winner. It rarely expands to the fifth low-handicap hole. Thus, I would, at a minimum, recommend scoring birdies (or an eagle on a five par) on the top three low-handicap holes, and possibly extend it to the fourth low-handicap hole. I believe that reflecting birdies on the top five low-handicap holes (unless your group actually does it, which I doubt) may attract unnecessary and unwanted attention to you and your group. It is also contrary to your goal of leaving everyone feeling good about winning in a faintly legitimate and non–ethically compromising fashion.

By somewhat misleading your playing partners (for their own best interest), you will encourage their confidence in you, allowing them to rest assured that you do not have complete disregard for your integrity—or most importantly, theirs. In this intentional fashion, you protect them from being complicit in a criminal act. By keeping them "innocent" of the circumstances, you protect them from any direct association as accomplices. You make them think there is a line you won't cross and won't allow them to cross. The last thing you want is for your playing partners to think of you as reckless, without regard or respect for boundaries. Of course, in the end, it's all theater for the good conscience, as the clients know deep down that they are cheating. They will wink at you but never admit to what they are undertaking—because at the end of a wonderful day, embellished by evening cocktails, they are more than okay with the transgressions of the day.

CHAPTER THIRTY-NINE

SOMETIMES YOU GET TIRED OF WINNING

I became so good at this charade that, after several years, some of the guys I usually played with wanted us to come in second because our group was winning everything we showed up for. We established such a dominant track record and reputation that everyone else who was anyone else who noticed us coming to any outing automatically assumed that they were playing for second place. We had become a sporting dynasty, like the New England Patriots, the Montreal Canadiens, the Chicago Bulls, UCLA basketball, the Celtics, the Los Angeles Lakers, UConn women's basketball, the Roman legion—you get the idea.

So, at the behest of some members of our usual outing ensemble, we collectively, albeit reluctantly, decided to lie low for a while. Runner-up wasn't as good as first place, but by that time, we had won so much that we began having a hard time finding items to pick up in the pro shop. Golf shirts and clothing, accessories, gifts for the spouse and children, clubs, gear, sunglasses, miscellaneous equipment—it was a never-ending cavalcade of golf-related prizes. In twenty-one years, I rarely purchased golf-related items in any golf retail store or my pro shop. I only have two shirts with my previous club's logo, and that's only because I won them at a golf outing held there. It got to a point where we would go into a pro shop, find absolutely nothing that we didn't already have or want, and just held onto the gift certificates until some new equipment would unveil itself. We were like conquering Vikings, pillaging everything in our line of sight—until there was nothing left to pillage.

CHAPTER FORTY

IF MAINSTREAM MEDIA CAN LIE, YOU CAN TAKE MULLIGANS (AND SAY YOU HAVEN'T)

The sad, funny, and brutal truth is that the ethical compass of this country has embraced deliberately fabricated white lies as standard vernacular. Current mainstream and social media properties have become complicit as the lead conductors of maintaining factual information in the shadows. These days, you are forced to act as a private detective to uncover the truth. It is now a requisite procedure to apply what used to be journalistic standards entrusted to the media to your efforts of acquiring information you can assess to be legitimate.

The mainstream media has resorted to normalizing misleading information to script their own biased narrative. Headlines are especially maliciously misleading. So, what's a mulligan here and there? Fiction is already part of the national fabric, contributing to the creation of alternate realities. Consequently, telling fishermen stories to either dramatize a point, shape a narrative, or advocate a disingenuous position has distressingly evolved into a commonly accepted and depraved activity. Most, if not all, traditional and electronic media communications today are framed or underpinned by unrepentant bias, depending on whose views or positions you want to advance. Sadly, the appetite for curiosity in our American popular culture is perpetually fueled by sensationalism and dramatically misleading news. Currently, there no longer functionally exists a media property that appeals to a broad range of the American population. All media news has been segmented to effectively maximize targeted commercial appeal for advertisers. This strategic tactic offers another example of using the science of marketing to target and *exploit* consumer population segments.

People are always longing to know, for whatever reasons, details—the more intimate and salacious, the better—about celebrities, sports figures, politicians, rich people, and other popular figures. The details need to be as outrageous as possible to motivate public interest and encourage the media's higher ratings—whether it's a personality's meteoric rise to the top or their catastrophic fall from grace. This type of media approach sells because the American public craves an unending and immediate social and media news cycle. We are a culture of "right here, right now!" The never-ending news feed delivered to our televisions and mobile devices all significantly contribute to our sound-bite attention spans and to the embracing of biases.

It is important to point out that political media, irrespective of your political alliance, is especially criminally irresponsible. If you pay attention to media outlets, whether print, broadcast, or electronic, you are distinctly left with the impression that the other side is potentially damaging to your lifestyle and well-being while posturing that their side is the best thing for you to believe in. You can't rely on any empirical, objective journalism anymore, with the explicit exception of just a few media properties. The journalists and the media companies have all staked out their ideological and political positions, and it is fairly transparent that editorial management manipulates the presentation of content and context to support those perspectives.

Regrettably, you have a team of specialists, with superior communication and social media engineering skill sets, framing issues with polarizing narratives to be served up to the American public. So, our whole culture is driven by the moment—by ideological and political junkets of propaganda disguised as information and skewed to represent contentious contrasting philosophies and ideologies that completely disrespect the art and science of functional compromise. Unfortunately, too much of the American populace ignores fundamental facts and relies on sensational rhetoric to drive their reasoning because they are too lazy and downright hostile toward confronting the rational exercise of critical thinking. It's a mindless methodology where the lack of accountability to think below the surface or engage in elemental thought is gleefully encouraged as normal behavior by malevolent pied pipers disguised as journalists.

As a result, the nagging premise is that our country is most often culturally and socially managed with white lies. It is a country where people will believe perspective over facts as long as it agrees with their perspective, irrespective of the facts. We are a country that tries to take factual information and turn it into misinformation with communication that manipulates a particular position that needs to be promoted or is being set up as a foundation for a future proposition. You may consider it a convenient suspension of truth, a time-out for inconvenient truths.

For example, you have no business meetings scheduled for a day, but instead of wasting a vacation or personal day to play golf, you call in sick. Who's going to get hurt? You tell a woman or man they are the greatest thing you have ever encountered, when in reality you have another date lined up for tomorrow. It's not a lie, and it's not the truth, because it is a fact at that particular moment versus tomorrow when you're with the other woman, or man. You find out that a colleague is about to get eviscerated by the boss for dropping the ball on a project, and when that colleague asks if you have heard anything so that he or she can prepare accordingly before meeting with the boss, you say, "Nope. I haven't heard a thing." because you want to avoid being associated with alleged misgivings that you had no part of. Is that a bad thing? Why would you want to inject yourself in business that has nothing to do with you?

A labor report comes out from the feds, and it's a whopper of a number, significantly exceeding the projection earmarked by experts. Can you imagine what happens next? One side says this is great and a sign of better things to come. The other side says it indicates a lack of progress; we're in stagnation and it's a sign of worse things to come *because* they're not the right kind of jobs. Two different perspectives on the same statistic. Who's right? They both know they are stating alternate realities, and they are both disingenuous so as to accommodate the purpose of their narrative. Deliberately misleading white lies? How many kids have played hooky and told their parents they were at school? You're late for dinner because you played some extra holes at the club, but you tell your wife that there is tremendous traffic on the highway that's delaying you for about an hour.

Did Bill Clinton have sex with Monica Lewinsky in the White House? Does the correct answer to this question derive from the traditional, bedrock interpretation of sex? Or is the archaeologically validated rendition of a sexual act revised to accommodate Bubba's definition of sex? Now, I guess, we could choose to ignorantly suspend facts and truth and accept the delusional narrative that any oral intimacies between a woman and a man involving sexual organs and sperm should not be considered a sexual act. And did you notice that this was deliberately and deceitfully profiled in the media as "Monica Lewinsky's affair" and not "Bill Clinton's affair?" White lies are the fiber of our culture and democracy in our country. But as all this relates to cheating in a corporate golf outing, making your partners think that they are not really cheating closes the circle with the Bill Clinton and Monica Lewinsky scenario. If experiencing an orgasm through oral sex is redefined as not having sex, then Clinton didn't have sex, and he didn't really cheat on Hillary, and you can definitely tee up a mulligan!

CHAPTER FORTY-ONE

YOU ARE THE HOST OF YOUR OWN REALITY SHOW

A primary form of etiquette and decorum that must be observed as the hostess with the mostest, in winning (mostly every time) and losing (almost never), is this: you must always be gracious, benevolent, and entertaining with your partners in the group to ensure repeat invitations by the senior executive or vendor who is sponsoring the outing and invited you as their guest. To accomplish this, you must constantly offer and provide meaningful on-course instruction throughout the round, combined with a gregarious and enjoyably engaging rapport. The immediate gratification associated with an on-the-spot lesson and the subsequent personal execution of a good shot realized by the player in your group will unquestionably result in that player thinking you're the guru of golf.

It is also important to stay considerate and fluid with the unfolding golf lesson situation. If the guest happens not to execute the shot after the lesson, don't hesitate to drop another ball or two until they hit the shot that meets the expectations of themselves and you. Then, to really impress them, hit exhibition shots throughout the round, explaining your instruction with shots they normally would only see while watching a tour event on TV. This simple little sportsman's (salesman's) gesture cannot be overstated and pays social and business dividends for years in the form of prime-time outing requests for your presence. What really drives your group crazy is when you start calling the shots you are about to hit and then execute them as described. You advise them of the trajectory, low ball flight, high flight path, right to left, left to right, running the ball up versus flying it to the hole—and proceed to fuck with their heads through the execution of the shot.

The most significant rule of thumb for managing your team and playing partners is to be flexible. You must possess the ability to switch gears on the fly as you respond to the format, circumstances, and distribution of publicized or showcased prizes. Corporate outings are a fluid environment in which you adapt to, and optimize all the variables you will encounter in the outing. And remember the underbelly of psychology that stresses you conduct your onsite assessment behavior in a subtle way so that your playing partners—and anyone else participating in the outing—don't really feel like you are attempting to cheat. The first order of business when attending an outing is to conduct an on-site assessment, much like a thief typically scouts a location before the theft.

When you arrive at the outing, you check your bag, park or valet your car, check in at the reception desk, buy some raffle tickets, collect your gift or gifts, drop them off in your assigned locker (if they are not put in the trunk of your car), and then move on to scout the outing. After you have conducted a couple of laps around the venue to confirm the landscape, it is time to shuffle off to the pro shop and consider the range of offerings you will get to select after the outing.

Check out the clothing and accessories, the equipment options, and prioritize items that you would want to walk away with after you collect your winnings. Make sure they have the sizes of the clothes you're interested in and the equipment you can land on as well. As you will note from the above sequence of activities and housekeeping chores, all of this movement consumes time.

And I haven't even confronted eating, socializing, warming up by hitting balls and putts, and, if any of your partners are also on the range warming up, extra time not only to give a lesson but to observe how the lesson you just gave plays out by visually evaluating them as they hit some balls. However, even though you are destined to cheat and don't necessarily even need to warm up, you can still go to the range with a purely theatrical intent. The idea is to take advantage of a packed, captive audience on the range and forewarn them about the type of scoring they can expect from you on the course.

By doing this, you are demonstrably setting the stage and managing expectations. This activity lays some meaningful groundwork as the range is going to be primarily filled with hackers and hackers' friends giving the hackers really bad hacker lessons. It is the perfect opportunity to embark on an attention-grabbing display of what you're capable of doing with a golf ball and, consequently, what you could very well accomplish on a golf course. So, you lay out your practice balls as you have done a thousand times over, stretch out, grab a wedge, and start hitting some crisp wedges at a target on the range.

That's all fine and dandy, but nothing will grab someone's fancy like the crack of a ball compressing on the face of a driver with a 112-mile-an-hour swing speed. You swing away, pummeling straight drives way down the fairway that are 275–300 yards away. You don't have to look around to know that you have accomplished your purpose. Most of the guys in proximity to you have taken note. Your thoughtful, meticulous practice regime and your ball-striking display strongly suggests, to most on the range, that you're not a rookie. In fact, they are now curious about which group this ringer will be playing with. It is also entertaining when other frequent flier outing participant colleagues approach you and start asking for lessons, or boisterously exclaim that there is a "ringer" among us and that everyone else is playing for second place.

The time comes to unassumingly move on and get back to your group and initiate the next stage of generating excitement and laying the foundation for a winning day with your playing partners.

It is now time to set the media narrative, which you will reinforce throughout the day. Start an unassuming conversation navigating the topic of ideological cheating by highlighting the fact that the rest of the field is filled with habitual, dastardly cheaters. A functional tactical option is to choose to replace the Rudy narrative with an air of "How come this particular group of guys wins it year after year?" This sublime maneuver will encourage philosophical skepticism and ramp up elements of anger and angst, ultimately resulting in a consensus that your group will not accept losing to a bunch of hackers who are using unscrupulous cheating methods to undermine your group's chances of success.

Moreover, it will lend credence and guilty-conscience cover for your group to adopt an adjusted sense of fair play with the rules of golf given the lawless and shameless nature of the cheating bastards, who are abusing the innocence of the outing organizers and some in the playing field. You continue to stick with the script, "How do you think they get these low numbers? Think about it. Do you think *that* short guy can hit the longest drive? How can that guy shoot par when he can hardly get out of the golf cart?" The trick is to get them engaged in the conversation while simultaneously volunteering suggestions on how to offset the cheating to give your group a "fair" shot at competing and winning. At this point in the conversation, you are in a position to maneuver and shape the discussion, ultimately having everyone agree to adopt a moderate level of cheating.

CHAPTER FORTY-TWO

SHOW ME THE DINERO

B e very conscious of where the money is. You don't want to win trophies. *Why the fuck do outings even consider rewarding players with trophies? Who the fuck wants to take home a trophy?* Do the event organizers actually think the winners will display them in their office or home as if they were legit PGA Tour event accolades? And please, at all costs, avoid looking like a moron by showing up at home with a trophy thinking that it will become a showcase home decoration above your fireplace mantel. You'd have to be an idiot to think that your wife will share your enthusiasm for making a stupid crystal golf ball fucking trophy, or a plastic reproduction of a golfer replicating a bad swing, part of the interior decor she has painstakingly assembled.

The trophy will rightfully end up in the garage, the garden room, or go straight into the garbage. I have had the distinct pleasure of depositing my outing trophies in the garbage cans by the first tee on my way to the car. So, if you are the person heading up an outing or leading the golf committee for an outing, lose the trophies and replace them with gifts and pro shop credits. That will increase golfer participation and customer satisfaction. The bottom line is, be cautious about attending golf outings that reward players with trophies rather than gifts (unless the golf course itself is the trophy) because the organizer of the event is a clueless apparatchik.

You need to be selective about which corporate outings to prioritize. The ideal way to prioritize where you plan to spend your time and golf talent is to establish functional criteria for consideration. But what are the fundamental rules for outing selection criteria that you must establish to ensure a successful run on the corporate golf tour? And if you are an organizer of golf outings, I suggest you also take notes. Here are a couple of fundamental rules for selecting the type of golf outing that is worth the effort to attend:

1) The outing takes place at a golf course that you normally do not have access to—a golf course or country club that is ultra-exclusive, or is an acknowledged and historical PGA or USGA tournament site. This creates an exceptional, once-in-a-lifetime golfing experience. The prize at these types of outings is the golf courses themselves. This means that the organizer of the outing has invested the largest chunk of their budget on the venue. At an outings like this, you are destined to receive a stupid, inconsequential goodie bag upon entry containing a sleeve of balls—nothing good—with some sunscreen, a cheesy towel, and a brown-bag lunch. The goodie bag will strictly be composed of an assemblage of donations. You might also receive a hat with the course logo, but that's it. The sub-par goodie bag won't matter because you're there for access to the course itself.

Only charitable organizations that are both very significant *and* plugged in to the highest levels of private golf club membership will be able to gain access to this caliber of golf course. You will invite your best clients to these outings and assemble your own selection of prizes, independent of the outing. You will expense the purchase of some additional logo apparel and top off the evening with reservations at an outstanding steak restaurant proximate to the course, to ensure your guests have an exceptional time.

2) Examine and establish a clear distinction between what represents "worthy" events to you in light of the fact that *all* corporate outings are designated as good, worthwhile causes.

My version of the worthy criteria may very well be thought of as more self-serving. I always aligned myself with outings that offered extravagant gifts and venues, disregarding the merit, cause, or ethics of the organization. There are golf outings whose cause is honorable and contributes to valid and purposeful efforts to help people—great. Then there are others that perform as posers. These types of foundations employ a smoke screen of goodwill disguising their real purpose of funneling donated funds to finance the capital budget of their aligned corporate mothership. In principle, not so great.

If a company wants to construct a new department or a new service line, their fundraising arm—their foundation—will try to raise funds to cover the project costs with tax-free donations earmarked for that project versus utilizing commercial financing methods. In reality, these poser foundations use golf outings to squeeze vendors and well-intentioned benefactors for donations, which enable them to expand their business assets, offset their operational capital needs, and help subsidize the foundation's magnanimous administrative expenses. Many corporate golf outings are the brainchild of a charitable foundation that performs at arm's length from, but is still integrated with, the mothership corporation. As a result, it gains another source of financing without having to tap into venture capital—capital which would otherwise require fiduciary reciprocation to investors or lenders. The corporation also capitalizes on avoiding taxes which would normally be due on capital investments. These are just some of the advantages of having an arm's length foundation to perform as a not-for-profit organization.

Oh, they say all the right things and shake (down) enough hands, acknowledging everyone's thoughtfulness and congratulating their inner spirit to serve humanity, but it's largely bullshit. In great part, these empty showcases of philanthropy are hedonistic celebrations for the senior executives in the illustrious corporate suite preying on vendors and mostly well-intentioned philanthropists looking for name recognition, networking opportunities, and tax incentives. I know for a fact that these foundations target unsuspecting benefactors with deviously manipulative tactics behind the scenes.

These corporate arteries, acting as foundations, are also heavily supported by vendors that are forced to participate so as to demonstrate good citizenship with their clients, reciprocating at a level commensurate with the amount of business that vendor does with the organization. And even though vendors are cognizant of the insincerity represented by this type of outing and are reluctant participants (in principle) in the affair, they nonetheless roar to take advantage of this self-serving boondoggle for all it has to offer. Philosophically and legally, a quid pro quo between organizations and their vendors is not supposed to exist, but this pay-for-play arm-twisting tactic is nonetheless ruthlessly imposed. And if they don't comply, they are inviting repercussions from their client. It's funny; the smart vendors, knowing this is going to occur, simply increase their invoices by about 10 percent to partially cover their costs associated with participating in these fundraisers.

However, despite these shameless maneuvers, you might have to put aside your cynical misgivings (like I did) because these outings can still prove to be more than a great event. They may, in fact, be considered a pretty damn great event! And this is where *my* distinction of worthy plays out for criterion numero dos. This factually experienced criticism of these poser foundations may be largely irrelevant if the outing significantly adorns its participants with lavish door gifts and winning prizes. If this proves to be the case, lovingly celebrate the corrupt activity in criterion number two and go vanquish the land!

CHAPTER FORTY-THREE

MIAMI LIGHTNING

I was at an outing in Miami, and this was actually one of those worthwhile altruistic causes I felt compelled to participate in after personally being invited by the CFO (who is also a friend) of an international broadcasting network. None of the gentlemen in the group knew what the prizes were, nor were they interested, because they were just looking to experience a nice day of golf that benefited a good cause. Not to be deterred by succumbing to a compassionate perspective, I scoured the whole club in an attempt to find prizes and was disappointed to conclude that there were none to be seen. Usually, an outing displays the prizes to jack people up, feeding their hopes for a victory.

I then moved my investigation to the pro shop. There is also a science and methodology to asking a pro about the prizes without exposing your intentions. So, don't just walk into the shop and directly ask what the prizes are. You need to be discreet. Stealthy. I lingered, looking at some items, and started a casual conversation with the pro. I asked him how things were going, asked about the outing, and finally worked my way to asking about the format and the prizes. Although I was disappointed by his response, I didn't let it show. I simply said, "Great! Thank you," and walked out.

This outing was giving trophies as prizes for low scores. I joined my group after loading up on the lunch buffet, and lounged around engaging in sophomoric conversations about how our wives vociferously complain when we fart in bed, under the sheets, because it takes so much longer for the odor and moisture to dissipate, and other antics that were just short of squeezing green Jell-O out of your mouth. We were having a good time in spite of the trophy prizes. Sometimes you still want to experience winning even if you trash the trophy.

My first challenge was to change the group's mindset from a passive "glad we're here" to a competitive and winning attitude. I wanted them to feel the edge to win for the sake of winning. Moreover, I had to convince the CFO of the company, whose guest I was, that it was OK to win at his own outing. From my perspective, I wanted to export my outing tactics to Miami. During the warmup session on the range, we discussed and agreed on playing to win. The next discussion was about strategic approach. The format was a four-man scramble where the group was required to use each of our drives at least three times, and each person had to take a turn hitting from their team's best shot on every shot. That meant all four of us would pick the best tee shot, hit from there, and continue to hit the best shot in the group until the hole was completed. No problem. It was a significant field, about 140 or 150 golfers. I estimated the winning score to be, as in most scramble fields, in the high fifties, maybe fifty-six or fifty-seven. At least fifteen to sixteen under.

I want to take a moment to put these scores in perspective. There aren't many amateurs with credible low-single-digit handicaps. In any given golf outing, there are a handful of players that have legitimate single-digit handicaps, and only a couple of those guys have handicaps in the low single digits. To have any chance of shooting fifteen or sixteen under par, the single-digit-handicap guys would all have to play together, and play well. But 99 percent of the time, they don't play together because, since there are not many of these single-digit guys to go around, most teams will have laid claim to one of those "ringers." This is the person who will be your ace and deliver the most incredible shots at the critical moments.

At best, the other three guys consist of mid to high handicap players. This is the team that 99 percent of the time, would best several other teams posting scores of twelve, thirteen and fourteen under, by incredibly scoring fifteen, sixteen or twenty under to win. That means the winning team has to birdie at least fifteen to sixteen holes and have an eagle or two to boot. It represents quite a statistical feat. The odds of pulling off a feat like that has the statistical probabilities of hitting a squirrel with a tee shot that is a worm burner, draining five forty-foot putts in a round, finding Jesse James's secret buried treasure on the sixteenth hole, or discovering a new law of physics. *Got it?*

So, how can these gentlemen, golfing Amazonians, actually achieve this miracle of miracles, this athletic masterpiece? They rely on cheating, of course. They justify that *it's not really cheating* because—after missing their first attempt at a putt or chip, they simply count the second putt, which is always made, or they count the second chip. Or they just pick up a missed five-foot putt because they obviously would have made that putt the second time. The reality of life and sports is that it is not about what you could or should have done. It's about what you do and what it is—the first time at bat, except on the corporate golf tour! The CGT encourages and honors those who live for the "second shot" or effectively counts the "what could have been" scenario scorecard. They turn the illusion of "what could have been" into a hallucinatory reality—and, most importantly, first place. It's a wonderful, idyllic world where all you want to happen, happens. It's Universal Studios. You always hit a great shot; the stars, the moon, and the putts are always aligned; and you always win.

I was happy with how our score was tracking as we made our turn, which happened to be on the back nine because we started on hole number one in the shotgun. I was especially happy with *how* we were accomplishing our score. All of us were hitting decent shots and felt we were playing well, so the "guilty conscience" of the players was not prevalent; they felt that they deserved that birdie putt because the first two shots were hit well by the team. That is a critical aspect of the psychology behind the perception that you are not really cheating. For example, if the group is hitting shots relatively well, then from their perspective, accepting the second attempt at putting for a birdie that is made, instead of the first putting attempt that was not made, is more palatable. After all, when you are soundly striking the ball and are hitting really good shots, don't you deserve that putt?

As we made the turn to go to the back nine, I noticed that all the prizes were finally being displayed. Apparently, they had put them up after everyone had teed off, and I noticed that, along with trophies, there were sets of clubs, drivers, fairway woods, putters, and golf staff bags. I walked over to take a closer look at the table of prizes and noticed the trophies were all for the team placements, but the good prizes were designated for the raffle and the skills contests—you know: longest drive, closest to the pin, straightest drive. I thought it peculiar that they would give away the most expensive stuff for these skill contests versus team scores. It was the only time I had ever experienced that kind of approach, which demonstrates that whatever management firm they hired to execute the event didn't know what the fuck they were doing. I mean, why would you give away top-tier prizes for one shot instead of what a team could accomplish with their joint effort through eighteen holes? I wish the pro would have revealed that there were golf prizes for the skills contests when I asked him before starting play. I now had to re-strategize our approach to winning some prizes and manage our team accordingly.

I no longer cared about the low net or gross team score. Not knowing that all the good prizes would be going to be dedicated to skills awards, we had wasted the first nine holes and had to put on a surge on the remaining nine holes.

We had to win every skills contest left on the back nine, which meant one closest-to-the-pin on a three-par and one long-drive hole. We ignored, on principle, the straightest drive hole. I explained our approach in detail to our group. It was a blunt discussion. No time for psychological massaging of politically delicate terms. So, we adjusted accordingly, hit our balls onto the designated par three hole, made note of the closest distance marked at that point, disregarded it, and recorded the closest proximity to the hole statistically relevant to the length and difficulty of the hole to hopefully ensure a winning result. When we came to our long-drive hole, we were a little more brazen and moved the longest drive marker to a location where no one could humanly reach the distance. The explanation? Gusty tail winds? The ball hit the cart path and rolled? The ball bounced off a metal or stone yardage marker or a sprinkler head? *The Bermuda Triangle?*

Incredibly, with a score of fifteen under, we finished the day in third place but walked off with two full iron sets from Titleist and Nike after capturing the long drive and closest to the pin contests. The CFO who invited me did not win anything, but after the round, I gave him the Nike iron set I won for the closest to the pin. I knew I was going to do that as soon as I had won it, and he happily accepted the offer. After all, at this point in my corporate golf tour career, I did not need or want anything related to golf merchandise. And guess what? I was invited again to play the following year, which we won simply for bragging rights.

Contrary to my policy edicts, I still have that winning trophy displayed. It's in my older son's room. He wanted it.

CHAPTER FORTY-FOUR

YOU JUST CAN'T MAKE THIS SHIT UP

In the tri-state area, there was a Hispanic not-for-profit 501(c)(3) foundation that ran an annual golf outing. The outing claimed to raise money for a local community college's programs and scholarships for Hispanic kids. On the surface, it was a noble enough concept, but below the surface existed a certain level of speculation on how the funds were actually used. Nevertheless, this program always received tribal support from key Hispanic, street-hardened business and community leaders. I was asked by the organizers to sponsor the event on behalf of my company.

The opportunity intrigued me, not so much because I would be participating and supporting an alleged worthy cause, but because I wanted to personally witness the den of thieves that were reputed to attend and play at this event.

And I was not disappointed.

I was witness to golf cheating at unparalleled levels. It was such a disgraceful exhibition of cheating that it disheartened my faith in humanity. The wolves were certainly in control of the hen house. The format was a scramble, and the winning score was twenty-two under par, and when it was announced, it was overtly, drunkenly celebrated. Prizes included golf clubs, golf sets, golf accessories, and many round-trip airline tickets provided by a major US carrier. All the king's men (friends of the boisterous patriarch, who was the host of the outing) won airline tickets, among other things. It was a preordained activity, with scores being rewritten on the announcement podium itself.

There was no possibility of out-cheating the cheaters at an event that lauded cheaters. The invitation should have headlined that "only shameless cheaters need participate." No humility was on display, as evidenced by my experience on a particular three-par hole that was marked as a closest-to-the-pin skills contest. As I approached the green on the par three, I focused on the measurement pad next to the putting surface, as I usually do. The measurement pad is where everyone posts their results after they measure the distance between the hole and their ball on the green, and logically post the distance if they are closer than the previous person who posted their distance from the hole. The names and distances are placed on the measurement pad in a descending order, from longest distance from the hole appearing first to shortest distance appearing last, indicating that person to be the winner of this "skills contest."

If other golfers couldn't beat the short distance displayed by a previous player, then they do not bother indicating their distance. Consequently, they will not win a prize. When I picked up the measurement pad, I saw a long list of names and distances on it. What I saw was the following (the word "Name" will replace the actual name of the person, followed by their distance from the hole): Name, 12'4", Name 10', Name 7'8", Name 6'3", Name 5'0", Name 4'1", Name 3'7", Name 3'2", Name 2'5", Name 1'6", Name 1'4", Name 1'1", Name 9", Name 7", Name 4", Name AND WINNER 1." The closest-to-the-pin prize on this hole was two first class round-trip tickets to anywhere in the continental United States, donated by a top airline carrier who was also one of the sponsors of the event.

Thinking this through logically: what do *you* think the odds are of twelve golfers, unquestionably hackers, hitting it inside of five feet on a 180-yard par three with a right-side tucked pin within a five-hour period? The pin was not staked out in the middle of the green. And, for the record, the wind was blowing about twenty miles an hour from right to left. It's probably the same statistical odds as getting a hole in one. Seriously.

The after-outing reception provided all the confirmation I needed that I had just participated in a hornet's nest of rogues. The reception's guests were celebrating and boasting about all of the incredible golfing feats they had performed throughout the day: holed-out bunker shots from the fairway, chip-ins, and dozens of putts that rolled in from another zip code. As I mentioned, the winning score was twenty-two under, and not one team shot worse than sixteen under that day. Every story was topped by another one. I had never been a part of an exhibition like this. At the podium announcing the winners, the host honored and laughed at the exploits of the cheaters throughout the announcements. It was an out-of-body experience, giving one the feeling that one had died and gone to a cheating pirate's paradise.

Discreetly cheating, as highlighted in this book, is one thing, but this was belligerently lawless. They were all rejoicing in their defilement of each other. I only stayed for a short time at the reception, pretending I was having good-natured fun overlooking all the sadistic rejections of ethical decency. But it reached a point where, frankly, I could no longer deal with the mostly buffoons trying to replicate Caligula reveling in one of his Roman feasts. I left for the evening and would never again sponsor, nor participate, in this event. Several years later, the event dissipated as its support faded.

Let's move on to a focused review of the CGT rules you will incorporate into future golf outings with your group.

CORPORATE GOLF TOUR (CGT) RULES [I.E. RULES FOR CHEATING AT GOLF OUTINGS]

CORPORATE GOLF TOUR RULE APPLICATION #1.

1-1. The Game, Player Conduct, and The Rules

A game of Scottish origin consisting of eighteen gopher holes, played over beautifully landscaped grounds, where you hit a one-, two-, or three-piece ball 1.68 inches in diameter that is constructed out of a combination of rubber and plastic materials into eighteen gopher holes from starting locations (tee box) that are hundreds of yards away with a converted field hockey stick. The gopher holes are so small that you can't see any of them from ten yards, much less four hundred yards, so you need flags to identify where the gopher holes are. Yup. That's the concept that has defined a revered sport. It's also the concept that led to the creation of a nineteenth hole where players go to the bar immediately after their round of eighteen to try to figure out what in the hell they were doing out there.

Standards of Player Conduct

There must be some honor amongst thieves. You have to play as if you are, in fact, not cheating.

Playing by the Rules

Hell, have some fun! Forget about the USGA for the day and abide by the CGT rules that are defined here. The main player, who is appointed as acting captain of the group, is responsible for knowing both the CGT rules and the format of an outing. Please recognize that there is limited flexibility within the CGT rules to ad lib as they are plenty permissive already. Just be discreet and maintain a professional sense of decorum. Definitely do not let the field suspect you of cheating.

CORPORATE GOLF TOUR RULE APPLICATION #2

2-1. Course Played as Found

A player may take any reasonable liberties ("reasonable liberties" defined in the next section) to improve the position of their ball. This does not solely apply to wayward shots that end up in the woods, sand bunker, or heavy rough. You can improve your lie even if you hit a shot in the fairway. Think about it: you may end up in a divot or an uneven lie—sidehill, downhill, uphill, whatever—after hitting a good drive. Why should you be subject to anything less than an inspiring and level ball position? It is just like being on a range mat, right? Isn't that fair?

2-2. Actions That Improve Conditions Affecting Your Stroke

The following actions to improve conditions that affect your stroke are considered "reasonable liberties." Preferred lies and angle improvements that enhance the opportunity to strike a good shot while optimizing scoring results are permitted—through the course—and within FOUR APPROXIMATE CLUB LENGTHS—from where your ball lies with the club of your choosing. Or you can eyeball five yards. If you are in the rough but within four club lengths or five yards of the fairway, you can place your ball in the fairway instead of playing from the rough. I mean, you're close enough to the fairway, and "close" counts in the CGT.

The one exception to this rule is if you are playing a "long drive" skills contest hole. If you are on this specific hole, then any drive coming to rest twenty yards left or right of the fairway is regarded as being on the fairway and is a valid contender for the "long drive" skills prize. So, if your tee shot is longer than where the present long drive is posted but twenty yards in the rough, the shot is considered to be in the fairway and you would represent the new longest drive. Please make sure you place the long drive marker in the fairway parallel to your ball, AND NOT IN THE ROUGH WHERE YOUR BALL ACTUALLY CAME TO REST.

You also have the flexibility to provide yourself with an open shot if you happen to be blocked out of your next shot. Given these circumstances, you are allowed to extend the four-club (or five yards) improvement until your ball comes to rest at a point that provides you with a clear shot to the green. For example, if your ball is in the rough and comes to rest directly behind a tree, thereby completely blocking your shot to your target, then you can move your ball until you have an unperturbed shot at the green. However, your ball must stay in the rough, with a preferred lie, of course. You are NOT permitted to blatantly improve your lie and move your ball thirty yards into the fairway. I mean, you should have some scruples.

If your ball is in a fairway or greenside bunker, you are allowed to place your ball in a preferred position within said bunker. YOU CANNOT REMOVE YOUR BALL FROM THE BUNKER. Please have some sense of decency. However, if your ball is on an uphill or downhill lie, up against the lip, or even plugged, you are allowed to take relief in another part of the bunker without incurring an unplayable penalty. You can even rake the spot where you will be placing the ball. Rake it nice and fluffy and give yourself a great placement.

You may also move your ball to realize a full swing. If your swing is impeded by tree limbs, shrubs, fences, stones, etc., then you are allowed to move your ball into a position that enables a full, clear swing at the ball along with a clear line of sight to the green. But you have to maintain your ball in the rough unless you are within four club lengths, or five yards from the fairway.

CORPORATE GOLF TOUR RULE APPLICATION #3
3-1. Lifting, Cleaning, and Marking Ball

A player may lift and clean a ball that is resting on the green, fringe, or anywhere else on the golf course at any time. A player may use a flat instrument of any kind to mark a ball on the green either directly behind it, on the side of it, directly in front of the ball, or just toss the marker up to fifty percent closer to the hole. When marking in front of the ball, a player may place his or her ball back in front of the ball mark. The player does not have to place a ball directly behind the mark. This will allow the player to place the ball closer to the hole by the length of a ball mark. And a player may mark their ball as many times as desired to decrease their balls' proximity to the hole.

A player may improve their proximity to the hole by up to fifty percent from where it lies on the green unless the ball is originally inside of ten feet to the hole from where it rests. Any ball that lies ten feet, or closer, to the hole is considered a "gimme" and the hole would be deemed completed. For example, if a player's ball is thirty feet from the hole (on the green), they can reduce the distance to the hole by up to fifty percent, making it a fifteen-foot putt. If a player is twenty feet from the hole, a player may reduce the distance to the hole by up to 50 percent, making it a ten-foot putt, which is now considered a "gimme." A player is not allowed to improve their proximity to the hole by more than fifty percent from where the ball lies on the green, and you must be on the green to employ the fifty percent reduction in length to the hole rule.

However, if a shot is not on the green but lies approximately ten feet from the hole, you have also entered "gimme" range.

Please note: the ball must be resting on the green to apply any CGT ball marking technique.

Also, the lead player must maintain their "theatrics" of advancing the ball closer to the hole inconspicuous to the rest of the team. Remember, it is the lead player's responsibility to assuage the team from having the perception that they are cheating excessively. As the lead player approaches the green, they may mark the ball closer to the hole (no more than fifty percent closer to the hole) by using one of the marking techniques described in a later segment. Your team will be pleasantly surprised that the ball hit onto the green is actually closer to the hole than anticipated. The lead player should reinforce the perception.

3-2. Ball is Played as You Want it to Lie

You are always playing "winter rules." If your ball is within five yards or four club lengths of the fairway, it is equivalent to being in the fairway. Any ball in the rough that is outside of the fairway by approximately five yards, or four club lengths with your longest club, must be played from the rough. However, you are still allowed to place the ball within four club lengths, or five yards, of your original lie in the rough (or more if you encounter a blocked line of sight for a shot to the green, or are impeded with your swing), and are allowed to fluff your ball up in the rough to realize an excellent lie. Remember, "winter rules" apply for any outing through the green. Always give yourself the best possible lie.

Oftentimes, the format of a corporate outing will be a scramble. It represents an opportunity for each player to take turns putting from the same location. When the team observes their putting line, the team is allowed the discretion to place the ball in what is agreed to be the straightest line possible towards the hole and proximate to the ball's original line. This calibration decreases, to the greatest extent, any right-to-left or left-to-right curvature of the green and the line of the putt leading to the hole.

3-3. Relief Without Penalty Allowed at any Time

A player may take relief from a penalty area without incurring any type of penalty. Makes sense, right? I mean, how often have you played this course? Did you know there was a water hazard there? Did you know that thirty yards to the right of the fairway was out of bounds? Why would you? If you did, you obviously wouldn't have hit it there. Do you think anyone else is taking any penalties? No. You get free relief anywhere, with no penalty. Enjoy your day.

3-4 Completing Play of Hole

You do not need the ball to come to rest at the bottom of the hole that you are playing to. The corporate golf tour rules specifically allow you to count the stroke and complete the play of the hole when you or any member of your group HITS ANY PART OF THE HOLE when putting or chipping to the hole. The ball does not need to go into the hole. If you hit the hole, IT COUNTS! A thirty-foot putt hits the diameter of the hole and spins away—it counts! A chip hits the flag and bounces away—it counts! This allows your team to statistically have the greatest opportunity to win by figuratively expanding the diameter of the hole, facilitating the ability to legitimately convert the team's putt, chip, or pitch by simply hitting the hole in your attempt. Additionally, if your ball is within ten feet from the hole, the next shot is considered good ("gimme), and the hole is completed.

CORPORATE GOLF TOUR RULE APPLICATION #4

4-1. Scoring

Whoever or whichever team (sometimes in corporate outings, they award both team and individual winners) turns in the lowest score wins. In particular, the first order of business would be to appoint a captain of the team. That person would manage on-course team play and be the final arbiter of any golfing questions, including, but not limited to, where to ultimately mark the location of where the ball comes to rest on a green, how many yards are added/ assigned to one of the teammates in the group for the long-drive hole, what lies to play on the course, how far a putt to give, best use of mulligans on tee shots, etc. Most importantly, the captain will be the gatekeeper of the group scorecard. The captain has the creative license to do what is needed to turn in the lowest score, but they also have the responsibility to make the score look plausible. For example, don't turn in a scorecard where your team records five eagles, two of which occurred on par-four holes. This is a statistically irreconcilable feat and will not carry any credibility with the pros monitoring the event or the other outing participants. Don't do it! And remember to post birdies, or an eagle (on a five par) on the first three to four low handicap holes!

4-2. Failure to Hole Out (otherwise known as a "gimme" in the corporate golf tour)

Failure to hole out in an outing is otherwise known as a "gimme." A "gimme" is permissible when you are within ten feet of the hole (whether the player is on the green, or not), where all shots and putts will be considered "good." The "gimme" does not incur a penalty or a disqualification and is as good as "holing out." If your group decides to putt or chip within the ten-foot "gimme" range and the ball hits any part of the hole and does not come to rest at the bottom of the hole, IT STILL COUNTS. Or, you can just count it as a "gimme." Let me repeat: the putt or chip does not need to fall in the hole to count. If your putt or chip hits any part of the hole, it counts, even if it does not come to rest at the bottom of the hole.

Note: the "gimme" and hitting the hole on a putt or chip without having the ball actually go in the hole does not incur a penalty or a disqualification and counts as "holing out." In fact, there are no penalties in the Corporate Golf Tour rule book.

4-3 Two Putt Rule

The two-putt rule for the CGT is very simple. As soon as anyone puts a putter in their hands to play the next shot, that player is granted a two-putt maximum per hole. This includes whether the ball is on the green or not. There are often times when a player may be just off the green on the first cut or fringe—or be ten or twenty yards from the green, but the grass is cut low enough and the ground firm enough that the putter is actually the best club with which to execute the next shot. If that is the case, the two-putt rule goes into effect here as well. Additionally, the second putt is always considered "good" irrespective of whether a player chooses to putt out. So, make sure you do not leave your first putt short!

4-4. Doubt as to Procedure

Play a mulligan or two, and use your best shot. Playing more than two mulligans per hole is not allowed, as you should conduct yourself with some level of competency or shame.

So, when you are on the tee box for a four or five par, you are always allowed to take mulligans. However, proper discretion should limit the number of mulligans you can use on one hole amongst your foursome. That limit is two mulligans per person, if needed, per hole. Using mulligans on multiple and continuous holes is permitted.

Please be advised that mulligans on three-pars are not permitted. You can hit an extra shot on a three-par (for practice purposes), but you are not allowed to put the mulligan into play. And why are mulligans not permitted on par threes? The simple reason is that ninety-nine percent of the time, the three-par holes in an outing field represent a backlog of groups waiting to tee off on those particular holes. This means there are witnesses observing you take multiple mulligans. You cannot have witnesses to your mulligan excesses, and you can't eliminate witnesses by killing them. If players observe you flagrantly disregarding basic golf rules, then the logical assumption by your competitors would be that you are engaging in reckless cheating throughout the course that day. And remember, you do not want to be suspected of cheating under any circumstances. The participants who consistently attend golf outings are a small circle of people, and word gets around quickly. So, do not take mulligans on three-pars.

4-5. Refusal to Comply with a Rule

So what? You are at an outing where many of the participants are cheating, either by taking mulligans, improving their lies, taking gimmes, or altering their scorecard. You will not be disqualified if you do not comply with traditional, established governing body golfing rules. However, you will be held to dubious, leering scrutiny if you do not abide by the Corporate Golf Tour Rules of Golf.

4-6. General Penalty
None.

CORPORATE GOLF TOUR RULE APPLICATION #5

5-1. Form and Make of Clubs

Players' clubs do not have to conform to any technical specifications or rules governed by any established governing body of golf. Any club that the established governing body of golf has outlawed for professional or amateur events is good to go for corporate outings. This includes clubs like the Juggernaut XXL, the Hammer X, Sooolong 750cc Big Custom Golf Driver, the Mazel wedge, the Smithworks wedge, any Anchor putter, and so on. If the club looks good on television or some type of promotion affirming it will add thirty yards to your drive or take ten strokes off your game, buy it, and bring it to the outing.

5-2. Maximum Number of Clubs Allowed During Competition

There is no minimum or maximum rule that governs the number of clubs you must carry in your golf bag to compete on the corporate golf tour. Hell, bring two drivers, several putters, and four wedges in addition to your normal complement of clubs. Shit, put as many clubs as you want in your bag. No one is going to check, much less tell you that you won't be allowed to play because you have too many sticks in your bag for the outing. No one.

5-3. Balls Allowed in Golf Outings

Whatever you want. Golf balls, otherwise considered illegal by governing golf bodies, are permissible. All manufactured golf balls are approved for play on the corporate golf tour. You know those balls you saw on infomercials promising the longest distance you've ever seen? They're legal. Use them to hit prodigious drives on the longest drive holes. The Polara, Band-it, Foo-King-Long—go for it, and unleash mulligan hell on those long-drive contest holes.

5-4. Ball Unfit for Play

You may change your ball at ANY TIME during the round or on the green, whether or not it has mud on it, has been scraped, cut, or has suffered any other damage that may impair its flight. In fact, you can use several balls on one hole. For example, you can use a hard ball like a Pinnacle, Top Flight, or even Band-it off a tee where you need the extra distance, then switch to a softer ball that has more spin control on your approach shot to the green.

5-5. Handicaps and Competition

Handicaps are prohibited in the CGT because if you follow the CGT rules, they aren't needed to score a win. Handicaps are useless instruments that are to be ignored by players at any golf outing, because most players will always play much better than the handicap they possess. Let's face it, in my experience, and mostly everyone else's, a player's handicap is probably already inflated for a number of reasons, including as a basic self-defense mechanism in an attempt to maintain an even and equitable playing field against other players who have inflated their handicap. This bizarre disregard of the rules regarding handicaps to game the system is mentally somewhat understandable, but ultimately, the posturing cannot logically or ethically sustain its position as a justifiable defense or its moral equivalence.

Notwithstanding the unintended irony related to the handicap system that is supposed to standardize fair play for all categories of golfers, and depending on the format of the outing, players may have to submit their handicap of record as a prerequisite for participation in some golf outings that they will attend. Please understand, inflated handicaps are not unusual. Many players' handicaps are unashamedly embellished, thereby granting those players the maximum opportunity to garner successful results in the "net scoring" portion of a golf outing. These exemplary golf citizens are known as "sandbaggers."

In a contrived way, "sandbaggers" who inflate their handicaps are, in great part, created out of a survival necessity in the recognition that there are a lot of people deviously driven to malign their handicaps for their own selfish reasons. It is an endless, tireless cycle of deceit.

In delusional contrast, you then have the knuckleheads with big egos who keep their handicaps in single digits when their real handicap is higher than what is recorded. I also don't submit to this type of deranged logic. Whereas the people with high handicaps don't submit low scores or increase the scores they post, the other guys don't post high scores, or they post scores lower than they actually achieve. These guys would rather protect their ego and lose money and lose at outings in order to maintain the illusion of being a member of an exclusive club of golf expertise known as the single-digit handicap player. Personally speaking, I cannot stand the handicap system due to its inherent flaws and the ease with which you can cheat the system—and, thereby, others. In conclusion, no one trusts "legitimate" handicaps in outings or club tournaments, so do not worry the least bit about them in the rules of the CGT.

THE CGT GUIDE ON HOW TO MANAGE YOUR SCORING POTENTIAL IN A CORPORATE GOLF OUTING [I.E. RULES FOR CHEATING AT GOLF OUTINGS CONTINUED]

Tee Shots

Have you ever been to an outing and noticed that one of the things they offer when you check in is the opportunity to purchase "mulligans"? This has got to be one of the stupidest things I have ever seen. Any outing that sells "mulligans" is being run by someone who doesn't know how to run an outing. I mean, everyone is using mulligans regardless of whether they buy one or not. I feel sorry for the schmucks who actually buy this shit.

Whether the outing is selling them or not, mulligans are *always* free! If your first tee shot is not as good as it could have been, then you must always take advantage of mulligans on four and five pars (no more than two mulligans per player, per hole) to ensure optimum ball position to play the next shot. However, there is no need to utilize a mulligan if you hit an excellent first tee shot.

Do not employ mulligans on par three holes because there are usually multiple groups on a par three (waiting for their turn to hit) that will take notice of your indiscretions and assume your group is cheating throughout the course of the outing. But don't despair. Chances are statistically on your side that someone from your group will hit the par three green, and then you can cheat by placing the shot that is on the green closer to the hole. And in the rare circumstance that your group does not hit the green, you have to suck it up and play the ball from where it sits—but not before marking down a three on the scorecard before your attempt to scramble for par. You *never, EVER* bogey a three-par.

Scoring and Tie Breakers

What you score on par fours is especially important for two significant reasons. You will note that any team that wins an outing will ultimately demonstrate birdies on short par fours. The propensity for scoring well on holes that are short of four hundred yards will dominate a winning team's scorecard. The logic behind this is simple: "If we don't birdie these short holes, someone else will. We won't win the outing if we don't birdie these short holes." Consequently, most short par fours will be birdied.

Also, par fours are important for tie-breakers. It is not typical for a course to recognize a par five or a par three as the low (hardest) handicap holes. This classification is usually reserved for very long par fours. Generally speaking, the number-one and the number-two handicap holes on most courses will be occupied by par fours. Why is this important? It's important in the event there is a tie for the low winning score. The tie-breaker criteria that the pros will likely revert to in most tournaments will be to compare, or "match," what the tying teams scored on the lowest-handicap holes.

So, it would go like this: If there's a tie for a low score, the pro will then go to the number-one handicap hole on the card and see how each team scored. If one team scores lower than the other on the number-one handicap hole, then the team with the lower score wins. If they both score the same—a tie—on the number-one handicap hole, then the pro would look at the team score for the number-two handicap hole to determine a winner. If the teams tie for low score on the number-two handicap hole, then the pro would proceed to compare, or "match," the scores on the number-three handicap hole, and so on until a winner is determined by which team scored lowest on the next-lowest-handicap hole. This technique to determine a winner in the event of a tie is referred to as a "match of cards," and it is the predominant and most expedient method by which to determine a winner for a golf outing. Essentially, it's match play by paper.

The other method to determine a winner from scores that are tied is to compare the total team score from either the front or back nine. The team that has the lowest score for whichever nine is selected by the pro is declared the winner. This method is not utilized as frequently as the low score on a low handicap "match of cards" criteria. Consequently, it is important for teams in an outing to score well on the low-handicap holes, as they could be the determining factor in whether a team wins or loses. A birdie on the three to four low-handicap holes will usually spell a win for your team in the event of a tie.

Skill Contests
—Closest to the Pin on Three-Pars

Par threes are interesting. They are interesting because if you were to conduct a survey on where or which holes are birdied, you would find that, aside from the short four pars, par threes and par fives are the leading opportunities where groups can reasonably expect to birdie. Unless it's a very difficult, long par three where they are giving away an extraordinary "hole-in-one prize," like a luxury vehicle. At an outing, a par three is usually set up a short*ish* distance where the players attending the event will expect to birdie, especially if you are playing in a scramble format.

There are usually four par threes on a course you are playing (which is the statistical average for golf courses). Some may have five par threes, and others may have three par threes, but the overwhelming majority of courses are designed with four par threes. Out of the four par threes, it is reasonable to conclude that those par threes will represent at least three birdies on your scorecard. That's three under par to start your round. It is conceivable and even acceptable to stretch that to four birdies, but if that were to be the case, then I would suggest that you at least birdie one of the par threes legitimately. If you think about it, if your team birdies at least three par threes and four par fives, then you are already starting your round at seven under. Now you just need to identify the par fours that will continue to augment your scoring.

The other interesting aspect—or opportunity, if you will—represented by par threes is that at least two of the par threes will be selected as a "skill contest." This means that the outing will usually designate two of the par threes as closest-to-the-pin and hole-in-one prize holes. What does this mean? First off, these designated holes afford you the opportunity to win a prize—whether it's a car, cruise, money, or set of clubs on a hole-in-one par three, or pro shop credits or a gift if it is a closest-to-the-pin par three. There is no way to win a hole-in-one prize other than actually getting a hole-in-one, so I won't waste any time on this. However, winning a closest-to-the-pin contest is another matter. It is an opportunity where extensive cheating occurs and fiction triumphs over truth.

There are two distinct techniques to consider to optimize your results on a par three. The first is to physically mark your ball fifty percent closer to the hole from your original ball position. The second is recording your distance on the measurement pad that you would find somewhere next to the green. Irrespective of where you ultimately physically mark your ball, when you record your distance on the measurement pad, you may improve the distance from where you physically marked your ball on the green. For example, if you mark your ball eight feet from the hole (even though your original position was sixteen feet after your tee shot), when you record your distance on the measurement pad, improve your distance by several more feet. The additional distance you deduct from where your ball physically lies strictly applies for recording purposes only with the measurement pad. So, even though your original tee shot landed sixteen feet from the hole, you have cut your physical distance from the hole by half, to eight feet (now a "gimme"), and decreased that even more when recording your distance on the measurement pad.

However, please be aware that you should record a distance on the measurement pad relative to what you feel will be the probable winning distance from the hole, irrespective of where your ball actually lies for the putt. For example, prior to marking the ball on the green on the par three, walk over to the measurement pad to see the closest measurement of another player's ball. Obviously, you must be closer to the hole than the last recorded mark that is closest to it. After you have finished marking your ball on the green, you will proceed to record your "new" distance to the hole on the measurement pad ensuring that the distance you record is shorter than the last recorded distance. If your physical length to the hole is longer than the shortest recorded distance to the hole, then just mark the measurement pad a shorter distance, placing you ahead of the previously recorded distance.

For the sake of argument, let's say the last and shortest recorded distance to the hole is eight feet, five inches. If you were to record a distance to beat the closest distance recorded on the measurement pad, how much closer would you record the distance? You can't record it as only eight feet, where your ball physically lies. First of all, it kinda looks deliberately stupid. Second, it's definitely stupid given the fact that there is a statistical probability that someone can get inside of you at eight feet. So, what are you to do? Your priority is not so much to get inside the closest shot before you as it is to reduce the statistical probability that someone else can get inside the distance *you* record from the hole on the measurement pad.

To avoid the prospect of consequently losing after applying the effort to cheat (which doesn't make sense, as you don't cheat to lose; you cheat to win), you must record the distance that provides you with the greatest statistical proximity for success. After you measure your ball from where you marked it, you will go over to record your distance on the measurement pad. Using the eight-foot distance from the hole as the basis for your assessment, you will make another mental adjustment to your distance before you record the distance. Ultimately, you may end up writing down a distance of five feet, five inches. Basically, when you record the distance of your ball from the hole on the measurement pad, you again decrease the physical distance by another 32–33 percent. The statistical probability of someone hitting a ball inside of five feet, five inches is much lower than having someone hit a shot inside of eight feet. Please note: the measurement pad decrease in distance strictly applies for paper recording purposes and is not to be applied to where your ball physically lies. You are not allowed to improve your physical distance to the hole by more than fifty percent when marking your ball on the green.

These tactics require fluidity in assessment and judgment. For example, if one of your playing partners hits their ball fifteen feet from the hole, then you may have to employ multiple techniques of marking and recording your distance. Perceptually, fifteen feet doesn't look that much different from seven-and-a-half-feet when marking your or your playing partners' distance. That reminds me: if your playing partner hits it closer than you do, you must repeat the marking and recording techniques you would have employed for yourself and apply them to your partner. If you are that distance (fifteen feet) from the hole, then unfortunately even if you shave off fifty percent of the distance, you are still seven-and-a-half feet from the hole, allowing the statistical probability of someone hitting a ball inside of you to increase significantly. So, when you record your distance from the hole, it should be five feet or less. Please keep in mind that the CGT rules prohibit anyone whose ball is on the green from physically reducing their distance to the hole by more than fifty percent (outside of ten feet) for a putt. However, that does not apply to recording the distance from the hole on the measurement pad on a par three. These are two separate and distinct tactics only allowed to be employed on par three skills contests. Part of the gentleman's code of the CGT requires a measure of integrity.

—*Long Drive*

The long drive is a fun skill test to participate in and an interesting one to experience. I am considered to have been someone who used to be able to hit the ball a reasonable distance. In my prime years, I would average about two hundred and eighty, two hundred and ninety, and occasionally, three hundred yards per drive—not prodigious by any stretch of the imagination, but nonetheless functional. I have been a professional golfer on the mini-tour, a scratch and scratch-plus golfer, and am currently a single-digit handicap player. These attributes allow me to be cognizant of what can realistically occur on a golf course as it relates to a player's performance and scoring. I have played with many great players, but I can also appreciate golfers who may not play or score very well but can launch their drives into orbit. This skill contest is primarily designed for them, but it does not cease to amaze me when I witness someone win who seems physically incapable of hitting a golf ball two hundred yards, much less the three hundred plus yards needed to win this skill contest.

It's especially interesting when you see a three-hundred-yard plus drive recorded by someone on a hole where there was a severe headwind of thirty miles an hour hit by a guy so uncoordinated you would have to wonder how he managed to generate the swing arc necessary to produce that kind of clubhead speed. To be in compliance with the official CGT rules and have the greatest chance to win this skill contest known as the "Long Drive Contest," you will need to implement the following tactics and considerations as necessary: If your ball comes to rest twenty yards off the fairway on either side, then your ball is considered in play, and you are eligible to contest for the longest drive. The first rule is that if you are within twenty yards of either side of the fairway on a long drive hole, but still possess the longest drive—*it counts*! The long drive hole is the only exception to CGT rule 2–2, where you are only allowed to move your ball four approximate club lengths, or five yards closer to the fairway.

Second, you are allowed two mulligans on the longest-drive hole if your first ball is either short of the longest drive or you hit a very wayward shot that exceeds the twenty-yard perimeter of hitting into the rough to the left or right of the fairway. If your mulligan balls exceed the distance of the current longest drive—*it counts*! The last method is a more direct and flagrant approach but still legal under CGT rules—and one I have employed in an outing. After your tee shot, drive your cart straight at the longest-drive marker in the fairway, pick it up while moving, and spear it into the ground about twenty to thirty yards ahead of where it originally lay. Then don't forget to go back to pick up your ball. As always, be aware of your surroundings, as you don't want competing groups to see you and incorporate your tactics for their own selfish use. When approaching a long-drive skill contest, all of these techniques should be considered.

—Straightest Drive

This has got to be the dumbest fucking skill contest ever invented, second only to the "Most Honest Golfer." Who were the anteaters that thought of this concept? The criteria used to determine a winner for this skill contest is at best murky. The straight-drive string only runs out at about two hundred yards. What happens to a two-hundred-and-sixty-yard drive when there's no string out that far? I mean, I really want to know how the fuck you determine a winner in this. And despite the fact that the straight drive string is only about two hundred yards long, outings deploy this stupid fucking skills test on a four-hundred-and-fifty-yard-long par four. Can't they put a two-hundred-yard string on a much shorter and tighter hole that maybe, just maybe, would only require a two-hundred-yard tee shot of precision? A hole where you have to put your ball in the fairway? Given the fact that I don't agree with this idiotic concept, it is a skill contest that is banned from the CGT and has no further dialogue with respect to information on tactics.

—Most Honest Golfer

Forget it. This takes the top prize for useless thought for morons and I won't have anything to do with this.

Marking Your Ball

There are four ways to mark your ball when on the green. The first and traditional way to mark your ball is to step up to where your ball is and place a marker directly behind the ball. This procedure is the established, rule-abiding manner in which to mark a ball on the green. The following three techniques for marking a ball are not legal or by any means sanctioned by any governing golf authority, except for the corporate golf tour. Consequently, the following techniques I describe are only permitted under the governing body of the CGT.

The second technique is fairly simple to execute. When you get to your ball on the green, ensure that you place your mark in *front* of the ball. Not behind it. This will allow you to shorten your putt by inches because when you place the ball back on the green (use a big ball mark like a poker chip), you will place the ball in front of the marker. Let me repeat: when you place the ball back on the green, you place it *in front of* the mark as if you had marked it from behind. Additionally, when you place your ball in front of the marker, do not put the ball directly in front of your ball mark. Mark it another inch or two in front of your mark. In other words, create some space between your ball and the mark when putting the ball down. You will want to repeat this process several times before you actually putt. It provides you with the opportunity to improve your distance from the hole by a couple of feet. For example, when you get to the green, you mark your ball in the indicated CGT manner. As your group is reviewing the putt, you should capitalize on the opportunity to re-mark your ball in the same fashion several more times. Employ this tactic in a discreet manner, pretending that re-marking your ball repeatedly will help you align the putting line better. Each time you do this, you eliminate multiple inches from the length of your putt. Depending on the audience you are playing with, replacing your mark with the ball to review the putt presents the appearance of behavior that is a completely reasonable and legitimate action.

The third ball-marking technique is much more aggressive and requires much more discretion on your part as it borders on criminal activity—and includes marking your ball multiple feet ahead of where your ball actually lies. This requires extreme visual sensitivity and discretion combined with reasonable calibration of how much footage to eliminate, *not exceeding a fifty percent reduction in length to the hole from your original lie on the green.* For example, you would usually consider employing this technique when you are approximately forty, thirty, or twenty feet away. This would enable you to turn a forty-foot putt into a twenty-foot putt, a thirty-foot putt into a fifteen-foot putt, or a twenty-foot putt into a ten-foot putt—which would be considered a "gimme" as it is within the ten-foot range.

How do you do this? You casually walk up to the green to get your ball and simply don't mark it when you pick it up. You pretend to mark your ball, except you don't put a mark down and walk over to your cart to do something. Then return to the general area of where you picked up your ball, except fifty percent closer, and proceed to place your ball down as if to line up a putt. Remember, you are only allowed to decrease the length of your putt by fifty percent. Obviously, this is a tactic that does not need to be employed when you are within ten feet of the hole because you can simply take a "gimme."

The fourth and final technique is the most belligerent and riskiest because you have to manage several elements. The first goal of this technique is to be the first player on the green. If you, or someone in your group, hit a ball onto the green, then you start to independently move toward the green with your golf cart. If your playing partner is not on the green, you advise them to take whatever clubs they need, along with their putter, (If you're playing in an outing that doesn't provide caddies, players will keep their putters in their respective bags. If the outing does provide caddies, then your foursome's caddie will hold all the putters for the group), and advise them that you will meet them up at the green. Let them walk while you ride up to the green. Employ this technique if they are not too far from the green in terms of walking distance—let's say inside around hundred yards or a distance that would not be cumbersome on your playing partner or rude from your perspective to have them walk up to the green.

When you arrive at the green, you approach your ball with marker in hand, and as you position yourself to pick up the ball and start to bend down, you instead toss your marker fifty percent of the distance to the hole from where your ball is lying and proceed to pick up your ball. If you are thirty feet out, you toss your marker to approximately fifteen feet. If you are twenty feet out, you toss your marker to about ten feet—which is a "gimme." There are two aspects to consider at this stage that will ensure the success of this technique and maintain the laughable notion that you are a golfer with some degree of integrity.

First of all, make sure that the other golfers are not in visual range or at an angle proximate to the green to take note or umbrage with what you are doing. Remember, it is the visual component that you must focus on. Someone could be physically near the green but not positioned well to visually notice the technique that you are deploying. Secondly, you must use a flat and heavy marker, as they tend to stick better to the ground or green. A flat, heavy marker is important because it enhances the efficacy of the "toss" technique that you must execute. I specifically refer to this as a "toss" rather than a "flip" because flipping a marker toward an area away from you will often result in a side-spinning, rolling motion by the marker that you will be unable to control.

For example, when you "flip" your marker away from you, it will generally land on the side of the marker and begin a rolling motion that can run amok, going left or right or boomeranging (in a rolling fashion) right back toward you. This results in you not having an effective mark that is not anywhere close to the spot where you want your ball to be. In order to avoid this mishap, you must toss your marker in the same fashion as you would a minuscule frisbee. This method of tossing will greatly improve the chances that your marker will fly straight and land flatly and squarely on the ground, significantly reducing your risk of having to chase down a ball marker that is rolling out of control, drawing everyone's attention to your maneuver and disqualifying your ability to discreetly eliminate the distance to the hole with your ball.

It is also important to take advantage of your group's awareness and perception of your ball's approach shot to the green as it relates to the final position of your ball on the green. For example, when someone sees you hit a ball onto the green, their perspective is to associate the line of the ball flight with the flag and background objects. Therefore, if you hit your ball to the right or left of where the flagstick is, players will be more sensitive to where you mark your ball relative to how far left or right from the flagstick they thought the ball had landed. However, people generally don't have the same awareness when it comes to depth perception. So, if someone hits an approach shot that is in line with the flagstick, they can't really judge how close the ball is to the flagstick. If an approach shot at the flag maintains its line of flight toward the flag, then a person will not be able to discern if the ball comes to rest five, ten, fifteen, or twenty feet in front of or behind the hole.

How many times have you hit an approach shot in line with the flagstick where you thought the ball would be a couple of feet away, only to find that you were a disheartening ten to fifteen feet away? But you thought you'd stuck it close! No matter, as the rest of the group thinks you hit the shot to a couple of feet from the pin. When your ball comes to rest between you and the pin, the technique of tossing your marker appropriately provides you with a welcome benefit because you are keeping your body directly in line with the pin and blocking the view of your toss.

Putting

As captain of your team, it is your responsibility to clearly communicate the two-putt rule to your team members at the beginning of the round so that they are aware of it and don't feel the pressure of having to execute excellent putting on greens they are not likely to be familiar with. This presents an optimum opportunity to be more aggressive with birdie attempts, as the next putt is always good. The classic phrase that works with this method is "Get it to the hole. The next one is good!"

—Gimme Range and Hitting the Hole with Your Putt or Chip

An acceptable "gimme" range is any putt or chip inside of ten feet from the hole. Any ball resting on the green, fringe, or rough within ten feet of the hole is an automatic "gimme" even if you choose to finish the play. A player can nonchalantly come up and swipe at his or her putt, or shot, without the need for over-reading and excessive concentration. This will help all players relax and enjoy their round. If you are outside the ten-foot range, it is also acceptable to count the putt, or chip, if the ball simply hits the hole. If your ball hits any part of the hole and does not fall in the hole (also applies to chips), it is still counted as if the ball had dropped in the hole. In the CGT, putts or chips simply have to hit the hole or the flagstick for it to count as good. It *need not* go in or come to rest at the bottom of the hole.

Keeping Score

How you record a winning score will greatly depend on how you manage your scoring. I know, it sounds like a stupid and simple thing to say, but it's still important to point out because of nuanced and customized approaches. To truly manage your score effectively, you must know the salient points of when to record good scores as they pertain to different holes, as well as how to optimize your scoring with different golf outing formats. Lastly, it is imperative to take command of the scorecard in order to implement what you believe will be a winning score for that outing.

—Scorecard

You have three options available to you to keep score: 1) You can keep an honest score; 2) You can adjust your scoring accordingly as you progress through your round; and 3) You can simply fill out the scorecard before you begin the round, not worry about it, and go on to enjoy your round.

—Recording Good Scores on Low-Handicap Holes Is the Difference between Winning and Losing

Although alluded to earlier in the book, it is important to reinforce the significance of recording birdies (eagles on par fives) on the top three or four low-handicap holes. At the conclusion of the outing, if teams have tied scores, the club pro will most often choose to use the tie-breaker methodology of matching the team scores on low-handicap holes to determine a winner. The pro will begin the tie-breaker with the number-one handicap hole, and if there is still a tie, then they will proceed to the number-two handicap hole and so on until the team with the lower score on a low handicap hole wins a hole, and the outing. It is a sudden-death playoff system by simply matching cards—match play—on a hole-by-hole basis, always starting with the number one rated low-handicap hole.

Scoring Formats

Several scoring format options are available for use by the head pro and the organizer of the outing. The scoring format ultimately utilized will be determined based on the goals of the organizer and the methodology to get the playing field to complete all eighteen holes (weather permitting) in an enjoyable and timely fashion. Also, the pro shop may request "legitimate" USGA handicaps from all participants in the event they apply handicaps for team and individual net scoring.

The scoring format criteria to implement a successful event are the following: 1) enjoyment factor, in which everyone in the field enjoys some level of participation; and 2) pace of play, in which all groups finish their round in, God willing, no more than five hours. This will ensure minimal waiting times for a participant to hit a shot, minimal waiting for a group's turn to play a hole, and efficiency in getting the majority of the groups off the course and into the scheduled cocktail reception.

The head pro has several scoring formats to offer the outing organizer. These are the primary formats used:

—Scramble

A scramble is the most popular scoring format to execute in an outing. It is a favorable format to use for inexperienced golfers, keeping the field engaged while maintaining a reasonable pace of play. In a scramble format, the group always selects their best shot to play for their next shot, including putts, until they hole out. For example, a group selects their best tee shot to hit, then they continue to select the best shot to play until they complete the hole. Essentially, it is four players playing "one ball" as they are always selecting to play their best shot in the hitting rotation. This format is the preferred choice to expedite play at a golf outing.

—Shamble

A shamble is a scramble hybrid where the group members pick the best tee shot to hit. They then each hit from that spot but continue to play *their own ball* until they each hole out. This format is popular in part because it allows players to play their own ball throughout the round after selecting the team's best tee shot to hit. This is a particularly appealing format when the outing takes place at an exceptional golf course venue, as the players will then be able to experience the course while playing their own ball, for the most part, throughout the round.

—Best Ball

The best ball format is the most labor-intensive format for the pro shop to implement as well as the most time-consuming one, significantly extending time on the course as every player is playing their own ball through all eighteen holes. And even though the rules are for a player to pick up his or her ball after double par, they ignore the rule and rarely do so. Very annoying. There are no shortcuts here, as each player will play as if they are in a regular foursome on the weekend. If you are participating in an outing that has a best-ball format, be prepared for a grueling six-to-seven-hour round. Ouch!

—Callaway

The Callaway scoring system for outings is strictly a "one-day" scoring methodology (equation) that helps facilitate golf outings in which players play their own ball (another long day on the golf course) on every hole until they complete the hole. Several caveats are involved: the highest score any player can record for any hole is double par. For example, no more than a six on a par three, no more than an eight on a par four—you get it. Pick up the fucking ball and keep moving. Also, depending on your gross score, you get to deduct some holes where you scored your worst; except for the seventeenth or eighteenth hole. For whatever reason, the Callaway scoring methodology doesn't accept those holes to be factored into the scoring. Those holes are discarded and inconsequential, no matter what goes on there.

Now for the actual scoring methodology. Tabulating your score is a multi-step process: 1) Based on your total gross score, you review the formal Callaway chart and take note of the handicap deduction column that tells you specifically how many "worst" holes you are allowed to use in the calculation; 2) You then refer to the handicap adjustment column (Callaway chart) and add or subtract the corresponding number (per your score) represented in the handicap adjustment column *from the sum* of your worst hole(s) applied from the handicap deduction column; and 3) You then subtract the total of that equation from your gross score to establish your final "net" score. An example is warranted. If you shoot a gross score of seventy-six, you would have a -2 represented in the handicap adjustment column. Then, based on your gross score (seventy-six), the handicap deduction column indicates that you would apply only one worst hole to the equation. Let's say your worst hole, on a score of seventy-six, is an eight on a par four hole (double par) that is not the seventeenth or eighteenth hole. You would then subtract two (-2 handicap adjustment column) from the eight (one hole from the handicap deduction column) for a total of six. You then subtract six from your original gross score of seventy-six resulting in a net score of seventy. Using the same example of a gross score of seventy-six; if your worst scoring hole is a ten (double par on a par five), then you would subtract two (-2 handicap adjustment column) from ten (handicap deduction column) resulting in an eight, and subtract eight from seventy-six resulting in a sixty-eight as your final score. Obviously, you would be better off using a double par on a par five to gain the extra strokes to deduct. And remember; you are not allowed to deduct the seventeenth and eighteenth holes even though they may be your worst holes. You have to select your next worst hole(s) other than seventeen and eighteen. Additionally, you are not allowed to apply more than double par on any of your worst holes. If you score a nine on a par four and it is your worst hole, you are only allowed to recognize it as an eight for your score.

Here is the Callaway chart for your reading pleasure:

Gross (using double par max.)					Handicap Deduction
		70	71	72	Scratch
73	74	75			1/2 of Worst Hole
76	77	78	79	80	Worst Hole
81	82	83	84	85	1 1/2 Worst Holes
86	87	88	89	90	2 Worst Holes
91	92	93	94	95	2 1/2 Worst Holes
96	97	98	99	100	3 Worst Holes
101	102	103	104	105	3 1/2 Worst Holes
106	107	108	109	110	4 Worst Holes
111	112	113	114	115	4 1/2 Worst Holes
116	117	118	119	120	5 Worst Holes
121	122	123	124	125	5 1/2 Worst Holes
126	127	128	129	130	6 Worst Holes
-2	-1	0	+1	+2	Handicap Adjustment

The trick with this system is to figure out which gross scores provide you with the ability to post a winning score that is two, three, or four under par for your group. Frankly, don't even bother with this shit and fill out the scorecard before the round even starts.

No Witnesses

Be mindful of what you are doing. Look around and make sure no other teams are witness to your actions. If you have A and B shotgun tee groups where you share initial tees, then be conscious of your position on the course, your shots, and the appearance of your shots to the group behind you. If you look like you are out of position or not in scoring position, and the group behind you notices where you are, then questions—suspicions—may be raised. You don't want anyone at the dining and awards activities after the outing saying,

"There's no way those fuckers shot eighteen under! They looked like they were barely making pars."

Outings that take place on courses that have the luxury of extensive acreage and allow the design of isolated holes are best suited to providing the greatest private environments to covertly achieve victories while maintaining a strong degree of comfortable anonymity. This secluded environment recalls the age-old philosophical question, "If a tree falls in the forest and no one is around, does it make a sound?" Well, it depends on your perspective, but you can easily argue that it does not—resulting in the thought that if a CGT foursome is surrounded by complete privacy in the woods, do they cheat? If they are playing in a golf outing and adhering to the CGT rules and guidelines, then they are obviously not cheating.

CHAPTER FORTY-SEVEN

HUMILITY, INTEGRITY, AND HONOR

[IF KIQUE PLAYED GOLF, HE WOULD NEVER CHEAT AT A CORPORATE GOLF OUTING]

One day, I am attending a function for work when, out of the blue, a gentleman draws my attention. He approaches me and asks if my name is Eurice Rojas, which I acknowledge. He then asks if I am the son of Eurice Rojas from Cuba. I mean, who the fuck else could I be? Does anyone think there actually is another person in the world with a name like Eurice, much less followed by a Rojas, and who was named after his father? What would the odds be on that? Although I am very proud of my name, what the fuck was my father thinking, smoking, or drinking when he named me?

We embarked on a conversation in which he tells me that he was good friends with my dad and often reminisces about how they would always be horsing around, back in the day, playing basketball and baseball together. It is a nice memory to share with me about my dad, but being in the cynical, paranoid, and often neurotic business of sales, marketing, and politics, I immediately start thinking that this guy is blowing smoke up my ass for a favor, or to hit me up to buy some ads for his newspaper. Also, if you don't know any Cubans and are unfamiliar with the Cuban culture, then you probably also don't know that we have been endowed with a gift—many think it's a genetic disease—to greatly exaggerate and dramatize our stories or anything we claim to have experienced.

It is, however, part of the formula that makes us great orators. Cubans are generally known for having the propensity to turn boring, mundane fishermen's stories into fisherman lore. The profane levels of exaggeration are akin to ingesting several doses of LSD, *and then* telling a fish story about catching a marlin the size of the Empire State Building that had just defeated a megalodon in a sea battle. What started out as an actual capture of a fish the size of a sardine will turn into reeling in the largest prehistoric marlin that ever existed, fighting barehanded with a machete in mouth ultimately securing the fish onto the side of the boat—à la Ernest Hemingway, replicating his novel, *The Old Man and the Sea.*

But unlike *Old Man and the Sea* where the fisherman docked with the skeleton of the fish he had caught, the Cuban guy would have brought the monstrous-sized marlin (in actuality a sardine) into port intact, along with the corpses of the sharks that he killed that were trying to feed off of the dead, mammoth sized marlin (sardine) on the way into the dock. Then he would have fed the whole village (in actuality just fed a little kid who ate the small sardine) with all the shark and marlin meat he had captured, and the town would have been saved and named after him. He would have transformed himself into a nautical legend and a hood ornament for a car. Think of it—Castro was able to do it, globally, with an island roughly the size of Tennessee. I left the business function hopeful that the warm and fuzzy historical throwback of my father and this gentleman was, first, genuine and sincere, and second, accurate. I mean, it's always rewarding, for the most part, to receive unsolicited insight into my father's life when he was a young man.

Two to three weeks later, I went to Miami on a business trip and took the time to visit with my mom and dad. During the visit, over dinner—something barely edible that my mother lovingly put together—I asked my father about this gentleman and whether he knew him. When I mentioned his real name—not his nickname—my father perked up, stretched out a big smile, and exclaimed his nickname, "Kique?" in an excited manner. He mentioned that he had lost touch with Kique and didn't know how he was doing. More importantly, he mentioned him by his nickname rather than the man's birth name. He was obviously happy to hear about him, which made me feel good, knowing that I had met someone who meant something to my father. His initial reaction also served to validate the gentleman's story.

So "Kique" wasn't blowing smoke up my ass after all.

I continued to recount my story about this gentleman to my dad, encouraged by his enthusiasm about me having met him, confirming his physical features and the fact that he told me about growing up playing basketball and baseball with him. I hoped this would fuel a conversation filled with significant stories about my father that would help me better understand his nature and character as he grew up in Cuba. It was also an opportunity that most families look forward to as a way to pass their memories on to their children.

However, when I mentioned to my father how this gentleman had remarked that they'd played sports together, something unexpected happened and my dad's reaction changed to one of surprise and confusion. *Shit. I knew it was too good to be true. The fucking guy was blowing smoke up my ass after all!* And with that, my opportunity to relive warm stories and gain insight into a man who was a resolute guardian of privacy regarding his life experiences subsided. To my surprise, our ensuing conversation about "Kique" would turn out to be much more meaningful than a warm and fuzzy anecdote. My father then responded with a sly smile, "Basketball? baseball? We never played baseball and basketball together!"

"He said you guys played all the time!" I countered.

I was disillusioned and somewhat confused as I saw my father contort his facial expression again into one of sternness.

Squinting his eyes, he asked, "Do you want me to tell you who this man really is and what he did for our family?" This was certainly a mysterious delivery and assertion. I was intrigued. "Kique was the man who provided me with the forged documentation to help me, and us, leave Cuba. He is the one who arranged for me to get that material." With that, my dad sat back and reflected. The room was silent as I also sat there, stunned at what he had just shared with me.

Of course, those documents turned out to be for naught because, as described earlier, when our family was confronted by the head of airport security in our attempt to escape, we were allowed to leave Cuba because of the relationship my father had forged with him earlier in his life. Nonetheless, the effort, risk, and danger that this gentleman, "Kique," undertook on our behalf—collaborating with an underground network to obtain falsified documents to aid my father's escape attempts—were profound. I sat there in disbelief and basically repeated the statement he had just told me. "He provided you with forged documents?"

My father just nodded. He then casually added to please give "Kique" his regards and to give him his contact information.

"*Coño. Que bueno saber de Kique.*" —"Damn. It's great to hear from Kique."

And that was the end of the conversation. The next time I saw my dad, he briefly mentioned that he had spoken to "Kique" directly, but nothing more or less was made of it. I couldn't wait to get back to Jersey to confront this man again. I wanted to thank him for risking his life for my father and my family. But I also did not understand why he hadn't been forthright in his initial conversation with me about the actual role he played in my father's life and our family's future. A lot was at stake from all sides.

Back in Jersey, I approached him at another function. He immediately and enthusiastically asked me if I had spoken to my father and given him his regards. I informed him that I had and that my father was very happy to hear from him. After a moment of joyous reconciliation, I then proceeded to tell him, "But my dad told me that he and you did not grow up playing sports together." He changed his expression from an excited one to a conciliatory one. "Yes. I know."

I asked him why he hadn't told me what he had done for my dad when we had first spoken. He looked at me with humble eyes, put his hand on my shoulder, and simply said, "Son, men don't talk about those things."

With tears welling up, I proceeded to hug him and thank him for what he had done. He wasn't seeking platitudes or recognition or special favors. Rather, the issue was a matter of three steadfast and valued principles that are grudgingly difficult to experience in this day and age: **humility, integrity, and honor**.

My father was reserved and humble, intelligent and curious. He was a person who passionately pursued knowledge and was steadfast in his commitment to his principles of freedom. Adhering to those values came to a flashpoint when Fidel and his communist intentions for the Cuban revolution became apparent. The commitment to his principles fueled our escape to America in anticipation of a new life that celebrated the principals of freedom instead of the suffocating government control of Cuba. Unfortunately, he could not escape the psychological scars that resulted from the revolution. Whether it was to avoid emotional anguish or to honor unspoken confidentiality between friends, my father was always wary of displaying or sharing his memories of Castro and the Cuban revolution.

Also worth noting were several additional concerns: 1) Fidel exported Cubans that posed as asylum seekers, but were in fact spies, that were dispersed throughout the U.S in Cuban population enclaves like South Florida, New York, and New Jersey. The role of the spies was to infiltrate and participate with anti-Castro organizations and report any relevant intelligence on proposed propaganda, including legislative and political activities against Castro back to Cuban officials; and 2) The Cuban Americans who had re-settled in South Florida vehemently and understandably detested Fidel. Their rabid loathing of Fidel was also accompanied by angry, uncompromising vitriol against Communism. And this community was also aware of the infiltration of Cuban spies in their communities, so they were highly suspicious of anyone with previous connections to the current regime in Cuba. My father believed that the people caught up in the political whirlpool of the South Florida Cuban community would not altogether understand, or respect, the fact that he ultimately turned against Castro. My father was arrested as a political prisoner for defending his anti-Castro principles. Consequently, he closely guarded his past relationship with Castro and would only reveal his experiences to an exclusive few. Fortunately, I was one of those few.

And as such, I received each detail with deep reverence and respect.

At the most, my father would share two to three memories a year with me, and those were usually when I (alone or with my wife) was in Miami for a trip.

When we would visit my parents, my dad would proceed to pull out a file, with the pictures that are displayed in this book, and proceed to reenact one of their (mom and dad) experiences. It was relegated to one story per visit to Miami. Then, he would pack up the pictures and go to another room and hide them. He never disclosed the location of the pictures, and he refused to tell me where they were hidden.

And that's the way he wanted it.

After my dad passed away, my wife found the file of pictures, amongst other things, in the drop ceiling of the room where my father would go after each storytelling session.

The creation of this book is in honor of the sacrifices endured by my father, mother, and countless other Cuban families in their quest for freedom. My father never sacrificed his integrity, honor, or humility. In fact, he was willing to die for them.

Those are also values which are demanded on the rolling fields of the golf courses I've spent half my lifetime on.

These rare human traits are what unwittingly contributed to my attraction to the captivating sport of golf, and which thankfully, continues to resonate with a majority of golfers to this day.

ACKNOWLEDGMENTS

I will be forever grateful to the following individuals for their contributions to my inaugural book, *Out of the Rough: The Cuban Revolution and its Effect on Golf.*

My wife and best friend, Norma, for her inspiration, selfless support, unconditional love, and fierce determination to overcome the improbable.

My good friend Angel Bernal for graciously dedicating significant time poring through a final draft. His constructive attention to detail, unique comical wit, and clever insights were a valued gift.

Fate favored me on the day I met the incredibly talented team at Life to Paper Publishing. I had the rare opportunity and good fortune to experience the amazing skill sets offered by Tabitha Rose and Jennifer Goulden. Their professionalism, heartfelt commitment, and tireless work ethic elevated my performance and contributed to a meaningful life journey.

My good friend Robert Cardenas for introducing me to Tabitha Rose at Life to Paper Publishing.

The impressive skills of friend and producer Carlos "Chaz" Acosta who, along with his production company Space Camp Studios, meticulously managed the audio recording of the book.

BIBLIOGRAPHY

I consulted with several credible website sources to collect and compare information and validate timelines related to the stories my father had shared with me. Obviously, my father was also a source. The following web sites provided meaningful and factual material along with other resources to research:

New York-New Jersey Cuba Sí Coalition: cubasinynjcoalition.org

US Department of Justice: justice.gov

The Brownsville-Herald: newspaperarchive.com/Brownsville-herald-apr-04-1958-p-1

The Militant: themilitant.com

The Cuban History: thecubanhistory.com

The New York Times: nytimes.com/1958/03/28/archives

Casa de las Americas: unacuba.org

Wikipedia: wikipedia.org

Britannica: britannica.com/biography/fidel-castro

History: history.com/topics/cold-war/fidel-castro

USGA: usga.org

Pew Research Center Fact Sheet, 9/16/2019

Eurice B. Rojas

Onelia Rojas

Latin American Information Network Information Center

African American Golfer's Digest

Rogers Park Golf Course

ABOUT THE AUTHOR

Eurice E. Rojas is a dynamic and visionary leader featuring a compelling career as a golf professional, an entrepreneur, an executive in the tobacco and health care industries, an elected councilman and now a thought-provoking author.

He is a first-generation Cuban American with a story unlike any other. With a keen eye for detail and a passion for storytelling, his debut book, *Out of the Rough: The Cuban Revolution and its Effect on Golf*, is a must-read for anyone interested in a compelling life journey. It reflects on his family's relationship with Fidel Castro and their escape from Cuba, the tenacity to survive the streets of New York city manifesting in the improbable partnership with the sport of golf, and the transformative power of sports within a corporate culture.

What's more, Eurice factually exposes the calculatingly audacious system of cheating in corporate golf outings, and the insidious little secret of golf handicap system abuse.

Whether leading healthcare organizations or crafting insightful and stimulating narratives, Eurice brings a unique blend of expertise, creativity and strategic thinking to everything he does. His unwavering commitment to excellence and innovation has made him a standout figure in business, sports, politics and beyond.

He possesses a bachelor's degree from DePaul University in Chicago and a master's degree in healthcare administration from Seton Hall University in New Jersey.

Made in United States
North Haven, CT
05 June 2023

37400514R00164